THE NORMS OF WAR

THE NORMS OF WAR

Cultural Beliefs and Modern Conflict

Theo Farrell

LYNNE
RIENNER
PUBLISHERS

BOULDER
LONDON

Published in the United States of America in 2005 by
Lynne Rienner Publishers, Inc.
1800 30th Street, Boulder, Colorado 80301
www.rienner.com

and in the United Kingdom by
Lynne Rienner Publishers, Inc.
3 Henrietta Street, Covent Garden, London WC2E 8LU

Library of Congress Cataloging-in-Publication Data
Farrell, Theo, 1967–
    The norms of war : cultural beliefs and modern conflict / by Theo Farrell.
        p.   cm.
    Includes bibliographical references and index.
    ISBN 1-58826-361-4 (hardcover : alk. paper)
1. War and society.   2. War and civilization.   3. Conflict management.   I. Title.
HM554.F37   2005
303.6'6—dc22
                                                            2005011001

British Cataloguing in Publication Data
A Cataloguing in Publication record for this book
is available from the British Library.

Printed and bound in the United States of America

The paper used in this publication meets the requirements
(∞) of the American National Standard for Permanence of
Paper for Printed Library Materials Z39.48-1992.

    5   4   3   2   1

For my parents,
Brian and Marie-Thérèse Farrell

Contents

Tables and Figures

Acknowledgments

This is a "quick book" that turned into a long labor of love. What was supposed to make some discrete interventions in IR debate turned into something much more ambitious in theoretical scope and empirical sweep. Such a transformation in this project would not have been possible without the support I received over the years from a number of quarters.

Special thanks to Tim Dunne and Ted Hopf for kindly providing constructive feedback on draft chapters of the book. Over the years numerous other colleagues provided comments and criticisms on material that one way or another has ended up in the book. With apologies for any omissions, I wish to thank Debbi Avant, Michael Barnett, Jeremy Black, Risa Brooks, Chris Demchak, John Duffield, Lynn Eden, Emily Goldman, Jeff Legro, Colin McInnes, Terry Terriff, and Nigel White. I am also grateful to the many colleagues at Exeter who provided sound counsel and welcome support throughout this project, in particular, David Armstrong, Tim Dunne, Mick Dumper, Andy Hindmoor, Iain Hampsher-Monk, and Bice Maiguashca. My thanks to Preslava Stoeva for producing the bibliography.

I am grateful to the Economic and Social Research Council, the Arts and Humanities Board, and the University of Exeter Research Committee for grants supporting the research and writing of the book. Work on the book was also aided by visiting fellowships at the Department of Politics at University College Dublin (UCD), the Department of Political Science at Trinity College Dublin (TCD), and the Center for International Security and Cooperation at Stanford University. For arranging these, my thanks go to Tom Garvin at UCD, Mick Laver at TCD, and Lynn Eden and Scott Sagan at Stanford.

Lynne Rienner Publishers deserves particular praise. My commissioning editor, Richard Purslow, approached this project with characteristic energy and enthusiasm. His successor, Elisabetta Linton, has shown much consideration and tact in steering the book through the review process. I am grateful to Karen Williams for efficiently managing the production of my book. My thanks also to the three anonymous reviewers who helped me kick the book into shape. I am especially grateful to one reviewer who read the whole manuscript twice, providing incredibly detailed reports on both occasions. I have since discovered this reviewer to be Thomas Berger—someone whose work I have long admired as one who sets the standard for scholarship on culture and war.

Finally, I wish to thank my wife and sometime academic collaborator, Hélène Lambert, for . . . well . . . everything. And our daughter, Eloise, for keeping it all real (in the most delightful way possible).

This book is dedicated to my parents, Brian and Marie-Thérèse Farrell. As youngsters, both found safety in Ireland during World War II—Dad was evacuated from Britain, Mum fled Switzerland with her family. They met and fell in love in postwar Dublin, and thereafter made their lives together along with their seven children in Ireland. In this roundabout way, the Great War that blighted the world is also the war that made my family.

*   *   *

An earlier version of Chapter 2 appeared in *European Journal of International Relations* 7, no. 1 (2001): 63–102. Some material from Chapter 3 was previously published in "Memory, Imagination and War," *History* 87, no. 285 (2002): 61–73. Likewise some material from Chapter 4 previously appeared in "Courting Controversy: International Law, National Norms, and American Nuclear Use" (coauthored with Hélène Lambert), *Review of International Studies* 27, no. 3 (2001): 309–326.

THE NORMS OF WAR

1

The Norms of War

Ideas shape the way humans make war. This is true for both individuals and communities. Ideas of who we are tell us why we should fight. To be sure, wars are fought over material things—the occupation of territory, the acquisition of resources, and to gain access to markets. But polities and people also go to war in order to enact particular identities. States may fight to gain recognition as a great power, a modern polity, or a loyal ally.[1] Equally, men may fight to affirm their place in society as the brave husband, grown-up son, or protective father.[2] Ideas about what is possible and proper also shape the way that wars are fought. Notions of what a professional army looks like can lead the very smallest of states to emulate the greatest military powers. Racist beliefs can lead some enemies to be treated more brutally than others, regardless of operational imperatives. And the selective banning of some military technologies (e.g., chemical weapons) owes far more to human sensitivity than strategic opportunity.

In this book, ideas that prescribe or proscribe behavior are called norms. Norms are beliefs shared by a community about who they are, what the world is like, and given these two things, what they can and should do in given circumstances. Note that these are not private ideas residing in the heads of individuals, but public beliefs that are institutionalized in community discourse, doctrine, policies, and practices.[3] Norms can comprise both identities and worldviews that collectively provide guides for action; at the very least, norms flow from identities and worldviews. A community's understanding of the natural world will determine what they believe to be possible, just as its view of the social world will determine what that community believes to be proper.[4] Norms function to regulate behavior by defining the rules of the game. For example, in ancient times it was perfectly acceptable for victorious armies to butcher captives. Today the rules have (thankfully) changed, and such behavior would be considered abhorrent and illegal. Norms may do more than constrain actors and legitimate action. Norms can also constitute actors

1

and the very possibilities for meaningful action. Thus, ancient armies could call on deities for support in their endeavors. Today, norms of modernity rule out the possibility of divine intervention in war.[5]

This book examines how norms have shaped modern warfare—from the way states organize for war, to how societies mobilize for war, to how wars are waged. It provides a theoretical framework to facilitate a synthetic overview of research on this topic from a range of literatures and disciplines. Thus, we go beyond the confines of political science to explore the work of historians, sociologists, and law scholars. At the same time, this book addresses the political science concern with showing causation. Accordingly, the main body of the book marshals empirical data and historical analysis to identify specific norms, and then uses process tracing to track their causal effect in selected case studies. The picture that emerges from this interdisciplinary overview and historical analysis is one that subverts the neorealist notion that war is a pure brutish test of strength in which beliefs and values have no place. Instead what we find are norms operating at multiple levels to profoundly shape modern military practice.

Of course norms are not new to International Relations (IR). Indeed this past decade has seen the dramatic rise of constructivism as a major US-led research program in the discipline.[6] Around the same time there has been a renaissance in cultural approaches to strategic studies.[7] Particularly striking is the different level of analysis pursued by these two literatures.[8] Constructivists have concentrated on norms operating in a range of policy areas at the level of the international system. Included here are studies on the evolution, diffusion, and impact of international norms of state sovereignty,[9] human rights,[10] as well as norms legitimating and limiting violence in world politics (e.g., international prohibitions against the use of military force by nonstate actors and against assassination as a tool of statecraft).[11] Culturalists, on the other hand, have been mostly concerned with norms located in national and organizational settings.[12] Thus, Colin Gray has argued that US and Soviet nuclear strategy diverged according to differing strategic cultures: the less casualty-sensitive Soviets being more prepared to contemplate unlimited nuclear war.[13] Equally, Elizabeth Kier has contrasted the technophobia in intrawar British Army culture with the technofriendly culture of the Royal Air Force (horse-lovers versus plane-freaks, to put it crudely).[14] Accordingly, constructivists tend to see norms producing system-wide effects in world politics where culturalists find norms shaping uniquely national military styles and organizational ways of war. *The Norms of War* builds on these two literatures and spans these levels of analysis.

This book also imports ideas from three specific literatures that are little used by IR scholars working on military culture. First is sociology's new institutionalism, which examines how norms are institutionalized in transnational professional and policy communities. There is an important difference here with much constructivist work, which tends to focus on international norms that are shared by states; new institutionalists look at norms that are shared by transnational communities operating from and across states (e.g., education, healthcare, and military professionals). New institutionalism thus provides insight into the dynamics of norm diffusion.[15] The second literature is the social and cultural history of warfare.[16] Most of these studies deal with single historical case studies, though some of this work is comparative. Perhaps reflecting mutual antipathy between the disciplines, this literature does not seek to engage IR.[17] However, it does have much to tell us about norm creation, in particular, with regard to the broad range of actors involved in constructing and contesting norms. This provides an important corrective to the narrow focus on elite beliefs that dominates IR scholarship on military culture. Third is public international law, in particular, studies on the development of legal norms intended to limit the occurrence and conduct of war. This literature also examines how norms are institutionalized in convention and custom, as well as revealing much about why states comply with legal norms and the consequences of norm violation.[18] By providing further insight into norm diffusion, creation, and institutionalization, these three literatures help substantiate the broad constructivist project. At the same time each suggests important modifications to IR scholarship that shall be explored in this book.

The general theme of how culture shapes warfare raises a host of questions regarding the origins, development, and impact of norms. Where do norms come from? Who creates them? How are norms institutionalized in international society, and within states and military organizations? Indeed, how do norms interact across these international and national levels in shaping military action? What happens when norms clash—that is to say, when they provide rival prescriptions for action? Equally, what happens when norms are violated? And given that norm violation is (by definition) exceptional, how does normative change occur? IR scholars do not have all the answers here; hence, we must also consider the work of sociologists, social historians, and scholars of international law.

I have, of necessity, narrowed my empirical focus to modern warfare as practiced by Western states. That said, I have tried to cover the main aspects of modern Western warfare. These I consider to be: the rise of Western military organization from the sixteenth century onward; the mass industrialized wars of the twentieth century; the nuclear revolution of the second half of the twentieth century; and the evolving legal framework for humanitarian use of force in the late twentieth century and early twenty-first century. Each chapter in this book introduces a new literature to IR scholarship on culture and war and deals in historical order with one of the above aspects of modern warfare. Chapter 2 covers the sociology of Western military organization, Chapter 3 considers the social and cultural history of mass industrialized war, and Chapter 5 looks at international law and humanitarian war. Chapter 4 does not introduce a new literature as such, but instead draws on and develops a recent constructivist account of the nuclear revolution.

This chapter considers four questions that collectively provide the theoretical framework for the book: (1) What are norms? (2) What are the levels of norm analysis? (3) How do norms work? and (4) How does culture change? It concludes with a discussion on methods and case selection.

Technical Scripts and Moral Codes

Constructivists commonly think of norms as *principled beliefs about moral action*. In part, this is due to a particular constructivist concern with the spread of human rights norms.[19] When it comes to war, constructivists are interested in how moral values impose international restraints on the conduct of war.[20] In contrast, culturalists in strategic studies tend to think of norms as *causal beliefs about effective action*. We noted how culturalists have explored this in studies on national and organizational belief systems regarding the effectiveness of certain forms of military action.[21] Combining these two perspectives, I consider the norms of war to be both *moral codes* and *technical scripts* that, respectively, tell actors what is right and what works in war.[22] Of course, I recognize the possibility for a norm to be both a moral code and a technical script. For instance, Victor Davis Hanson argues that the horrific frontal assaults that were characteristic of hoplite battle in ancient Greece were the embodiment of a belief in the efficiency of this form of warfare (landowning warriors wanted short and decisive battles so they could get back to their farms) combined with a belief in its moral value (the landowning class affirmed their place in the polis through personal valor and sacrifice in bloody battle).[23]

As noted earlier, I try to identify and examine specific norms in this book (see Table 1.1). In Chapter 2, I examine two transnational norms that shape national military action—norms of conventional warfare and civilian supremacy. The former is primarily a technical script for war that prescribes conventional force structures on the grounds of military effectiveness. The latter is a moral code that prescribes military obedience of civilian political leadership on ethical grounds. Chapter 3 explores state-society relations, and the role of collective memory and imagination, in the creation of moral codes and technical scripts for mass industrialized war. It suggests that two norms have made such warfare possible by Western states: a norm of military mobilization rooted in the moral purpose of war, and a norm prescribing the technical effectiveness of machine warfare. Chapter 4 considers cultural beliefs about nuclear war. My particular focus is on the first and largest nuclear power, the United States, and on the evolution and impact of two norms on US practice. First is the "nuclear taboo," a moral code prohibiting nuclear first-use, and second is a norm of countercity targeting, a technical script for nuclear war. Chapter 5 looks at two

Table 1.1   Norms Examined in This Book

Moral Codes	Technical Scripts
Civilian supremacy	Conventional warfare
Military mobilization	Machine warfare
Nuclear taboo	Countercity targeting
Humanitarian intervention	
Humanitarian law	

moral codes for humanity in warfare—norms of humanitarian law and an emerging nonlegal norm of humanitarian intervention.

In this book, I treat military organizations and policy communities as the primary agents of norm creation, enactment, and change. This ontology reflects the concentration of expertise and legitimacy on military matters in these communities. Indeed, I argue in Chapter 2 that norms of conventional warfare and the norm of civilian supremacy are central to the identity of what is a transnational military profession. That is not to say, however, that agency is confined to policy and military elites. As I show in Chapter 3, a range of secondary agents in civil society are also involved in norm work—these include cultural and commercial elites, as well as wider public opinion. In reproducing and even changing norms, military organizations and policy communities often reach out and try to recruit these secondary agents in order to mobilize civil society behind state visions of wars—past, present, and future. The social history of warfare literature strongly suggests that state agents do not always have it their own way; that cultural elites and public opinion can hold their own ideas about war. But, as Chapter 3 also shows, often these secondary agents think and act (and can be made to do so) in accordance with military and policy views about war. In Chapter 4, I find that secondary agents are irrelevant when it comes to nuclear targeting norms, an immensely technical area of military activity that is dominated by military and policy communities. However, cultural elites and public opinion were roped into an attempt by policymakers to transform (i.e., water-down) the nuclear taboo. Chapter 5 does discuss the role of nonstate actors and of transnational processes of legal norm diffusion. However, when it comes to war, international law is still mostly created by states for states.

Levels of Analysis

Obviously, norms exist at multiple levels of analysis—this much is suggested by the earlier discussion. Norms are institutionalized at the systemic level: formally in international law (including international regimes and organizations), as well as in less formal institutions of interstate practice. Norms are also institutionalized in state policy and practice (i.e., in strategic culture), and below the level of the state in military doctrine and activities (i.e., in organizational culture). Two additional levels often missed by IR scholars working on war are transnational and domestic civil society. As explored in Chapter 2, transnational and international norms differ in who and how they target: international norms connect with states, transnational norms connect with actors within states; therefore, international norms operate externally to shape state behavior whereas transnational norms penetrate states to shape their internal workings. Chapter 3 critiques the elite bias in IR theorizing about norms and force in world politics. Strategic culture comprises beliefs shared and practiced by national communities of policy and military elites. However, as suggested earlier, beliefs about war also develop in civil society and these beliefs may also impact on state practice. This points to the need for an expanded concept of strategic culture, one that takes account of broader social relations in the domestic sphere.

If then norms exist at international, transnational, national (broadly conceived), and organizational levels, which norms matter when it comes to the culture of war? Jeffrey Legro raised this question in 1997 in comparing the impact of international legal prohibitions and organizational culture on military restraint during World War II. Empirically, Legro sought to explain variation in military restraint and, therefore, lack of conformity to international law. He concluded that norms institutionalized in organizational culture had more force than those institutionalized in international law. In other words, restraint was a function of consistency between international law and organizational culture. But does it have to be a question of either/or? In fairness to Legro, he was the first to explicitly compare the causal effect of norms at two different levels (up to then, constructivists were busy trying to prove to IR colleagues that norms mattered at all, at whatever level). Legro does end up recognizing the need to examine the interaction of international and domestic norms, and to develop "synthetic cross-level ideational models."[24]

This is the approach taken in this book. Figure 1.1 situates the various levels of analysis. Some norms are carried through transnational networks to penetrate states and impact on military organizations directly. Also above the state are international norms, some of which will be institutionalized in international law. Some of these legal norms connect with states but, as discussed in Chapter 5, some legal norms are also transmitted through transnational networks and connect directly with actors inside states.[25] At the state level is national strategic culture, the production and enactment of which may involve domestic civil society. Finally, below the state are military organizations, whose cultures may be informed by strategic culture as well as by transnational norms. Note that the norm traffic is two-way: military culture may shape national strategic culture as well as vice versa; likewise international norms are constitutive of and constitute state beliefs, form, and practice. According to this pic-

Figure 1.1   Levels of Norm Analysis

ture of cross-level norm activity, states and organizations are "open systems" in that the norms encoded in strategic and organizational culture may originate from outside.[26] Equally, norms may travel out from states and organizations and shape higher-level normative orders. This is represented in Figure 1.1 by broken lines for state and organization boundaries.

Table 1.2 shows the levels of analysis applicable to the norms examined in this book. Chapter 2 examines two transnational norms—conventional warfare and civilian supremacy. It also develops a cross-level ideational model to explain how transnational norms interact with local norms in shaping national military behavior. In Chapter 3, I infer the existence of two generic norms of mass industrialized warfare—military mobilization and machine warfare—from Western trends and discourse of the mid-nineteenth century to mid-twentieth century. However, these norms are national specific, in that they are given specific form by domestic cultural dynamics. I stay within states for Chapter 4, looking at the development of two US nuclear norms. The nuclear taboo may be located in US strategic culture, while the norm of countercity

Table 1.2   Levels of Analysis in This Book

	International	Transnational	National Strategic	Organizational
Chapter 2		Conventional warfare, civilian supremacy		
Chapter 3			Military mobilization, machine warfare	
Chapter 4			Nuclear taboo	Countercity targeting
Chapter 5	Humanitarian law (international and transnational) Humanitarian intervention			

targeting develop within the organizational culture of the US Air Force. In Chapter 5, I examine the institutionalization and impact of international legal norms of humanitarian law (which also have transnational effect), and the evolution of an international norm of humanitarian intervention.

How Norms Work

How do norms take effect? In other words, how do they shape military action? Norms work in two fundamental ways. They may *regulate* actors by proscribing and prescribing action. This is a rationalist perspective, whereby norms operate at a shallow level to channel utility-maximizing activity. For constructivists, norms also go "all the way down" to *constitute* the situations and identities of actors.[27] By providing the rules of the game, norms actually constitute the game itself—in other words, rules give meaning and form to social situations. Some rules also specify roles for players in social games—in this way, norms may define the identity of actors. At this deeper level then, norms shape the ends (i.e., self-interests and preferences) as well as the means of social action.[28] Related to this fundamental ontological distinction are two logics of action and three analytically distinct causal mechanisms (see Table 1.3).

First is the "logic of consequentialism" whereby actors follow norms for instrumental reasons. Here a norm is adhered to either because it benefits the actor or because it is enforced by sanctions.[29] This is the rationalist view of norms as "roadmaps" and binding rules, that is to say, as devices for regulating social interaction.[30] Second is the "logic of appropriateness," whereby actors have been socialized into accepting certain values, routines, and roles that, once internalized, are taken for granted and are acted out automatically.[31] As

Table 1.3 How Norms Cause Action

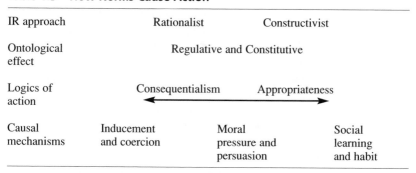

IR approach	Rationalist		Constructivist
Ontological effect	Regulative and Constitutive		
Logics of action	Consequentialism		Appropriateness
Causal mechanisms	Inducement and coercion	Moral pressure and persuasion	Social learning and habit

Martha Finnemore points out, this is a different type of reasoning from that involved in consequentialist action, one involving analogy and metaphor rather than ends and means. "Actors may ask themselves, 'What kind of situation is this?' and 'What am I supposed to do now?' rather than, 'How do I get what I want?'"[32] This then is constructivism's deeper function of norms in defining the identity and social situations of actors.

The logics of appropriateness and consequentialism are not mutually exclusive. As James March and Johan Olsen observe, "any particular action probably involves elements of each."[33] This is shown in Table 1.3. Theoretically and ontologically, these logics are poles apart. At the same time, they comprise a scale of real-world social activity. An actor may follow a norm both because it is the appropriate thing to do and because there is utility in doing so. Indeed, actors can be "skilled users of culture," and may seek to promote norms that confirm some material advantage.[34] Thus, we may expect militaries to favor norms of conventional warfare because these prescribe expensive force structures. Moreover, we must recognize that norms will be most effective when they serve and are supported by material forces.[35] Thus the norm of civilian supremacy will be more secure in mature than emergent democracies, because it is institutionalized in legal and political institutions that create barriers to military disobedience.[36] However, that is not to say that norms require material power to take effect or to exist. The whole point of the logic of appropriateness is to recognize that norms can have a life of their own in the social identities and practices that they create and are therein themselves recreated. Given that both logics may be present in any social action, the empirical question becomes which logic "captures more of the action in a given situation"?[37] Or toward which end of the scale do we plot the social action? These questions may be answered by looking at causal mechanisms.

According to Alexander Wendt, "norms are causal insofar as they regulate behavior."[38] Note that norms can do this through constitutive as well as regulative effects, in that prescriptions and proscriptions for action are attached to identities and social situations. But note also that norms do not provide the motive for action. Put another way by Friedrich Kratochwil, "rules and norms can become causes in that they determine, but only *probabilistically* so, outcomes (decisions)."[39] Actors may still be able to exercise choice within normative injunctions, and may even occasionally choose to ignore norms altogether. Thus, as Kratochwil notes, the use of norms as explanatory variables must contend with "norms remain[ing] valid in spite of their violation in actual practice."[40] This issue is discussed in Chapter 5. For the moment, we need to recognize how norms cause military action, which is to provide moral codes and technical scripts that, assuming there is norm compliance, will channel, constrain, and constitute action. Norms so shape action through three mechanisms: inducement and coercion, moral pressure and persuasion, and social learning and habit.

The role of inducement and coercion is suggested by the logic of consequences. In those cases where norms are protected by material structures, actors' preferences will be manipulated by the promise of payoffs for norm compliance and/or pain for noncompliance.[41] Of course, carrots are unnecessary if the stick is big enough. In such cases where actors have no choice but to comply, inducement is replaced by raw coercion. Inducements and coercion may be exercised through the relations between states, within states in state-society and civil-military relations, and in hierarchical structures within military organizations. Since dominant norms tend to be reflected in material structures, inducement and coercion can prolong norm persistence within defined communities.[42] However, as discussed below, cultural change is possible and does occur even when material structures remain constant.

At the other end of the scale is learning and habit. As suggested by the logic of appropriateness, this is where a community accepts and internalizes the norm in question, and socializes community members into norm adherence. Social networks play an important role in transmitting the content of norms throughout the community.[43] Social learning may be a reiterative process, as incoming members are socialized into community culture. Once norms are fully internalized, they are enacted automatically and embodied in habit.[44]

The third causal mechanism applies when actors seek to advance rival norms, and each uses moral pressure and persuasion to win over the other(s). This can involve negotiation between two or more states over, say, the rules of a trade or arms control regime, or pressure from nongovernmental organizations (NGOs) to get states to internalize and comply with, say, environmental protection or human rights norms. It can also involve a clash of norms within a policy community or military organization, with rival groups mobilizing support within their community for their own norm. This causal mechanism is distinct from coercion and inducement because it is the more persuasive norm and not the more powerful actor that determines the outcome. Hence, the pressure is moral not material (e.g., using shame rather than sanctions) and persuasion rests on the force of argument.[45]

At the same time, any such interaction is bound to be conducted under the shadow of power disparity in one form or another: either in unequal material power between the actors, or in rules embedded in the social situation that produce inequities in social power. This is illustrated in debates in the United Nations (UN) about the normative standing of humanitarian intervention. All states are sovereign equals in the eyes of the UN. Small states can and often do oppose the more powerful states on this issue. But that does not mean that their voice will carry as much weight. Also, the rules of the UN give disproportionate social power to the permanent members of the Security Council (UNSC): the United States, Russia, China, France, and Britain. The UNSC has played a leading role in assigning normative value to the practice of humanitarian intervention. While power is almost always present in social interaction, with this causal mechanism the assumption is that power is not overtly used in an argument over norms. Hence, the outcome is attributed to pressure and persuasion and not coercion and sanctions. This condition will exist when the powerful are not able or willing to force the weaker side to give in. As Neta Crawford points out, coercion is costly and often not as efficient as persuasion (especially in long-term relationships). Hence, she notes, "politics is thick with places where arguments can and must be persuasive."[46]

This causal mechanism is, therefore, located midway between the logics of consequentialism and appropriateness in Table 1.3 in recognition not of the resources of actors (i.e., power disparities) but of their motives. Are actors engaging in argument over norms for strategic or normative reasons? One needs to distinguish here between rhetorical action and truth-seeking argument.[47] Rhetorical action is "the strategic use and exchange of arguments to persuade others to act according to one's preferences."[48] Rhetorical action thus follows the logic of consequences, and actors who engage in it see the situation as a straight battle of ideas. Rhetorical action can be a means for weak actors to win norm battles against more powerful actors. Frank Schimmelfennig has shown how in seeking admission to the European Union (EU) and the North Atlantic Treaty Organization (NATO), the Central and Eastern European states were able to use rhetorical argument to entrap and silence more powerful opponents of EU and NATO enlargement.[49] With truth-seeking argument, "actors try to convince each other to change their causal or principled beliefs in order to reach a reasoned consensus about validity claims." In contrast to rhetorical action, actors engage in argument not to advance self-interests but to reach agreement about the validity of rival norms. Social action here follows the logic of appropriateness, as actors try to figure out what is right as opposed to what will pay off. Thus, in truth-seeking argument, "actors' interests, preferences, and the perceptions of the situation are no longer fixed, but subject to discursive challenges." As Thomas Risse notes, this means "that the participants in a discourse are open to being persuaded by the better argument and that relationships of power and social hierarchies recede in the background."[50] In sum, moral pressure and persuasion can serve strategic and normative goals. Where all actors involved are engaged in truth seeking, this causal mechanism falls under the logic of appropriateness; though it still differs from social learning because norms are being contested. Where all the actors are deploying rhetorical action, this mechanism falls under the logic of consequences. Analytically, it still differs from inducement and coercion provided power is not being exercised to determine the outcome. Empirically, power may be exercised in subtle (even undetectable) ways, and so the two causal mechanisms may run into one another. One final empirical complication we need to recognize is that moral pressure and persuasion may involve a mix of motives, forms of argumentation, and therefore logics of action.

Cultural Change

An understanding of normative change is integral to any complete account of how norms shape social organization and activity. This is evident in causal theorizing about norms and action. The causal mechanisms above explain change (as well as continuity) in normative orders. Coercion and inducement may serve to preserve a norm hierarchy, but equally this mechanism can be used to force cultural change upon a community. Moral pressure and persuasion provide a mechanism for determining the validity of rival norms, in other words, in situations ripe for cultural change. Habit is obviously a mechanism for cultural continuity, as norms are routinely enacted. But social learning provides a mechanism for incremental cultural change, whereby new norms that accord with existing ones are assimilated and learned.

It so happens that the literatures examined in this book all tackle the issue of normative change. Sociological institutionalism explores the growth of culture at the world level, in that many transnational norms and networks have global reach. Normative change occurs both at a global level with the diffusion of transnational norms, and at a local level as national norms are altered to fit or are displaced by transnational norms. The social history of warfare focuses on the development of military culture at the local level. Change is central to these histories as they examine the interplay within and between state authorities and civil society in producing, reproducing, and revising norms of war. International law returns our focus to norms operating at the international level. Two of the main themes that this book explores concerning international law regard change: namely, the role of agency in creating legal norms and the role of norm violation in affecting legal change.

In this section, I want to identify three generic enabling conditions of cultural change, drawing on IR scholarship on norms, military culture, and military innovation: these conditions are norm entrepreneurs, external shock, and personnel change. These literatures suggest that enabling conditions are especially important in situations where cultural change is problematic. In other words, when change is radical in nature—either because it involves replacing one norm with another or even changing a norm hierarchy—cultural change cannot be enforced. That is to say, the community undergoing change does so freely. Coercion and inducement can by itself explain radical cultural change: new norms are backed by force. Equally, there is nothing that remarkable about the social learning of new norms that fit existing normative orders. But moral pressure and persuasion is puzzling: Why should communities freely undertake radical cultural change? This is where the enabling conditions are particularly significant.

Norm Entrepreneurs

Actually norm entrepreneurs are something of a master enabler of cultural change. They pop up in most accounts, regardless of the causal mechanism. Whether normative change is radical or incremental in nature, and associated with power, persuasion, or learning, there is invariably a norm entrepreneur behind it. For constructivists, norm entrepreneurs may be states, intergovernmental organizations (IGOs), NGOs, or individuals working from within states, IGOs, and NGOs.[51] Entrepreneurs as individuals also loom large in the military innovation literature.

Studies on military innovation suggest that an entrepreneur's power or proximity to power is critical to success. The closer entrepreneurs are to the decisionmaking apparatus of the target community, the better placed they will be to communicate and push through new ideas. Better still is if the entrepreneur is in a position of power within the community. For Stephen Rosen successful entrepreneurs are visionary leaders able to mobilize change within their own organizations; here Rosen was countering Barry Posen's view that innovation was led by outsiders—military mavericks backed by civilian leaders.[52] For Kimberly Zisk and Matthew Evangelista, civilian reformers only became effective when they gained access to Soviet defense policy communities in the mid- to late 1980s.[53] In contrast, constructivists focus on the ability of norm entrepreneurs to interpret events, frame the discourse, and construct a new consensus. Constructivists recognize that occupying positions of authority can aid norm entrepreneurs by conferring legitimacy on their cognitive observations and normative pronouncements.[54] In some constructivist accounts, power also matters: the entrepreneurs are reform-minded powerful states.[55] However, many constructivists do not make power or proximity to power a condition of success. For instance, constructivists have produced a number of studies where the norm entrepreneurs have been nongovernmental actors and the target communities are states.[56]

External Shock

Scholars working on military culture uniformly identify external shock to the local normative system—in the form of wars, depressions, and revolutions—as an enabling condition of voluntary, radical cultural change. Shocks of such a profound nature are widely seen as necessary to undermine the legitimacy of existing norms, shift power within communities, and enable cultural entrepreneurs to construct a new consensus around alternative norms.[57] For some scholars, the development of antimilitaristic strategic cultures in postwar Germany and Japan was triggered in this manner by the utter defeat of these states in World War II.[58]

Legro rightly points out that, "We must understand what it is about a 'shock' or event that is likely to undermine an existing orthodoxy and enable a society to reach a new orthodoxy." He goes on to suggest two things. First, "the fit between social expectations (generated by collective ideas) and events": the more unforeseen and/or inexplicable an event is for a cognitive or normative frame, the more undermining it will be for that norm. Second, "whether subsequent experience is socially desirable": events with undesirable effects are more likely to generate support for change than events with desirable outcomes.[59] Legro's useful analysis can be refined by noting that events may also be shocking for their *anticipated* social undesirability. In other words, communities may be shocked into changing their ways of thinking and doing in order to prevent or ameliorate an event anticipated to have disastrous effects. According to Posen, "simple fear of defeat" provides an important motivation for civilian-led military innovation.[60] Aaron Friedberg offers a similar explanation for the creation of instruments of US military power in the face of its antistatist ethos: "periods of accelerated state-building have generally been preceded either by the anticipation or actual onset of war, or by a growing sense of impending domestic economic and social crisis."[61]

Personnel Change

New beliefs and ideas can travel with people into and out of communities. The literature on military innovation suggests that this can result in radical norm change when there is a turnover in key people or in a large portion of the community membership. Failing organizations typically seek to turn things around by bringing in new managers. This is as true in war as in business: thus, the US Navy sought to improve the effectiveness of its submarine fleet during World War II by replacing overcautious submarine commanders with young aggressive officers.[62] Large-scale changes in community membership can also affect cultural change. Zisk notes that preceding Soviet military innovation in the late 1980s, "there was almost a complete turnover in top-level Soviet officers." For Zisk, "such an influx of young officers to top positions and a high level of personnel turnover are bound to bring in people who are receptive to innovative thinking."[63] Naturally, at a national level, personnel change may occur as a consequence of electoral defeat or (in nondemocracies) regime change by other means. This involves not only change in leadership, but also usually large-scale turnover in policymaking personnel.

Putting the Conditions Together

Cultural change is most puzzling when it involves more than social learning and is not backed by inducements or coercion. The literature on military culture identifies external shock as an enabling condition for change under such conditions. However, in itself, external shock does not explain cultural change. Change does not follow automatically in the wake of shock. For this reason, Legro conceives cultural change as a two-stage process: shock-induced cultural collapse followed by consolidation of cultural change. In the absence of consolidation, new norms may not take root and, when the effects of shock have worn off, cultures may change back. The phenomena of transitory cultural change are illustrated in Friedberg's study. He records each crisis-induced state-building episode in the United States as being followed by a period of congressional-enforced state shrinking when the crisis has passed.[64]

What is needed, therefore, is a more dynamic model that restores agency to cultural change. This can be achieved by incorporating the role of norm entrepreneurs and personnel change. Most accounts of shock-induced change assume that shock takes effect by creating political space for entrepreneurs to challenge the existing norm hierarchy. The above discussion suggests that the critical attributes of successful norm entrepreneurs are proximity to the decisionmaking apparatus and effectiveness in framing debate and achieving closure. Changes in personnel may also come about as a direct consequence of external shock (e.g., war losses, resignations/reassignments following organizational failure, or electoral defeat) and this too may be expected to impact on cultural change where there is turnover in key or large numbers of people. These enabling conditions of cultural change are explored in Chapters 2, 4, and 5.

Chapters and Cases

This book seeks to develop our understanding of the relationship between culture and war. Its main purpose is to build on constructivist accounts of war by importing ideas and argument from sociological institutionalism, social history, and international law.[65] Accordingly, I have selected case studies that enable me to apply and develop the ideas borrowed from these non-IR literatures and, by so doing, to illustrate how norms evolve to shape military organization, military mobilization, and military operations. Chapters 2, 4, and 5 have a similar format. In each, two norms are examined using a single case study, and particular attention is paid to identifying cultural causal mechanisms and, where relevant, enabling conditions for cultural change. Chapter 3 adopts a different format. This is because it explores two central themes in the social history of warfare—state-society relations in norm creation and the cultural landscape of the two World Wars—both of which are too complex for my causal theory. If I am to engage this literature I must address these themes. Moreover, I consider these themes to be too important to be omitted from a book on culture and war in the twentieth century. I have, therefore, opted for theoretical eclecticism, as discussed below.

Two specific criteria have also guided case selection in Chapters 2, 4, and 5 (Chapter 3 is different for reasons discussed below). First is the possibility of alternatives to the case outcome, thereby necessitating an explanation as to why things turned out as they did. For example, as Kier argues, that it is pointless claiming that a military's organizational culture shaped its choice of defensive doctrine if it lacked the resources or freedom to chose an offensive doctrine.[66] In all the case studies I examine in these chapters I show that alternative outcomes were physically possible (even if they were "inappropriate" or "unimaginable" for the actors concerned). Second is for the case outcome to present a challenge for rationalist approaches to IR—approaches that assume that the world is populated by rational actors and that action is all about the advancement of self-interest. Neorealism exemplifies this way of looking at the world, focusing on how the structure of the international system creates overriding security imperatives for rational action. In the self-help anarchical world, balancing if not maximizing power is and must be the primary purpose of state activity.[67] Rationalists also look inside states at how military and policy actors manipulate state policy in order to maximize their own organizational autonomy and resource levels.[68] When it comes to the study of war, it seems reasonable to assume that states and militaries will act rationally for the sake of national survival. Precisely for this reason constructivists have been called upon to address "important international puzzles and phenomena and thereby demonstrate the empirical value of their approach."[69] Accordingly, in Chapters 2, 4 and 5, I show why rationalist explanations for case study outcomes are inadequate.

However, with this second criterion we need to recognize that there is a tension between theory and methodology. Addressing empirical puzzles for rationalist approaches makes methodological sense, in terms of validating constructivist scholarship. But theoretically speaking, norm-directed action may involve both logics of consequentialism and appropriateness (as argued in this chapter). Moreover, some norms "prosper" because "they are sponsored by powerful interests."[70] Therefore, a full account of the causal effect of norms must encompass both logics of action and recognize the real-world role of material power in supporting norm hierarchies.[71] An additional risk in concentrating on puzzling behavior is that the constructivist approach will come to be viewed as an "explanation of last resort," that is, "one to be turned to when more concrete factors have been eliminated."[72] This tension is evident in the gap between what Kier says and does. On the one hand, she cautions that "cultural explanations are not about explaining dysfunctional behavior."[73] Yet Kier herself sets out to explain why the French and British armies adopted doctrine that served them poorly on bureaucratic and real battlefields.[74] Accordingly, even though I concentrate on cases that are puzzling for rationalist approaches, I also incorporate power and self-interest in my causal account of how norms work.

Chapter 2 examines how transnational norms shape national military organization by looking at military development in early-twentieth-century Ireland. This is an excellent case for exploring the causal impact of norms of conventional warfare and civilian supremacy, since the Irish Army grew out of a guerrilla force that did not recognize higher civilian authority. Moreover, this case is puzzling. As I show, faced with the threat of invasion by an overwhelming British force, it would have made more strategic sense for the Irish Army to organize for guerrilla warfare in the lead-up to World War II; instead it put up a conventional defense. Civilian supremacy in Ireland is also curious, given that the army had won statehood for Ireland and in return the new civilian government drastically cut army resources.

In Chapter 3, norms of military mobilization are examined by looking at how Germany went to war in 1914 and again in 1939, while norms of machine warfare are considered in the conduct of the US campaign against Japan in World War II. The two world wars represent the zenith of mass industrialized war. And these cases usefully demonstrate how norms are formed from collective memory and imagination, and from the interplay of state and civil society. Chapter 3 differs from the others in that I do not seek to explain the outcomes of my case studies but rather I seek to understand how such outcomes were possible. This involves a different kind of explanatory theory—constitutive as opposed to causal theory. Constitutive theory asks, "What is a thing?" and "How is a thing possible?" whereas causal theory asks, "Why or how did a thing occur?" These theories explain things in different ways—the former by inquiring into the structures by which a thing exists, the latter by identifying the mechanisms or processes that generate a thing.[75] Constitutive theory, therefore, examines the cultural context of military action: how norms function in temporal and spatial settings to make some actions possible and others impossible.[76] The cases in Chapter 3 do raise questions (especially of an ethical kind), albeit ones that can be answered by rationalists as well as constructivists: How could Germany carry out massive invasions of Russia twice in 25 years? How could the United States firebomb Japan's cities to the ground, killing hundreds of thousands of Japanese civilians?

As the oldest and largest nuclear power in the world, the United States is an obvious choice for a case study on norms of nuclear use and nonuse. Chapter 4 also concentrates on the United States for two other reasons. First, because US crisis behavior and US nuclear war planning have both been extensively studied by historians and IR scholars.[77] Thus there is a rich secondary source literature to draw upon. Second, while nuclear norms do not stand outside the Cold War deterrence framework, the nuclear taboo does provide an alternative explanation for nuclear nonuse. Again, the US case is useful for exploring this because the United States enjoyed a period of nuclear monopoly and fought three major wars against nonnuclear opponents. These are all instances where the United States could have used nuclear weapons with little fear of nuclear retaliation. The fact of nonuse by the United States is, therefore, puzzling. Also somewhat baffling is the persistence of the norm of countercity targeting in US Air Force culture, especially when the Soviets had sufficiently built up their nuclear arsenal to destroy US cities in return.

Chapter 5 concentrates on NATO's war with Yugoslavia over the humanitarian crisis in Kosovo in 1999. This is an excellent case to explore norm violation and norm change in international law. Forcible intervention by NATO in the Kosovo crisis was not authorized by the UNSC and so was illegal under international law: hence it violated the nonuse of force and nonintervention norms. However, the intervention was widely seen as responding to an urgent humanitarian imperative, and so this is a crucial test case for the emergence of a new norm of humanitarian intervention. This is also an exceptional case study to examine the impact of norms of humanitarian law. The remarkable thing about humanitarian law is that states have agreed to abide by rules that will restrain them in war (when restraint can be self-defeating); the temptation must be to break such rules in practice. Yet, this case clearly shows the great effort NATO put into complying with humanitarian law. It also shows how humanitarian law operates both at international and transnational levels, by connecting with states and military organizations. Finally, the Kosovo case is puzzling, both in respect of the intervention itself and the restraint exercised by NATO: the intervention cannot be explained in terms of self-interest (it was costly and risky for NATO and promised no material benefit in return); likewise, restraint was exercised in the face of growing strategic imperatives for escalation as the campaign dragged on.

Chapter 6 concludes the book with a discussion of the processes and content of normative change in modern Western warfare.

Notes

1. For a case study of a state going to war to defend its identity as a great power, see Erik Ringmar, *Identity, Interest and Action: A Cultural Explanation of Sweden's In-*

tervention in the Thirty Years War (Cambridge: Cambridge University Press, 1996). For a case study of war in defense of a "loyal ally" identity, see Tim Dunne, "'When the Shooting Starts': Atlanticism in British Security Strategy," *International Affairs* 80, no. 5 (2004): 811–833.

2. Women are almost totally excluded from combat forces. In an exhaustive study of this phenomenon, Joshua Goldstein finds that gender norms function to get men onto the battlefield and keep women off it. Joshua Goldstein, *War and Gender* (Cambridge: Cambridge University Press, 2001).

3. Alexander Wendt, "Constructing International Politics," *International Security* 20, no. 1 (1995): 73–74.

4. Jan Golinski, *Making Natural Knowledge* (Cambridge: Cambridge University Press, 1998); Friedrich V. Kratochwil, *Rules, Norms, and Decisions* (Cambridge: Cambridge University Press, 1989).

5. On warfare in ancient times, see Robert L. O'Connell, *Ride of the Second Horseman* (Oxford: Oxford University Press, 1995); M. Kathryn Brown and Travis W. Stanton (eds.), *Ancient Mesoamerican Warfare* (Lanham, MD: Altamira, 2003).

6. The major work here is Alexander Wendt, *Social Theory of International Politics* (Cambridge: Cambridge University Press, 1999). For literature reviews, see Jeffrey T. Checkel, "The Constructivist Turn in International Relations Theory," *World Politics* 50, no. 2 (1998): 324–348; Ted Hopf, "The Promise of Constructivism in International Relations Theory," *International Security* 23, no. 1 (1998): 171–200; Jeffrey T. Checkel, "Social Constructivisms in Global and European Politics," *Review of International Studies* 30, no. 2 (2002): 229–245.

7. For literature reviews, see Alastair Iain Johnston, "Thinking About Strategic Culture," *International Security* 19, no. 4 (1995): 32–65; Theo Farrell, "Culture and Military Power," *Review of International Studies* 24, no. 3 (1998): 407–416; Jeffrey S. Lantis, "Strategic Culture and National Security Policy," *International Studies Review* 4, no. 3 (2002): 87–114.

8. These two literatures are compared in Theo Farrell, "Constructivist Security Studies: Portrait of a Research Program," *International Studies Review* 4, no. 1 (2002): 50–72.

9. J. Samuel Barkin and Bruce Cronin, "The State and the Nation: Changing Norms and the Rules of Sovereignty in International Relations," *International Organization* 48, no. 1 (1994): 107–130.

10. Audie Klotz, *Norms in International Relations* (Ithaca, NY: Cornell University Press, 1995); Thomas Risse, Stephen C. Ropp, and Kathryn Sikkink (eds.), *The Power of Human Rights* (Cambridge: Cambridge University Press, 1999).

11. Janice Thomson, *Mercenaries, Pirates and Sovereigns* (Princeton, NJ: Princeton University Press, 1994); Ward Thomas, *The Ethics of Destruction* (Ithaca, NY: Cornell University Press, 2001).

12. One recent study contrasts national military culture with the "universial instrumentalist logic of survival in international anarchy." Alan Macmillan, Ken Booth, and Russell Trood, "Strategic Culture," in Ken Booth and Russell Trood (eds.), *Strategic Cultures in the Asia-Pacific Region* (New York: St. Martin's, 1999).

13. Colin S. Gray, *Nuclear Strategy and National Style* (Lanham, MD: Hamilton, 1986).

14. Elizabeth Kier, *Imagining War: French and British Military Doctrine Between the Wars* (Princeton, NJ: Princeton University Press, 1997).

15. Walter W. Powell and Paul J. DiMaggio (eds.), *The New Institutionalism in Organizational Analysis* (Chicago: University of Chicago Press, 1991); W. Richard Scott, John W. Meyer, and Associates, *Institutional Environments and Organizations:*

Structural Complexity and Individualism (Thousand Oaks, CA: Sage, 1994); John W. Meyer, John Boli, George M. Thomas, and Francisco O. Ramirez, "World Society and the Nation-State," *American Journal of Sociology* 193 (1997): 144–181. Few constructivists draw on new institutionalism. For an exception, see Martha Finnemore, "Norms, Culture, and World Politics: Insights from Sociology's Institutionalism," *International Organization* 50 (1996): 325–348.

16. For literature review, see Theo Farrell, "Memory, Imagination and War," *History* 87, no. 285 (2002): 61–73.

17. On relations between these disciplines, see Ian S. Lustick, "History, Historiography and Political Science: Multiple Historical Records and the Problem of Selection Bias," *American Political Science Review* 90, no. 3 (1996): 605–618; Colin Elman and Miriam Fendius Elman (eds.), *Bridges and Boundaries: Historians, Political Scientists and the Study of International Relations* (Cambridge, MA: MIT Press, 2001).

18. Useful overviews include Christian Reus-Smit (ed.), *The Politics of International Law* (Cambridge: Cambridge University Press, 2004); Michael Byers (ed.), *The Role of Law in International Relations: Essays in International Relations and International Law* (Oxford: Oxford University Press, 2000); Rosalyn Higgins, *Problems and Process: International Law and How We Use It* (Oxford: Oxford University Press, 1994).

19. Kotz, *Norms;* Risse, Ropp, and Sikkink, *The Power;* Margaret E. Keck and Kathryn Sikkink, *Activists Beyond Borders* (Ithaca, NY: Cornell University Press, 1996); Rodney Bruce Hall, "Moral Authority as a Power Resource," *International Organization* 51, no. 4 (1997): 591–622.

20. Jeffrey W. Legro, *Cooperation Under Fire: Anglo-German Restraint During World War II* (Ithaca, NY: Cornell University Press, 1995); Richard Price, *The Chemical Weapons Taboo* (Ithaca, NY: Cornell University Press, 1997); Thomas, *The Ethics.*

21. Gray, *Nuclear;* Kier, *Imagining;* Alastair Iain Johnston, *Cultural Realism* (Princeton, NJ: Princeton University Press, 1995).

22. For a study that combines these two understandings of norms, see Neta C. Crawford, *Argument and Change in World Politics* (Cambridge: Cambridge University Press, 2002).

23. Victor Davis Hanson, *The Western Way of War: Infantry Battle in Classical Greece,* 2nd ed. (Los Angeles: University of California Press, 2000).

24. Jeffrey W. Legro, "Which Norms Matter? Revisiting the 'Failure' of Internationalism," *International Organization* 51, no. 1 (1997): 31–63; see also Legro, *Cooperation Under Fire.*

25. Anne-Marie Slaughter, *A New World Order* (Princeton, NJ: Princeton University Press, 2004).

26. W. Richard Scott, *Organizations: Rational, Natural, and Open Systems,* 3rd ed. (Englewood Cliffs, NJ: Prentice Hall, 1992).

27. Wendt, *Social Theory,* pp. 92–138.

28. Kratochwil, *Rules, Norms, and Decisions,* pp. 21–28; Alexander Wendt, "Anarchy Is What States Make of It: The Social Construction of Power Politics," *International Organization* 46, no. 2 (1992): 392–425. See also John R. Searle, *The Social Construction of Social Reality* (New York: Free Press, 1995), pp. 42–51.

29. Robert Axelrod, "An Evolutionary Approach to Norms," *American Political Science Review* 80, no. 4 (1986): 1095–1111; Aaron Widavsky, "Choosing Preferences by Constructing Institutions: A Cultural Theory of Preference Formation," *American Political Science Review* 81, no. 1 (1987): 3–21.

30. Judith Goldstein and Robert O. Keohane (eds.), *Ideas and Foreign Policy: Beliefs, Institutions, and Political Change* (Ithaca, NY: Cornell University Press,

1993); Anthony Arend Clark, *Legal Rules and International Society* (Oxford: Oxford University Press, 1999).

31. James G. March and Johan P. Olsen, *Rediscovering Institutions* (New York: Free Press, 1989).

32. Martha Finnemore, *National Interests in International Society* (Ithaca, NY: Cornell University Press, 1996), p. 29.

33. James G. March and Johan P. Olsen, "The Institutional Dynamics of International Political Orders," *International Organization* 52, no. 4 (1998): 952.

34. Ann Swidler, "Culture in Action: Symbols and Strategies," *American Sociological Review* 51, no. 2 (1986): 273–286.

35. Douglas V. Porpora, "Cultural Rules and Material Relations," *Sociological Theory* 11, no. 2 (1993): 212–229.

36. The importance of such barriers to military disobedience is explored in Peter D. Feaver, *Armed Servants: Agency, Oversight, and Civil-Military Relations* (Cambridge, MA: Harvard University Press, 2003).

37. Thomas Risse, "'Let's Argue!': Communicative Action in World Politics," *International Organization* 54, no. 1 (2000): 18.

38. Wendt, *Social Theory*, p. 82.

39. Friedrich Kratochwil, "The Force of Prescriptions," *International Organization* 38, no. 4 (1984): 705.

40. Ibid., p. 686.

41. Thomas, *The Ethics*, pp. 27–45.

42. G. John Ikenberry and Charles A. Kupchan, "Socialization and Hegemonic Power," *International Organization* 44, no. 3 (1990): 283–315; Ian Hurd, "Legitimacy and Authority in International Politics," *International Organization* 53, no. 2 (1999): 379–408.

43. Joseph Nye, "Nuclear Learning and US-Soviet Security Regimes," *International Organization* 41 (1987): 371–402; Peter M. Haas, "Epistemic Communities and International Policy Coordination," *International Organization* 46 (1992): 1–35.

44. Ted Hopf, *Social Construction of International Politics: Identities and Foreign Policies, Moscow, 1955 and 1999* (Ithaca, NY: Cornell University Press, 2002), pp. 10–16.

45. Risse, "'Let's Argue!'"

46. Neta C. Crawford, *Argument and Change in World Politics: Ethics, Decolonization and Humanitarian Intervention* (Cambridge: Cambridge University Press, 2002), p. 15.

47. This distinction is from Risse, "'Let's Argue!'"

48. Frank Schimmelfennig, *The EU, NATO and the Integration of Europe: Rules and Rhetoric* (Cambridge: Cambridge University Press, 2003), p. 5.

49. Ibid.

50. Risse, "'Let's Argue!'" pp. 7, 9.

51. On the role of states as norm entrepreneurs, see Klotz, *Norms;* Ethan A. Nadelmann, "Global Prohibition Regimes: The Evolution of Norms in International Society," *International Organization* 44, no. 4 (1990): 480–525. On the role of IGOs, see Finnemore, *National Interests.* On NGOs, see Risse, Ropp, and Sikkink, *The Power;* Keck and Sikkink, *Activists;* Ann Marie Clark, *Diplomacy of Conscience: Amnesty International and Changing Human Rights Norms* (Princeton, NJ: Princeton University Press, 2002). Most of these studies also identify individuals as entrepreneurs.

52. Stephen Peter Rosen, *Winning the Next War: Innovation and the Modern Military* (Ithaca, NY: Cornell University Press, 1991); Barry R. Posen, *The Sources of Military Doctrine* (Ithaca, NY: Cornell University Press, 1984).

53. Kimberly Martin Zisk, *Engaging the Enemy* (Princeton, NJ: Princeton University Press, 1993); Matthew Evangelista, *Unarmed Forces* (Ithaca, NY: Cornell University Press, 1999).

54. Andrew P. Cortell and James W. Davis Jr., "Understanding the Domestic Impact of International Norms: A Research Agenda," *International Studies Review* 2, no. 1 (2000): 76.

55. Nadelmann, "Global Prohibition Regimes."

56. Finnemore, *National Interests,* pp. 69–88; Keck and Sikkink, *Activists;* Richard M. Price, "Reversing the Gun Sights: Transnational Civil Society Targets Land Mines," *International Organization* 52, no. 3 (1998): 627–631; Thomas Risse and Kathryn Sikkink, "The Socialization of International Human Rights Norms into Domestic Practices: Introduction," in Thomas Risse, Stephen C. Ropp, and Kathryn Sikkink (eds.), *The Power of Human Rights* (Cambridge: Cambridge University Press, 1999).

57. Deborah D. Avant, "From Mercenaries to Citizen Armies: Explaining Change in the Practice of War," *International Organization* 54, no. 1 (2000): 48–49; Thomas U. Berger, "Norms, Identity, and National Security in Germany and Japan," in Peter J. Katzenstein (ed.), *The Culture of National Security* (New York: Columbia University Press, 1996), pp. 326–327; Duffield, *World Power Forsaken: Political Culture, International Institutions, and German Security Policy After Unification* (Stanford, CA: Stanford University Press, 1998), p. 251; Evangelista, *Unarmed Forces,* p. 7.

58. Peter J. Katzenstein, *Cultural Norms and National Security: Police and Military in Postwar Japan* (Ithaca, NY: Cornell University Press, 1996); Thomas U. Berger, *Cultures of Antimilitarism: National Security in Germany and Japan* (Baltimore: Johns Hopkins University Press, 1998); John S. Duffield, *World Power Forsaken.*

59. Jeffrey W. Legro, "Whence American Internationalism," *International Organization* 54, no. 2 (2000): 263.

60. Posen, *The Sources of Military Doctrine,* p. 77.

61. Aaron L. Friedberg, *In the Shadow of the Garrison State* (Princeton, NJ: Princeton University Press, 2000), p. 19.

62. Rosen, *Winning,* pp. 130–147.

63. Zisk, *Engaging,* pp. 173–174.

64. Friedberg, *In the Shadow,* pp. 30–32.

65. This book does not seek to prove the constructivist approach through competitive theory testing as this has been done in previous studies. See, for example, Katzenstein, *The Culture;* Katzenstein, *Cultural Norms;* Legro, *Cooperation Under Fire;* Kier, *Imagining War;* Johnston, *Cultural Realism;* Duffield, *World Power.* And so this book does not generate and test hypotheses from rival theoretical approaches (though it does critique them at the case study level).

66. Kier, *Imagining War,* p. 37.

67. Kenneth N. Waltz offers the classic neorealist account of states as power balancers in *Theory of International Politics* (Reading, MA: Addison-Wesley, 1979). The most prominent neorealist take on states as power-maximizers is offered in Randall L. Schweller, *Deadly Imbalances: Tripolarity and Hitler's Strategy of World Conquest* (New York: Columbia University Press, 1997); John J. Mearsheimer, *The Tragedy of Great Power Politics* (New York: W. W. Norton, 2001).

68. Graham T. Allison, *The Essence of Decision* (Boston: Little, Brown, 1973); Morton H. Halperin, *Bureaucratic Politics and Foreign Policy* (Washington, DC: Brookings Institution, 1974).

69. Checkel, "The Constructivist Turn," p. 328. A similar call is made in Andreas Hansenclever, Peter Mayer, and Volker Rittberger, *Theories of International Regimes* (Cambridge: Cambridge University Press, 1997), pp. 173–174, 190.

70. Lawrence Freedman, *Deterrence* (Cambridge: Polity, 2004), p. 71.

71. This is emphasized in Margarita H. Petrova, "The End of the Cold War: A Battle or Bridging Gound Between Rationalist and Ideational Approaches in International Relations," *European Journal of International Relations* 9, no. 1 (2003): 147.

72. Eric Herring, "Nuclear Totem and Taboo," paper presented at the British International Studies Association Conference, Leeds, United Kingdom, December 1997, p. 8. Put another way by Michael Barnett: "Research designs that attempt to address the 'irrational' through cultural models inadvertently concede the regularities to more utilitarian models, and thus cultural models get the twigs while these utilitarian models get the trunks." Correspondence with Michael Barnett (1 July 1999).

73. Elizabeth Kier, "Culture and Military Doctrine: France Between the Wars," *International Security* 19, no. 4 (1995): 74.

74. Kier, *Imagining War.*

75. Alexander Wendt, "On Constitution and Causation in International Relations," *Review of International Relations* 24, Special Issue (1998): 101–117.

76. The distinction between culture as a cause and culture as a context of military action is explored in Colin S. Gray, "Strategic Culture as Context: The First Generation of Theory Strikes Back," *Review of International Studies* 25, no. 1 (1999): 49–70.

77. Nuclear war planning of other countries has not been so well studied because scholars have had very limited access to primary source material on this highly sensitive area of state activity. In the US case, scholars have been able to make use of the Freedom of Information Act to obtain declassified material.

2

The Modern Military

Two features characterize the modern military. First is a common template of military organization—modern militaries throughout the world are formed of state-based, standing, standardized, and technologically structured forces. Second is an increasingly common pattern of civil-military relations, as modern militaries throughout the world follow the Western example in submitting to civilian rule. These features are somewhat puzzling. Many states do not require and/or cannot afford conventional force structures, but almost all states have them nonetheless. And why do militaries—particularly in newly democratic states—surrender power to civilians?

In this chapter I explore these questions in the context of a historical case study, namely, the army in postrevolutionary Ireland. Ireland achieved a degree of independence from Britain in 1921, after a 2-year guerrilla campaign by the Irish Republican Army (IRA) against the British authorities. The Irish Army was formed by the leadership of the IRA. Whereas the IRA largely ignored the revolutionary government, the Irish Army completely submitted to harsh civilian rule. Whereas the outnumbered and outgunned IRA relied on unconventional means to defeat the British, the Irish Army prepared a wholly conventional defense in the 1930s against expected invasion by an overwhelming British force. Thus, the Irish case is especially puzzling.

Essentially, I argue that the Irish Army acted according to dominant norms encoded in organizational culture at the time of its birth. Theoretically speaking, what concerns me is how norms held and practiced by military officers shape military choices about organizational structure and strategy, and military responses to civilian policy. I draw on sociology's new institutionalism, which argues that many forms of social organization and state activity are shaped by transnational norms that define professional identity, standards, and conduct. This approach suggests that military officers in different organizations and states may share core beliefs about the identity and appropriate behavior of military professionals. My account of Irish military development concentrates

25

on two such transnational norms of military professionalism: norms of conventional warfare and norms of civilian supremacy. In short, in submitting to civilian control and abandoning unconventional warfare, the new army behaved as it believed a professional army should act and organize itself. As noted in Chapter 1, many culturalist accounts of military behavior have focused on norms that are specific to national communities and military organizations. However, the Irish case demonstrates the inadequacy of cultural accounts of military behavior based solely on concepts of organizational or (national) strategic culture. As I show, the transnational military norms embodied in Irish Army practice were not indigenous to Ireland. For the IRA (the army's predecessor) practiced military sovereignty and unconventional warfare in its fight against the British. Constructivists in IR have concentrated on examining the evolution of international norms and their impact on world politics. However, constructivists have been criticized for failing to show *how* international norms "connect" with local agents.[1] Some constructivists have recently argued that it is only through institutionalization in national policies, laws, and practices that international norms take effect, and that this process is mediated through domestic political culture and interests.[2] This suggests a need for "synthetic cross-level ideational models" to show how systemic and unit-level norms interact to shape military behavior.[3] In this chapter, I close this constructivist-culturalist gap by offering such a model. The Irish case is interesting, not only because it nicely highlights the national impact of international norms, but also because it illustrates shock-induced radical cultural change in action. IRA ideas about unconventional warfare and military supremacy did not survive long in the new Irish Army. This chapter explains why.

Rationalist Theories and Ireland's "Irrational" Army

Two rationalist approaches have dominated the IR literature on military behavior: neorealism and bureaucratic politics. Both have difficulty in explaining why states acquire conventional force structures they can ill-afford nor need, and why militaries obey civilian rule.

Creating an All-Conventional Army

For neorealism, the logic of anarchy drives state practice in military affairs. The competitive nature of the international system generates the imperatives for state action, forcing states to balance power externally through alliance formation and internally through national mobilization and military organization.[4] Neorealism adopts an explicit market analogy in predicting that the need to survive will lead states to organize for war as efficiently as possible. This may involve military innovation by great powers, but lesser powers will rely on emulation of best military practice.[5] Best military practice is determined and observed through success in battle. Thus, "it is the victorious military system of every great war that sets the standard by which all others measure themselves and which acts as the model imitated by all."[6]

At first glance, neorealism appears to provide a powerful theory of military development. States will emulate the militaries of victorious great powers and this will especially occur at times of great need, in particular, following defeat in war. However, there is empirical evidence to suggest that military emulation may occur at times of little need—in particular, following victory in war—and that the model for imitation may be chosen for its familiarity rather than its proven success.[7] With the Irish Army, emulation was driven by desperate need, namely, to form an organization to defeat IRA rebels in the civil war that preceded the formation of the Irish Free State. Lacking the time and expertise to invent their own system of organization, Irish officers decided to adopt a foreign system and after looking around they opted for Britain's system. However, the British model was not chosen for its military success (after all, the British Army had itself failed to crush Irish rebellion) but for its familiarity.[8] Initial emulation of the British Army was arguably instrumental, all the same. The Irish Army did need to quickly adopt a military system so it could get on with fighting the rebels, and the British Army was mostly easily assimilated.

From a neorealist perspective, continued Irish emulation of the British Army should have been driven by security needs. However, the historical record shows otherwise. The Irish Army was literally starved of resources throughout the late 1920s and 1930s by civilian policymakers obsessed with controlling governmental expenditure. The army had little over 5,000 troops and an annual budget of around £1.5 million throughout the 1930s (in comparison to a budget of £11 million in 1924).[9] Fatally underresourced, the Irish Army was in no shape to mount a conventional defense against foreign invasion, which from the mid-1930s onward was expected to come from a Britain desperate to secure Irish ports for its naval campaign in the next great European war. The Intelligence Branch (G-2) of the Irish General Staff warned that the invading British would easily overwhelm and destroy any force that blocked their path into Ireland. G-2 recommended "that badly armed, ill-trained Irish Brigades should [not] be permitted to sit down to be battered up to pulp by vastly superior British forces," and that the Irish Army should instead deter invasion by promising a guerrilla-style campaign of organized resistance that would raise the cost of British military occupation.[10] Organizing along these lines would have involved a serious effort to train and arm the populace. The Irish Army view was that this would not have created an internal security problem. Indeed, as early as 1925, the army chief of staff called for the creation of a reserve force of up to 90,000-strong.[11] Moreover, by 1932, the Republicans who had rebelled against the state in 1922–1923 had already seized power by being elected into government.

Yet such an unconventional defense, which would have drawn on the army's guerrilla warfare heritage, was roundly rejected by the rest of the Irish General Staff. As discussed later in this chapter, army leaders instead pushed ahead in the 1930s with a massive program of modernization and expansion that ultimately failed for lack of funding. By 1940, the predicted threat of a British invasion seemed imminent to the Irish General Staff. However, in preparing to meet this threat, officers in the Plans and Operations Branch (G-1) dismissed (without reason) the earlier recommendations of their colleagues in the Intelligence Branch as having "no practical application" in 1940.[12] Instead, the main body of the Irish Army plunked itself down on the inter-Irish border, and awaited the unwelcome arrival of a vastly superior British force from Northern Ireland.[13]

Even at the time, it was clear that the Irish Army had no hope of repulsing the British invasion force. Against a British force of 80,000, the Irish were able to muster 40,000 troops. At first glance, this is a respectable force ratio from a defender's point of view. But the fact is that the British enjoyed vast superiority in skill and quality. Facing a well-trained British Army was an Irish Army that had undergone a massive and rapid expansion the year before, taking in tens of thousands of raw recruits. The British were also expected to have an advantage of over 10-to-1 in armored fighting vehicles (1,000 versus 73) and an 8-to-1 advantage in artillery (400 versus 51).[14] As one Irish Army planner acknowledged, "in the nature of things unless the enemy blunders badly or we happen to be extremely lucky, the odds are against us."[15] Reports of divisional exercises carried out by the Irish Army in 1942 indicate that it was the Irish who were likely to blunder, and blunder badly. They reveal a catalogue of basic tactical errors by Irish troops that the better-trained and better-equipped British Army would have been able to exploit with devastating effect.[16] With overwhelming British military superiority, preparing a fluid defense that avoided direct military engagement with the main British force (as suggested by G-2) was simply prudent. Indeed, such a strategy would have offered a considerable deterrent to British attack, given that Britain would not have wanted to have five army divisions bogged down in Ireland in the midst of a world war. In short, Irish security would have been better served had the Irish Army modeled themselves on their guerrilla predecessors rather than their once and future enemy.

The organizational politics approach provides one possible explanation for why states acquire military structures they cannot afford and/or do not need. In contrast to neorealism, it presents state practice as the product of incessant bureaucratic warfare.[17] Here it is the competitive nature of the domestic political system that generates the imperatives for organizational action. Military organizations, like other bureaucratic players, will seek to adopt structures and strategies that promise to confer prestige, increase resources, and secure autonomy.[18] This translates into military preferences for more forces, newer equipment, and offensive strategies (which require more resources and military autonomy than defensive strategies).[19]

However, the Irish Army's rejection of a guerrilla-style defense cannot be explained in terms of organizational politics either. Plans for a conventional force posture did not promise to increase army prestige, resources, or autonomy. Officials in the all-powerful Irish Department of Finance were staunchly pro-British (indeed many were former British civil servants) and, seeing little threat from Britain, had consistently refused to fund any expansion and modernization of the army.[20] Finance officials never deviated from their view, stated in 1923, that "a small infantry force well armed and with adequate transport would suffice and that many semi-spectacular services such as the Air Force and Cavalry should be omitted."[21] This was precisely the kind of lightly armed and mobile force called for by the army's Intelligence Branch in the mid-1930s.

One final approach developed by Barry Posen combines neorealism and organizational politics. Posen draws on organization theory to argue that outside intervention is needed to force major change on recalcitrant conservative militaries. Neorealism suggests that states do respond to security imperatives, and Posen sees this as occurring via civilian intervention in military affairs. In essence, worried about impending war or shocked by defeat, civilians force militaries to change their ways.[22] However, a conventional force posture was not forced upon the Irish Army by civilian direction. Civilian policymakers were not all that interested in how the army organized for war; they were only interested in how much it would cost. Indeed, the army had to plead for civilian guidance on defense policy some 3 years after the creation of the Irish Free State. To the extent that policymakers and politicians gave any thought to Irish defense, they harked back to the Anglo-Irish War in envisaging some kind of guerrilla campaign.[23]

Submitting to Civilian Rule

Rationalist IR theories of military behavior are particularly unhelpful in explaining military subservience to civilian rule. Neorealism is a systemic theory and is not designed for looking inside the state. Thus, it is unable to explain the structure of civil-military relations within states. The organization politics approach suggests that militaries will act to increase their resource base and protect their autonomy. However this approach starts from an assumption of military obedience of civilian government, and proceeds to explore how military organizations act to secure their interests within the boundaries of democracy.[24] One variant on this approach, principal-agent theory, has been applied to examine "how institutionally conditioned civilian choices as to the setting up and monitoring of military organizations affect the strategic relationship between civilians and military organizations over time."[25] However, with its emphasis on civilian choice, this model also assumes democratic rule to start with. As will be discussed later, there is a well-developed literature on civil-military relations in military sociology, some of which suggests that overly firm civilian rule may trigger a backlash by militaries seeking to assert their authority and/or defend their resources.[26]

However, the Irish Army did little to resist harsh treatment by the civilian government of the newly formed Irish Free State. This was curious given that Irish statehood had been secured by the army's predecessor, the IRA, in the War of Independence (1919–1921), and defended by the new Irish Army in the civil war that followed (1922–1923). As one leading historian of the Irish Army notes, "in such circumstances one might expect to find the military revered and cosseted by deferential ministers."[27] Instead the Irish government immediately demobilized most of the army (cutting it in size from around 48,000 in 1923 to just over 16,000 in 1924) and reduced army pay. Some officers felt so aggrieved by the government's harsh treatment of them that they mutinied in early 1924. The Irish cabinet used this crisis to force military leaders on the Army Council to resign, despite the fact that the army had, once again, come to the rescue by firmly suppressing mutiny. That the Irish government showed little gratitude, let alone deference, to its army is less puzzling than the Irish Army's failure to stand up for itself. The army chief of staff, General Richard Mulcahy, allowed the government to pass legislation in 1924 that greatly reduced his influence in favor of civilian policymakers and gave Finance officials complete control over army expenditure. In addition to acting against their own organizational interests, military chiefs enforced strict obedience to unpopular civilian policy within disgruntled army ranks.[28]

The point is that army leaders had enough support in their own organization and sympathy from the country at large to resist measures by the government designed to vastly reduce the size and influence of the army. Significantly, the Irish Free State emerged from the civil war without a civilian leader to match the stature of Mulcahy. This war did away with Ireland's two great revolutionary leaders: Éamon de Valera rebelled against the new state, while Michael Collins was killed in action. Those left behind were "a ragbag of obscure lightweights . . . who had come to prominence only when the British were leaving and it was safe to do so." By contrast, Mulcahy enjoyed considerable national status as former chief of staff of the IRA.[29]

The Irish Army undermined its own self-interests by submitting to harsh civilian rule, and state interests by adopting a wholly conventional force posture. This was not the utility-maximizing behavior predicted by rationalist IR theories, and in this sense it acted irrationally. In other words, army behavior was guided by the logic of appropriateness rather than the logic of consequentialism.

Transnational Military Norms: Evolution and Diffusion

I begin this section by discussing new institutionalism, the criticisms of this literature from IR scholars, and how this chapter addresses these criticisms. New institutionalism examines norms that are institutionalized in transnational professional fields. I go on to examine two such transnational norms shared and practiced by military professionals around the world: norms of conventional warfare and norms of civilian supremacy. I then return to constructivist theory to produce a causal model to explain the end point of norm diffusion, that is, how transnational norms actually take root in national settings. I call this process norm transplantation. In other words, how transnational military norms become encoded in the cultures and embodied in the practices of military organizations.

New Institutionalism and Its Critics

There are, in fact, three new institutionalisms. Two come from political science and concentrate on the role of interest-bearing institutions in shaping policy outcomes. These are respectively called historical institutionalism and rational choice institutionalism, and neither concerns us here.[30] The third new institutionalist literature is from sociology and concerns the role of ideational institutions (what are called norms in this book) in creating and expressing policy interests, actors, and outcomes. Of particular interest to us here is the way this literature locates norms in transnational professional networks.

Sociology's new institutionalism treats actors as "open systems," in that the norms encoded in organizational culture and embodied in organizational practice are seen as coming from the environment in which the organization operates.[31] In this way, the environment "penetrate[s] the organization, creating the lens though which actors view the world and the very categories of structure, action, and thought."[32] Norms, in turn, travel out of organization to shape the environment. Thus, organization and environment are mutually constituted. Significantly, these environments are defined in terms of organizational fields that are roughly coterminous with the boundaries of industries or professions. By defining organizational environments in professional and industrial terms, as opposed to national or geographical, new institutionalists focus attention on norms that are, by definition, transnational and increasingly worldwide. As noted above, some new institutionalists place particular emphasis on the role of world cultural models (of Western origin) in shaping global patterns of social organization, such as bureaucracies, states, corporations, and markets.[33]

New institutionalists argue that organizational fields start out displaying considerable diversity, but once a field becomes established "there is an inexorable push toward homogenization."[34] Actors in a particular organizational field gradually develop understandings of appropriate form and behavior. Professionalization is the process whereby these understandings are formed, reinforced, and spread, and thereby organizational fields stake shape. Understandings of organizational form and behavior are legitimated through codification in professional literature and the setting of professional standards, and propagated through profession-based formal education and social networks.[35] As organizations fall into line with the prescriptions that flow from these understandings, a prevailing template for organizing emerges and isomorphism occurs within organizational fields.[36] New institutionalists have produced studies of isomorphism in a range of state-organized activities, including education, environmental protection, and social welfare.[37] By comparison, little has been published on isomorphism in state-organized violence. An important exception here is the work of Dana Eyre and Mark Suchman, who produced the seminal paper on worldwide isomorphism in military organization. This paper, which focused on weapons procurement and drew on new institutionalized theory, was published in a much-cited collection on constructivism in world politics.[38]

New institutionalists probably overplay the scale and depth of worldwide isomorphism. The picture they present of global norms overwhelming local actors leaves little room for agency. Missing is any sense of actors as "strategic users of culture"; after all, actors are not complete "cultural dopes"—at least, not all of the time.[39] Actors may adapt global templates to better suit local sensibilities and imperatives. In other words, global norms may undergo some modification as they become embedded in national settings.[40] When it comes to world culture, what may we expect to find then? At a surface level, we may expect there to be worldwide adherence to global norms. But isomorphism will not be complete. In the process of "localizing" global norms, states may interpret and enact them in slightly different ways and this will result in some variance in national organization and behavior.[41] Consistent with new institutionalism, we may expect such strategic use of culture to be greatest in embryonic and early organizational fields. As professions mature it will be more difficult for organizations to resist the gravitational pull of global norms and to modify well-developed and established norms.

So far, new institutionalists have concentrated on producing correlative studies of the effects of transnational culture. Martha Finnemore points out that the "detailed process-tracing and case study analysis to validate and elaborate the inferences based on correlation are missing." Finnemore argues that this leads new institutionalists to pay insufficient attention to the role of power and politics in their portrayal of "world culture march[ing] effortlessly and facelessly across the globe."[42] Jeffrey Checkel makes a similar complaint about constructivists in IR who, to his mind, "fail to specify diffusion mechanisms and thus cannot offer a causal argument, verified through process tracing, of how norms are transmitted to states and have constitutive effects."[43] This criticism applies to the current institutionalist work on global military isomorphism, including Eyre and Suchman's important study on world culture and the proliferation of conventional weapons, and Ann Hironaka's promising work on the evolution of worldwide "scripts" that define and legitimate reasons for war. Janice Thomson's fascinating history of the rise of state-based monopoly on violence does examine the politics of this process. However, Thomson does not develop a theory of how the norms that delegitimize nonstate-based military actors were diffused and embodied in state action.[44] My theory of norm transplantation provides a causal account of transnational norm diffusion, one that accounts for the role of power and politics. As noted, this chapter also provides detailed case study analysis, that is, of the hapless Irish Army.

The norms that concern me are transnational norms of military professionalism. These are beliefs held by military officers, expressed and codified in military literature, reinforced in military education, and embodied in military practice about how militaries that aspire to be professional should organize themselves and act. I am not referring here to beliefs about specific military practices, precise makeup of military units, or use and usefulness of particular military technologies.[45] Rather, I mean core beliefs that underlie transnational military practice about the fundamental possibilities of professional organization and action. I distinguish between two core beliefs shared by military professionals: norms of conventional warfare and norms of civilian supremacy. The former functions to rule out the possibility for states (including poorer and less threatened states) to *depend* on labor-intensive militarization, irregular military forces, and guerrilla strategies for their external security requirements. The latter operates to severely limit possibilities for military disobedience of civilian authorities. The hypothesized causal impact of transnational norms on military behavior is represented in Table 2.1.

Norms of Conventional Warfare

Norms of conventional warfare prescribe military organizations that are standing, standardized, technologically structured, and state-based. In addition to these core norms are subsidiary norms regarding the precise makeup of con-

Table 2.1   Causal Impacts of Transnational Military Norms

Independent Variable	Dependent Variable	Hypothesized Impact
Norms of conventional warfare	Military choices about strategy and structure	Prohibits reliance on irregular forces and guerrilla strategies
Norms of civilian supremacy	Military responses to civilian policy	Prohibits military disobedience of civilian authorities

ventional militaries. For example, the triservices structure, the basic unit of organization (army divisions, navy fleets, and air force squadrons); functional specialization (logistics, communications, etc.); and the cutting-edge military technologies of the day. In the case of land warfare, roughly speaking, these technologies include: chemical weapons in the 1910s–1920s, mechanized warfare in the 1930s–1940s, nuclear weapons in the 1950s–1960s, electronic systems in the 1970s–1980s, and information technology from the 1990s onward. Organizing for conventional war requires long-term capital investment by states in military structures, personnel, and major weapon systems. The existence of such norms is strongly suggested by the extraordinary worldwide predominance of capital-intensive militarization, quite out of keeping with the differing resource and security circumstances of states.

Most of the 193 states in the world have standing (and standardized) military forces.[46] Only 33 states do not. Many of these are microstates, that is, states in name only. Of the more sizable states, three—Grenada, Haiti, and Panama—had their militaries disbanded following US military intervention. Haiti and Panama, as well as Costa Rica and Gambia, now depend on paramilitary forces for their security.[47] Moreover, 146 have adopted the Western triservice structure of army, navy, and air force. Exceptions include the small Caribbean states of Antigua and Barbuda, Bahamas, Barbados, and Trinidad and Tobago, which do not have air forces. The landlocked African states of Botswana, Burundi, Central African Republic, Chad, Lesotho, Niger, and Rwanda do not have navies (in addition, Gambia and Burundi do not possess air forces). None of the landlocked states in Europe—Armenia, Austria, Bosnia, Czech Republic, Hungary, Luxembourg, Macedonia, Slovakia, Slovenia, and Switzerland—have navies either.[48] These 22 exceptions would support a neorealist explanation for military development: tiny states can ill afford air forces, and landlocked states have no need for navies. The triservice structure also makes sense for the large military powers. There are, however, plenty of puzzling cases of small states that maintain three *independent* services: states such as Ireland, which has an air force but no combat aircraft, and the Democratic Republic of Congo, which has a navy with just four boats.[49] This point is further illustrated in Table 2.2, which lists five states that each have tiny but independent navies and air forces.

The state bias toward technologically structured forces is also very much in evidence. In an empirical study of the ratio of major weapons systems (artillery, armored vehicles, aircraft, etc.) to personnel in all the world's militaries in the late 1980s, Alexander Wendt and Michael Barnett conclude, "most Third World states have sustained levels of military capitalization comparable to all but the most heavily militarized advanced industrialized states."[50] The most recent data support this finding. Table 2.3 shows the level of capital-intensive militarization in 12 African states. These states have been chosen on two criteria: poverty and security. All are relatively poor; that is, none are in the top 100 states for gross national income (GNI).[51] All are rela-

Table 2.2   The Triservice Structure: Puzzling Cases

Country	Army	Navy	Air Force
Benin	4,300	100	150
Cape Verde	1,000	100	< 100
Djibouti	8,000	200	250
Equatorial Guinea	1,100	120	100
Suriname	1,400	240	200

Source: Data from International Institute for Strategic Studies, *The Military Balance, 2003–2004.*
Note: numbers = military personnel.

tively secure, that is, none have faced threat of invasion since independent statehood. Guinea-Bissau and Mali have experienced civil conflict in recent decades, but nothing on the scale witnessed in Angola, the Democratic Republic of Congo, and Mozambique, where rival armies fought for control of the state. Moreover, Benin, Burkina Faso, Ghana, Guinea, Mali, Senegal, and Togo are all members of the Economic Community of West African States—

Table 2.3   Capital-intensive Militarization in Small African States

Country	Gross National Income (world rank)	Defense Expenditures (US$ million)	Defense Expenditures (percentage of GDP)	Army Size	Personnel/ Weapons Ratio
Benin	144	46	1.8	4,300	66/1
Burkina Faso	139	41	1.5	6,400	96/1
Central African Republic	171	20	2.1	1,400	28/1
Gabon	123	75	1.7	3,200	28/1
Ghana	111	30	0.5	5,000	85/1
Guinea	137	57	1.8	8,500	57/1
Guinea-Bissau	203	3	1.6	6,800	59/1
Mali	142	68	2.3	7,350	54/1
Mauritania	175	16	1.7	15,000	90/1
Madagascar	124	45	1.0	12,500	86/1
Senegal	119	65	1.3	11,900	132/1
Togo	161	23	1.8	8,100	66/1
Average of African states	146	41	1.6	7,540	70/1
Average of European powers[a]	4.75	32,180	2.0	140,255	24/1

Sources: Data from International Institute for Strategic Studies, *The Military Balance, 2003–2004;* and World Bank, *World Development Indicators 2004.*
Note: a. France, Germany, Italy, and the United Kingdom.

which is, in effect, a regional security community.[52] In short, none of these 12 African states have the resource levels or security requirements to sustain capital-intensive force structures. Following Wendt and Barnett, I use the ratio number of personnel to major weapon systems as the key indicator of capital-intensive militarization.[53]

Table 2.3 compares the average figures for the 12 African states with those for four European powers—France, Germany, Italy, and the United Kingdom. We may expect these European states to have the resources (if not the requirements) for capital-intensive force structures. Immediately obvious are the wealth differentials (average GNI world rank of 4.75 versus 146 for the 12 African states). Predictably, the European powers spend more on defense, both as a percentage of gross domestic product (GDP) (2.0 percent as opposed to 1.6 percent) and vastly so in terms of US dollars (32.18 billion as opposed to an average of 41 million for the African states). Understandably, the European powers have larger armies (averages equaling 140,255 versus 7,540). The average personnel-to-weapons system ratio for the European powers is also lower than for the small African states (24/1 versus 70/1). However, this final crucial statistic must be interpreted in the context of relative levels of defense expenditure. On average, the European powers spend 78 times as much as the 12 African states, but have only three times as many major weapons systems per soldier.[54] Viewed thus, it becomes apparent just how remarkably capital-intensive are the 12 African armies.[55]

Wendt and Barnett identify labor-intensive militarization as the logical alternative for less developed states. Labor-intensive militarization generates military power "primarily by the mass mobilisation of lightly-armed militias." Such forces compensate for the lack of major weapon systems by "organising for territorial defence and guerrilla warfare, and cultivating ideology to create a highly motivated force."[56] Switzerland illustrates a wealthy state adopting a relatively labor-intensive form of territorial defense: the Swiss Army does have over 3,000 major weapon systems but it also has only 3,300 full-time soldiers—in other words, Swiss defense depends on mobilizing its army of over 300,000 reservists.[57] For poor states, a guerrilla defense is probably the best hope against wealthier aggressors. Empirical evidence suggests that conventional defense in such circumstances is hopeless as the poorer army will lose in a straight clash of arms. In contrast, a guerrilla defense is likely to be successful (provided the aggressor does not wage an unrestrained barbaric counterinsurgency campaign).[58] Labor-intensive militarization may also better serve the interests of those states that are struggling with internal civil conflict. Troops on the ground are far more important than tanks and artillery in waging counterinsurgency operations.[59] This is illustrated by the Colombian Army, which has for many years been waging a counterinsurgency war against left-wing rebels and has a personnel-to-weapons ratio of 353/1. Switzerland and Colombia are exceptions: few states rely on labor-intensive militarization for their defense needs. Even North Vietnam combined large-scale conventional offensives with guerrilla operations in its war with the United States.[60]

Arguably, it is tautological to point to the capital-intensive pattern of global military development as evidence of norms that are supposed to explain such military behavior. However, these correlative indicators of norm-driven global military isomorphism may be triangulated with historical analysis of the development of norms of conventional warfare. Norms of conventional warfare are derived from a Western model of military organization that produced, and was reproduced by, the professionalization of war.[61] This model may be traced back to the introduction of standing and standardized armies in seventeenth-century Europe, which enabled the development of professional skills leading, in turn, to the establishment and emulation of professional standards in warfare.[62] All of this was underpinned by long-term capital investment in state-based military forces in early modern Europe, first by the Dutch, Swedes, and English, and then by the Catholic powers.[63]

The "inexorable push toward homogenization" predicted by new institutionalists, may also be seen in the worldwide spread of this Western military model, the emergence of which was intimately linked to the rise of the modern state. As Charles Tilly famously put it, "war made the state and the state made war."[64] The development of state bureaucracies, scientific knowledge, and mass education in Europe were shaped by, and in turn shaped, the development of the modern military organization.[65] The Western model of modern military organization gained further definition in the mid-eighteenth century, with the invention of army "divisions" by the French, and in the mid-nineteenth century, with the development of the Prussian General Staff system and increasing functional specialization (especially, in logistics and artillery) in a number of European armies. Thus, by the twentieth century, modern armies were all structured into divisions, had specialized corps, and were led by staff officers expert in planning and organization.[66]

The Western military model was imposed by European imperial powers on their colonies, and was voluntarily adopted by extra-European states seeking to resist European expansion, and thereby it spread throughout the world from the eighteenth century onward. However, emulation of Western armies was often imperfect. Developing states tried to be "strategic users of culture," and initially just took those bits of the Western military model that they fancied. There were also material obstacles to perfect emulation: developing states generally lacked sufficiently skilled populations to man Western-style armies, and were reluctant to bear the political and financial costs necessary to fundamentally transform their militaries along Western lines. Military emulation in eighteenth century–nineteenth century India combined colonial imposition and voluntary importation.[67] The first states outside of India to adopt the Western military model were Egypt and the Ottoman Empire in the early nineteenth century. In both cases, transformation was only possible when the existing military elites were replaced and brand new armies were raised. Egypt's new army was very well equipped with modern weaponry and received French military training, but it lacked the skill and discipline of a European army (and indeed, was decisively defeated by the British in 1882). The Ottoman sultan, Mahmud II, wanted Western military technology but not ideas: he distrusted Western military advisers and did not let his army maneuver for fear of mutiny. In contrast to the Egyptians and Ottomans, Japan was far more successful in achieving complete emulation of the Western military model: more precisely, emulation of the German Army and British Royal Navy. This was because it was better prepared—culturally, politically, and financially—to undertake necessary fundamental military reforms.[68]

Professionalization of the officer corps played an important part in this isomorphic process, and continues to do so. The military revolution in seventeenth-century Europe professionalized war for soldiers, but not for their officers. Officers continued to be nobles and mercenaries. Professionalization of the officer class only occurred over the next two centuries. By the end of the nineteenth century, the officer class throughout Europe—with Prussia, France, and Britain leading the way—and in the United States had become fully professionalized, with entry and advancement by commission and social class being replaced by merit and competence.[69] Professionalization of the officer class led to the worldwide institutionalization of collective beliefs about appropriate military forms and practices. Professionalization remains a central mechanism whereby norms of conventional warfare are diffused worldwide and reproduced by the militaries of developing states. In practical terms, this diffusion process involves officers being sent to be trained in foreign military academies, and foreign military advisers, military literature, and equipment being received.[70] Many developed states (the United Kingdom, Germany, France, and Canada included) run schemes to educate foreign military officers but the biggest exporter of professional military knowledge is, by a long shot, the United States. The US International Military Education and Training (IMET) program has provided military instruction to 98,000 students from 105 countries between 1976 (when IMET was founded) and 1994. The global scale and reach of the IMET is simply unprecedented.[71]

Chris Demchak has found evidence of accelerated worldwide emulation of the latest variant on this Western model, namely, "the highly electronic, precision-guided military under construction by the United States in its modernization program." In short, "the US Revolution in Military Affairs is driving the images of what 'modern' means." She notes how "extraordinary" it is "for so many distinctly different defense leaders to espouse so similar vision of what a future 'modern' military would entail." According to Demchak, a "process has accelerated among the world's militaries especially [since 1995], redefining the taken-for-granted minimum in military capabilities to mean intensive use of information technologies (IT) and precision munitions." She produces evidence of many nations, such as Burma and Botswana, that are planning to modernize along US military lines, despite the fact that "they have, even in worst case scenarios, few sophisticated enemies and suffer from pressing economic problems." Demchak concludes that "the spread of modernization has no readily available explanation other than a broad structuring of the global community via a widening consensus on what constitutes a modern military."[72]

One hundred thirty new states have emerged since 1945. It is hard to imagine that all of them have the resources and requirements to undertake capital-intensive militarization. And yet, as I have already noted, almost all states in the world have standing and standardized armies based around major weapon systems. Many are now seeking to emulate the most technologically advanced military force in the world, namely, that of the United States. It is through professionalization of the militaries in these new states—whereby officers are sent to be trained in foreign military academies, and foreign military advisers, literature, and equipment are received—that the Western military model has taken root and is perpetuated.

Norms of Civilian Supremacy

The development of Western democracy has depended on military recognition of civilian supremacy. This norm is expressed through military nonintervention in domestic politics. By political intervention, I do not mean seeking to influence civilian government through normal constitutional channels or in collusion with actors within government for the purpose of shaping national security policy. Such behavior is the stuff of organizational politics, consistent with the concept of civilian supremacy, and, therefore, legitimate within democracies. Political intervention refers to the use or threat of violence for the purpose of replacing the policies or members of a civilian government. Taken to extremes, it can result in the supplanting of the entire civilian government in a military coup. Between the legitimate practice of exercising political influence and illegitimate political intervention is a gray area whereby the military may seek to blackmail the civilian government into changing policy. When this involves threats of violence, it must be treated as political intervention; when it involves threats of noncooperation, it may be considered as legitimate exercising of political influence depending on circumstances (e.g., where the military are seeking to reverse an illegal or unconstitutional civilian policy).[73]

In his classic study, *The Soldier and the State,* Samuel Huntington sees the withdrawal of the military from politics as a direct consequence of the rise of military professionalism. Huntington argues that military professionalism depends on the military maintaining a shared technical competence, a high sense of social responsibility, and a corporate identity, which distinguishes officers from civilians. This civilian-military distinction leads officers to concentrate on the business of war and leave government to the civilians. Thus, military professionalism produces and perpetuates norms of civilian supremacy.[74]

Huntington's conception of professionalism is problematic. For a start, by including social responsibility to a client, in this case the government, this definition of professionalism could lead to tautological generalizations when it is used to explain military nonintervention. This problem is easily rectified by excluding social responsibility, and emphasizing technical competence and distinct corporateness in the definition of military professionalism.[75] However, when professionalism is defined in these terms, some scholars argue, it may actually fuel military intervention in domestic politics. For Samuel Finer, this may occur should professionalism lead the military to see themselves as servants of the state rather than of the government, should civilians ignore military expertise, and/or should the civilian authorities seek to use the military for domestic political purposes. In addition, Eric Nordlinger argues that professionalism may lead the military to consider themselves better qualified to govern the state than incompetent or corrupt political elites. In a recent study on civil-military relations in Latin America, Samuel Fitch finds that military professionalization has affected the pattern but not the propensity for military intervention in politics: intervention has become more institutionalized but no less likely.[76]

Many of these scholars look at external factors in seeking to explain political intervention (or lack thereof) by the military. They see civilian action as providing the incentives and opportunities for military intervention in politics. Thus, firm civilian rule can lead to a military backlash. Equally, the military may intervene to fill a political vacuum created by weak civilian government. In a later work, Huntington, too, seems to have shifted to this position, finding no correlation between the level of foreign military training and political intervention by militaries in developing states. He concludes that "the most important causes of military intervention . . . reflect not the social and organizational characteristics of the military establishment but the political and institutional structure of the society."[77]

But ignoring the characteristics of the military is not satisfactory either. Because they are armed, what the military think does matter. As Fitch rightly argues, "military beliefs about their political role are thus central to the conflict over alternative models of civil-military relations."[78] Similarly, in a study of Russian civil-military relations in the 1990s, Brian Taylor concludes that "the most important obstacle [to military intervention in politics] has been the continuing commitment to a norm of civilian supremacy in the Russian officer corps."[79] How else are we to explain nonintervention in cases where the military have reason and are able to intervene in domestic politics? As we shall see, the army in postrevolutionary Ireland represents just such a case. Clearly, sometimes professionalism does produce military restraint.[80]

Crucial here is the distinction, originally missed by Huntington, between professionalization as process and professional norms as content. In some cases, when a military professionalizes it adopts norms of civilian supremacy as part of its professional identity and practice. Just as, in some cases, it does not. Established militaries may also change their professional identities over time so as to encompass a normative prohibition on political intervention (e.g., Russia) or even to exclude previously accepted norms of civilian supremacy (as happened in post–World War II Latin America).

Again, the existence of this norm is suggested by transnational military practice. The spread of democracy throughout the Western world from the nineteenth century onward rested on military subservience to civilian rule. In many cases, this norm was not expressed in law but rather was shaped by circumstances often peculiar to the state in question. For instance, in Britain it was fostered by a system that relied on retarding the emergence of a separate officer class, whereas in the United States it grew out of the military's largely self-imposed isolation from society in post–Civil War America. In both cases, the constitutional power-sharing arrangement between head of state and legislature gave plenty of scope for military intervention in politics. Thus, norms of civilian supremacy emerged despite, and not because of, the overarching legal framework.[81]

This picture of transnational norms growing from a variety of national roots is wholly consistent with new institutionalist and constructivist approaches. Just as norms of conventional warfare developed from circumstances peculiar to certain European states in the seventeenth century, so norms of civilian obedience owe their origins to various national historical experiences. In both cases, these norms were homogenized and institutionalized in a transnational military field, and were spread through interstate emulation of professional military practices. For most of the postwar period, military intervention in domestic politics was the norm in non-Western states just as nonintervention was the norm in the West. All this has changed with the recent wave of democratization. In his explanation for the transition of some 40 states from authoritarianism to democracy, Huntington emphasizes the "broad diffusion and acceptance of the norms of military professionalism and civilian control by militaries around the world."[82]

In conclusion, it should be noted that transnational military norms provide cognitive and normative frames that are *history contingent* in two senses. First, there is nothing natural, in the Darwinian sense, about the evolution of norms of conventional warfare and civilian supremacy. They did not evolve by trial and error as the intrinsically "best" way for militaries to organize and act, but rather they are the result of an ongoing process of culturally framed collective learning and social interaction; within the transnational military sector as a whole, this process stretches back centuries.[83] Second, the content and application of these norms have evolved over time. For instance, where standardization of conventional armies once meant common weapons, munitions, and uniforms, it now means integrated command, operations, and logistics. There is also a sense in which these norms have strengthened in application over time, both in particular cases and across the world.[84] Where military doctrine and practice in revolutionary China once placed as much emphasis on "people's war" as on conventional warfare, China is now bent on acquiring modern regular forces.[85] Overall, norms of conventional warfare seem to have gained almost universal application with the spread of the Western state form, from the sixteenth century onward. Equally, the successive waves of democratization in the latter half of the twentieth century are suggestive of an ever greater international diffusion of norms of civilian supremacy.

Transplanting Norms

How do these transnational military norms spread and take effect around the world? My particular concern here is with the end point of the norm diffusion process; that is to say, the empowerment of transnational norms in new national and organizational contexts, or what I call *norm transplantation*. Constructivist scholars in IR have recently begun to explicitly examine the modes and methods of norm diffusion in the international system. I draw on this literature to identify the context, process, and mechanism for norm transplantation.

First, however, how do we know when norm transplantation has occurred? We may use Andrew Cortell and James Davis's concept of "norm salience" to investigate when transplantation has occurred. "When [an international] norm is salient in a particular [national] discourse, its invocation by relevant actors legitimates a particular behavior or action, creating a prima facie obligation, and thereby calling into question or de-legitimating alternative choices." They suggest a threefold way of measuring norm salience through the international norm's appearance in domestic political discourse, domestic institutions (procedures and law), and state policies. Of the three measures, they prioritize political discourse as it may be expected to precede institutional and policy change, and because it can provide insights into how norms shape "nonevents" (paths not taken). The extent to which an international norm appears in discourse, institutions, and policy, and the degree of conditionality attached to them, determines whether the norm has high, moderate, low, or no salience.[86]

As I am interested in how the military profession conceives itself, my main concern is with *military* beliefs about strategy and civil-military relations. Thus, my Irish case study focuses on the organizational cultures of the IRA and the Irish Army. In measuring norm salience, I look for evidence of norms of conventional warfare in Irish Army discourse, training (which I take to be an army institution), and policy (especially on weapons procurement). Later on in this chapter, I draw on recent historiography to construct a picture of IRA beliefs and practices. I do likewise for the Irish Army, this time drawing on a wealth of primary source documents—training manuals, professional journals, planning documents—to supplement the limited range of secondary source materials. At the same time, I locate IRA and army norms within the broader political culture of Ireland, and I do this by examining domestic discourse, administrative procedures, national law, and state policies. At both levels of analysis, organizational and national cultures, I assume the possible existence of dichotomous normative structures. In such circumstances, the culture of the community in question (the benchmark for measuring transnational norm salience) is defined by a dominant set of norms, while challenging (sometimes dormant) norms provide possibilities for subversive cultural change.

For Jeffrey Checkel, "the degree of 'cultural match' between global norms and domestic practice will be key in determining the pattern and degree of diffusion." He notes that "diffusion is more rapid when a cultural match exists between a systemic norm and a target country, in other words, where it resonates with historically constructed domestic norms."[87] In our terms: norms of conventional warfare may suit or offend indigenous strategic norms; and local political culture may be consistent or in conflict with the transnational norm of civilian supremacy. Studies on strategic culture suggest that common national circumstances and experience can lead a national community of actors to construct and practice shared military beliefs.[88] Since "the poor and weak and peripheral [tend to] copy the rich and strong and central," transnational professional norms are most likely to reflect the strategic culture of developed states and have the potential to be inconsistent with the strategic culture of developing states.[89] My account of the rise of the modern military suggests that this has certainly been the case with norms of conventional warfare. Studies on civil-military relations suggest that local political culture is crucial to the empowerment of the norm of civilian supremacy.[90] This point is emphasized by Finer, who argues that the "levels to which the military press their intervention (running in our terms from legitimate political influence to illegitimate political intervention) are related to the level of political culture of their society."[91] His basic point is that local political culture may help or hinder the transplantation of the norm of civilian supremacy in new states. Checkel points out that "cultural match is not simply a dichotomous variable (yes, one has it or not): rather, it scales along a spectrum" running from a positive to negative match.[92] For instance, in the Irish case study examined below, I look for consistency between transnational norms of military professionalism and IRA culture. I do not aim to precisely plot the degree of consistency between transnational and national norms, but rather seek to determine whether they mostly match or mostly clash with each other.

Norm transplantation may involve nesting transnational norms alongside local norms in existing cultural structures. When the new norms match existing ones, the former may be "grafted" onto the latter.[93] Note that norm grafting may include some modification of the transnational norm by norm entrepreneurs in order to make it match local norms: in this way, transnational norms may undergo some "localization." When transnational norms clash with local norms, transplantation involves the former pushing the latter out of the cultural nest. In such situations, localization is not possible, as no amount of modification will disguise the fact that the transnational norm challenges local culture. Put another way, norm grafting "supplements, rather than supplant[s] an existing norm hierarchy."[94] As we shall see in the Irish case study, the transnational norms directly challenged the existing strategic and political culture of revolutionary Ireland. Norm transplantation involved supplanting these norms within new transnational ones in the organizational culture of the new Irish Army.

We may see the norm grafting and norm displacement processes at play in the evolution and spread of the Western military model in the early modern world. This model of state-funded, standing armies originated in the Dutch Republic at the turn of the sixteenth century. It was rooted in the notion that ordinary men could be trained and disciplined for war, and depended upon to serve the state. Ideas of discipline and duty were central to Protestantism, and the idea that ordinary men could be educated in technical subjects grew out of Dutch humanism. Critical to the Europe-wide spread of the Dutch military model was Sweden's adoption of it. The Dutch seldom went into battle in the early seventeenth century, and so it was left up to the reformed Swedish Army to dramatically demonstrate the advances of the Dutch model through a string of impressive victories in the Thirty Years War. Norm grafting helps us understand why the Swedes adopted the Dutch model: Dutch ideals of discipline, duty, and education found a receptive home in Sweden because it was a Protestant state, whose bureaucrats were educated in Dutch humanism.[95] As we noted earlier, the spread of what became the European military model to the extra-European world did not go so smoothly. There were successive attempts at norm grafting by the Ottoman rulers. Sultan Selim III tried to raise a Western-style army, but this failed in the face of stiff resistance by the traditional Ottoman warrior elite, the Janissaries. His successor, Mahmud II, got rid of the Janissaries, but he was not prepared to see a professional force develop in its place, for fear of a coup; thus, his new army was Western in appearance but not in attitude. In both cases, the sultans were unable to "localize" transnational military norms because these norms were completely at odds with local military culture. In contrast, Japan successfully adopted the Western military model in the late nineteenth century because the Japanese feudal military system was dismantled and dumped in favor of the Western one. Japanese warlords did experiment with Western military methods from 1853 to 1871. But the restoration of the Japanese emperor put an end to any attempt at norm localization. The emperor proceeded straight to norm displacement. Indeed, it was very much in his interest to adopt the Western military model; he needed a state-based, standing army in his struggle against the warlords and their samurai.[96]

There are three basic mechanisms for norm transplantation. These are the same three causal mechanisms for culture in military action: coercion and inducement, moral pressure and persuasion, and social learning.[97] In practice, norm transplantation is likely to proceed via two or more mechanisms. Power confers both coercive capabilities and legitimacy.[98] A target community that is coerced into complying with transnational norms may in time be socialized into accepting these norms and internalize them.[99] Similarly, Martha Finnemore and Kathryn Sikkink suggest that norms have a life cycle in which moral pressure and persuasion naturally lead to social learning. They argue that once sufficient support has been mobilized within the target community for a new norm, it crosses a tipping point, after which it is widely accepted and learned by the rest of the community: a process they call "norm cascade."[100] In contrast, Thomas Risse and Kathryn Sikkink suggest that social learning and moral pressure occur simultaneously. Actors learn about new norms in the very process of resisting them, and, as this resistance is overcome, so learning proceeds in pace.[101] Generally speaking, we may expect the primary mechanism of norm transplantation to be determined by context. In cases of cultural match, it will be social learning because the target community will be receptive to new transnational norms, and their adoption merely involves additions or adaptations to existing local norms. In cases of cultural clash, the primary mechanism is likely to be either coercion or, where the transnational norm is not enforced by powerful sanctions, moral pressure and persuasion: such leverage is necessary because the new norms contradict and threaten to replace existing community beliefs and practice.

We may distill two basic patterns of norm transplantation—one incremental, the other radical—from the above discussion (see Table 2.4). The incremental form of norm transplantation involves grafting new transnational

Table 2.4   Patterns of Norm Transplantation

Pattern	Context	Process	Primary Mechanism	Social Networks	Necessary Conditions
Incremental	Cultural match	Norm grafting	Social learning	Transmitting content	None
Radical	Cultural clash	Norm displacement	Coercion; political mobilization	Not important; mobilizing support	Power hierarchy; effective sanctions; shock and effective entrepreneurial and/or personnel change

norms onto existing local norm hierarchies. This requires social learning of these new norms by the target community, with content of transnational norms being communicated via a social network. Here there is nothing much to explain. Norm transplantation is uncontroversial and uncontested. As Cortell and Davis argue, "when such a cultural match exists, domestic actors are likely to treat the international norms as a given, instinctively recognizing the obligations associated with the norm. Domestic salience under such conditions is *automatic*."[102] The radical form of norm transplantation is an altogether different matter. It requires displacement of local norms by transnational norms, involving a much more profound cultural change than norm grafting. This raises the question of what causes norm displacement.

Two possible mechanisms have been identified. The first is coercion by an outside agency in forcing the target community to buckle under and comply with the new norm. Here we need to look for evidence of such coercive power being exercised in some way—either through power hierarchies or sanctions. The second mechanism is a campaign involving moral pressure and persuasion that is likely to be controversial and contested. Here we are talking about a process of radical cultural change as identified in Chapter 1, and we need to look for evidence of the three enabling conditions for such change: external shock, effective norm entrepreneurs, and personnel turnover.

The Making of a Modern Irish Army

How did Ireland end up with a modern army? Put another way, how did transnational norms come to shape Irish military development? As it happens, military and political leaders of the Irish Republican movement attempted to socialize the IRA into norms of conventional warfare and norms of civilian supremacy. This effort at radical norm transplantation failed because there was nothing to shock the IRA into abandoning its own norms of unconventional warfare and norms of military sovereignty. Norm transplantation succeeded in postrevolutionary Ireland when the new state was plunged into civil war. The struggle to defend the new state against IRA rebels produced the necessary shock, which, combined with large-scale personnel change and effective entrepreneurial leadership, mobilized support for the new norms.

Cultural Clash in Revolutionary Ireland

Initially, transnational norms of military professionalism clashed with the strategic and political norms of revolutionary Ireland (the period from 1916 to 1921). The IRA did not recognize civilian supremacy, and its field units did not practice conventional warfare.

The IRA considered themselves to be a moral elite who, by their struggle and sacrifice, had earned the right to govern Ireland. These themes of heroic struggle and blood sacrifice may be traced in Irish Republican mythology back to the Easter Rising of 1916, which was launched by Irish rebels in Dublin against impossible odds in order to ignite a revolutionary impulse in the Irish people.[103] The IRA was also elitist in attitude, in part, because it was elitist in membership. Ireland was predominately rural, working class, and landed. IRA members were mostly young, urban, skilled, middle-class men who were unmarried, unpropertied, and socially mobile.[104] As an elitist organization, the IRA did not always enjoy popular support. Indeed, often public support was given reluctantly, if not under the barrel of a gun.[105] In addition, the IRA financed and fought their war independent of political control. The first Dáil (Irish parliament), set up in 1918 during the revolutionary struggle against Britain, and the first Irish minister of defense were largely ignored by the IRA. Indeed, IRA members resisted taking an oath of loyalty to the Dáil that the minister of defense sought to impose on them and, in return, the Dáil did not take responsibility for IRA actions until 1921.[106] Since there was only mixed support for the Republican cause throughout Ireland, it is small wonder that the IRA distrusted the ordinary Irish voter.[107] Equally, it is not surprising that "the guerrillas thought of themselves as sovereign," since "they had organized and armed themselves and paid their own way."[108]

Ironically, the Irish rebels who rose up in 1916 wore military uniforms and acted like regular soldiers. This was their undoing: the British had little difficulty in locating the rebels and blasting them out of their static defensive positions. The Anglo-Irish War was a whole different ball game. The IRA were harder to find because many were part-timers who blended easily into the populace, while full-timers in IRA Active Service Units formed highly mobile "flying columns." Instead of directly engaging the British military, IRA units favored assassination, sniper attacks, and hit-and-run raids. Notwithstanding this mix of unconventional units and tactics, the IRA General Staff attempted to professionalize the organization by establishing standards of dress, conduct, training, planning, and operations. In so doing, it promoted military practices more closely associated with conventional (rather than guerrilla) armies, such as the Close Order Drill.[109] Driving this was a norm entrepreneur, in the shape of General Mulcahy. As chief of staff, Mulcahy was particularly concerned with developing a professional officer corps for the IRA. Mulcahy's own commitment to creating a professional army would have been forged by his experience in the Irish Volunteers, the predecessor of the IRA. Between 1913 and 1916, the Irish Volunteers were the military wing of the nationalist movement. The purpose of the Volunteers was to visibly demonstrate the nationalist commitment to achieving self-governance, and to this end they self-consciously adopted the appearance of a regular army. At this stage, the idea was to impress the British, not to fight them. Indeed, it was a splinter group of the Volunteers that had launched the 1916 uprising. The Volunteers reorganized themselves in British prisons following 1916, and in 1917 Mulcahy was appointed director of training for the Volunteers.[110] From this position, Mulcahy could exert most influence over the organization by turning Volunteers into professional soldiers. The mechanism for exerting centralized control became even more important to Mulcahy when he assumed command of the IRA as it drifted into war with the British authorities.[111] Accordingly, he ordered all IRA field divisions to set up training camps for the purpose of providing uniform training for IRA officers, as laid down by General Headquarters (GHQ).[112] The volume of directives flowing from IRA GHQ in Dublin out to field units certainly lent the impression of a unified and cohesive fighting organization.[113] In reality, however, the responsiveness of IRA field units to GHQ directives varied greatly from unit to unit, and from directive to directive. Certainly, nothing like a standard officer corps was achieved. In many cases units kept the incompetent and lazy officers they had elected precisely because these officers kept their units out of action. As well, the most militarily active and hard-pressed IRA field units in the south and west of Ireland were also unresponsive to GHQ direction because they were resentful of the lack of material support from Dublin.[114]

The process of norm transplantation in revolutionary Ireland was one of failed rhetorical action. Coercion did not apply because there was no power hierarchy through which the political leadership of the Republican movement and the military leadership of the IRA could act. Nor were there any sanctions that could be imposed on IRA field units for ignoring civilian and military direction from Dublin. Instead, the Dáil and the minister of defense attempted to persuade the IRA to recognize civilian supremacy. Equally, the IRA General Staff formed the social network through which pressure was exerted on IRA field units to adopt and comply with professional military norms. In both cases, this action was one of rhetorical action, not truth-seeking argument. Republican civilian leaders were not prepared to concede on the principle of civilian supremacy, just as the IRA General Staff were totally committed to turning their organization into a professional army. This effort at rhetorical action failed because the Dáil was not taken seriously by the IRA leadership, and IRA field units were either not bothered or too busy to professionalize themselves along the lines of conventional armies. And there was nothing to shock them into changing their ways.

Radical Norm Transplantation in Independent Ireland

In contrast to the IRA, the army of the Irish Free State practiced norms of civilian supremacy and conventional warfare. The norm of civilian supremacy led army leaders to accept unfair and harsh treatment by the civilian government. Norms of conventional warfare led the army to adhere to a wholly conventional force posture in circumstances that strongly suggested the efficiency of an unconventional strategy and force structure. The pressure for cultural change came from the same sources in Free State Ireland as in revolutionary Ireland: civilians sought to impose norms of civilian supremacy on the new army, while the army General Staff promoted norms of conventional warfare within their own organization. Only this time, they succeeded.

The national political discourse of postrevolutionary Ireland shows a firm belief in the norm of civilian supremacy. Typical of the dichotomous structure of most cultural systems, Irish political culture contained two traditions: one revolutionary, the other constitutional. Clumsy British reprisals following the failed uprising of 1916 reinforced public support for the revolutionary tradition, and with it the IRA. With statehood, however, the constitutional tradition reasserted itself once again, leading to the creation of constitutional democracy in Ireland.[115] The government was quick to institutionalize civilian control of the army in administrative procedures and national law. From 1922 onward, the army had to first seek permission from the Department of Finance before spending any money (even on something as minor as a couple of extra telephone lines) or making any appointments. This procedure was encoded in the Ministers and Secretaries Act of 1924. This act also emasculated the army leadership in a number of other ways. It designated the minister of defense "commander in chief" of the army, and made the three other senior army generals directly accountable to the minister instead of to the army chief of staff. Furthermore, it limited the army chief of staff to a 3-year term of office; as a result there were a dozen chiefs of staff in the first 35 years of the Irish state, as opposed to only two ministers of defense. Civilian control was further enhanced in 1924 in another procedure whereby the army could only communicate with ministers through civil servants.[116] To be sure, army leaders complained bitterly about these various measures, but they accepted them nonetheless.[117]

The norm of civilian supremacy is evident in national policy in the government's handling of the 1924 Mutiny Crisis. In public, the government pursued a tough line and did so with widespread public and political support: here policy reflected discourse. In private, it attempted to negotiate a settlement with the leaders of the mutiny, but the Army Council went ahead anyway and arrested the mutiny ringleaders. Up to this point, norms of civilian supremacy were embodied in government and army words but not deeds. The government entered into secret talks with the mutineers in order to minimize the political fallout from the crisis in an election year, while the Army Council's tough action breached ministerial instruction and was motivated by the desire to remove a faction that threatened its control of the organization. However, what happened next dramatically illustrated norms of civilian supremacy in action. Infuriated by the army's independent action, the government demanded the resignation of the Army Council: three of the four members resigned with little fuss, including Mulcahy, leaving only one general to be dismissed.[118]

Norms of civilian supremacy are illustrated both in the government's expectation that the army leadership would resign, and in the resignations themselves. It so happens that most army officers were surprised at the deference of the Army Council; some suggested that the Army Council ignore the government's order—a suggestion met with sharp rebuke by Mulcahy. Instead, in resigning, the Army Council ordered army officers to "stand loyal to the Government and forget us."[119]

As noted earlier, politicians and policymakers gave little thought to how the army should organize and fight. For the first 15 years, policy on national defense, insofar as it existed, amounted to keeping the army small and obedient. This contrasted sharply with the army's own policy, stated boldly in 1925, for national defense to be based on "a standing Army of infantry supported by artillery, armoured cars, tanks," and including an air force, chemical warfare service, and coastal defense system, possibly equipped with submarines.[120] Given the government's unwillingness to fund any such force, staff officers in the intelligence branch toyed with the idea of incorporating guerrilla warfare into Ireland's defense posture.[121] However, as already noted, these ideas were roundly rejected by the General Staff. The head of one army directorate later complained that he had not even been consulted about the idea of a guerrilla defense, while another said he was "not bothering" with G-2's plan since it bore "no relation to reality."[122]

The bias toward norms of conventional warfare is evident in army discourse and training from the 1920s to the 1940s. Of the approximately 300 substantive articles on military matters published in the Irish Army's professional journal, *An t-Óglách,* only two were on guerrilla warfare: one was reprinted from the British Army's journal, and the other was an unfinished paper originally written shortly after the Irish War of Independence.[123] Equally, in preparing Ireland's defenses at the outbreak of World War II, army planners studied carefully the recent experiences of foreign armies (particularly in mechanized warfare), all the while ignoring Ireland's own experience in guerrilla warfare.[124] This neglect of guerrilla warfare in favor of conventional warfare was institutionalized in army training. Of the 140 hours of training prescribed to infantry in 1923, not 1 hour was allocated to guerrilla tactics (whereas 3 hours were spent on learning how to salute!).[125] By 1926, guerrilla warfare had disappeared altogether from infantry training.[126] The focus remained firmly on conventional operations in training memoranda for reserves and full-timers throughout the 1930s and into the early 1940s.[127]

Finally, norms of conventional warfare were clearly enacted in the Irish Army's procurement plans. This is most evident in the army's 15-year plan, submitted to the civilian government in 1932, to develop a 75,000-strong force that could field a corps of three divisions well equipped with artillery, tanks, armored cars, and aircraft.[128] The army chief of staff told the minister of defense that the purpose of the program was to provide for "the systematic building up . . . of a Field Force suitable to the defence requirements of this country . . . organized in a self-contained, properly balanced whole . . . [and] equipped with all the modern weapons required."[129] The massive scale of this program can be appreciated by noting that, at the time, the army had only 13,000 troops, little artillery, a handful of armored cars, very few aircraft, and one tank. Needless to say, this modernization program was vetoed by the Department of Finance.[130]

How did transnational norms of military professionalism come to displace IRA norms? The Irish Civil War provided the necessary external shock for radical norm transplantation to take place. While the IRA General Staff was pro-treaty, most IRA field units were opposed to the treaty with Britain and the Free State that was born of if. Thus the IRA General Staff, which formed the General Staff of the Free State Army, had to urgently pull together a new army to defend the infant state against IRA rebels. The British model was adopted out of necessity, and this provided the primary mechanism through which professional norms were encoded in Irish Army culture. Lacking the expertise to devise their own organizational structure and routines, the General Staff later explained that "it was essential that we adopt some foreign system as a model, to train and experiment with, and as our armament and equipment was British this was as good a model to adopt as any other."[131] As this suggests, the Irish General Staff intended to use the British model as the basis from which to evolve a military system suitable for Irish strategic circumstances. As it turned out, however, the British model provided the blueprint for the enduring pattern of Irish military organization and behavior.

The Civil War also produced a large-scale turnover of army personnel with key beliefs, in that it led to the exclusion of those members of the IRA with the highest commitment to norms of military sovereignty and norms of unconventional warfare. These were the most active fighting units of the IRA in southern and western Ireland who rebelled against the Irish Free State. Consequently, less than one-tenth of the new army were former IRA members. Furthermore, many officers with IRA experience were demobilized following the Civil War, while at the same time a number of ex–British officers, valued for their professional expertise, were commissioned in the Irish Army.[132] The change in personnel brought a change in attitude: these new recruits did not consider themselves to be sovereign but rather servants of the state, and were not particularly attached to guerrilla warfare given that they had no experience of it.

The urgency of the Civil War, combined with the formation of a new army, gave Mulcahy the political space to act as an effective norm entrepreneur. Mulcahy was not as powerful within the IRA as suggested by his formal office of chief of staff. As we noted, the appearance of a centralized decisionmaking hierarchy in the IRA belied the reality of a highly decentralized organization. In fact, most field units owed loyalty to and took direction from local commanders before the Dublin Headquarters. With only 4,000 former IRA troops staying loyal to the Free State government, a brand new army of over 50,000 was raised to fight the Civil War. The General Staff of this new army comprised the same staff officers who had worked under Mulcahy in the GHQ of the IRA. Accordingly, they formed an effective social network through which Mulcahy was able to exert control, frame debate, and mold a professional organization.[133] Mulcahy's added authority within the new Irish Army would also have enabled him to exercise some degree of coercion and inducement. There was still a fair degree of informality in the new and young Irish General Staff. Many senior officers also owed allegiance to a secret organization called the Irish Republican Brotherhood (IRB): the IRB had wielded great influence within the IRA and continued to throw a shadow over GHQ control of the army.[134] For these reasons, Mulcahy still had to rely on pressure and persuasion (i.e., rhetorical action) to get his organization to professionalize.

The social network supporting norms of conventional warfare in the Irish Army was reinforced when the Irish General Staff sent a military mission to the US Military Academy at West Point in 1926. The purpose of this mission was to learn more about foreign military systems, ostensibly to enable the army to devise its own doctrine and training. To this end, returning officers formed a temporary Defence Plans Division (DPD) 2 years later. However, rather than coming up with a new force posture, the DPD concluded, "it seems that the doctrine laid down in the British Field Service regulations has sufficient in common with the doctrine suggested to us to warrant the adoption of the war organization evolved in England."[135] Since it also emphasized conventional warfare, US training confirmed the validity of the British military model. Ten years on, the Irish Army was still thoroughly British in character. One founding member of the DPD noted, "much of our present organisation, and almost all handbooks and manuals approved by the [Irish] Department of Defence, are British."[136] It was around this time that the Intelligence Branch proposed that the army prepare an inventive scheme of national defense that drew on its past experience in guerrilla warfare. It is noteworthy that the chief authors of this proposal, Colonels Liam Archer and Dan Bryan, had received no foreign military training beforehand. Given that conventional warfare norms were so well entrenched in Irish Army culture, it is no wonder that their proposal fell on deaf ears.

Radical norm transplantation took place in postrevolutionary Ireland because external shock, personnel change, and effective entrepreneurship operated in synergy to effect rapid and profound cultural change in the Irish Army. The norm of civilian supremacy is evident not only in Irish law and government policy, but more importantly in Irish Army practice during the 1924 Mutiny Crisis. Norms of conventional warfare are evident in army discourse (as recorded in its professional journal) as well as army modernization programs, war plans, and training policy. These norms were not homegrown, but rather were imported by army leaders seeking to professionalize the organization. By itself, external shock would probably not have been enough to effect radical cultural change; had the IRA split differently in the Civil War, and most of the IRA including those from southern and western Ireland remained loyal to the state, then there would have been a considerable body of support for norms of military sovereignty and norms of unconventional warfare within the new army, and more resistance to Mulcahy's leadership as well as to harsh civilian rule. The Irish case suggests an important correlation between personnel change and effective entrepreneurship, even if it does not provide conclusive evidence that both are necessary for external shock to produce cultural change. When it comes to norms of conventional warfare, this case also illustrates how cultural causal mechanisms may change over time.

Conclusion

Transnational military norms provide both technical scripts and moral codes for military professionals, telling them what action works and what action is right when it comes to organizing for war and dealing with civilian leaders.

Norms of conventional warfare are, first and foremost, technical scripts. The worldwide adoption of the Western military model embodies a belief, shared by all military professionals, that military power is most effectively generated through capital-intensive militarization, producing standing, standardized, and technologically structured organizations. For many cases, particularly for great powers, this is a perfectly reasonable belief. But in some cases, such as early-twentieth-century Ireland, this norm has blinded officers to a more efficient and effective, if less conventional, option: namely, labor-intensive militarization resulting in militia-style forces. The same may be said of the current emulation of the latest variant on the Western military model—that of the IT-intensive US military—by a host of small states that neither need nor can afford US-style armies. The stunning success enjoyed by US forces in the UN-sponsored war against Iraq in 1990–1991 has fueled this latest round of transnational military isomorphism. The premise now is: modern militaries must be high-tech to succeed. However, as Demchak points out in her work, most militaries seeking to emulate the United States have vastly underestimated the cost and difficulty of integrating new technologies into battlefield systems and organizational structures.[137] In their rush to be modern, these militaries have been too keen to embrace new software over tried and tested hardware. Such behavior exhibits a technical script in operation: military faith in what works before experience of it working.

To a lesser extent, norms of conventional warfare incorporate a moral code about who may legitimately employ violence and how they may do so. One by one, the various nonstate military agents—mercenary groups, privateers, and mercantile companies—were abolished by states between the fourteenth century and nineteenth century. The result was to invest states with a monopoly on the moral right and legal authority to exercise military force.[138] International law not only favors state-based militaries, it also sides with standing and standardized forces. Guerrilla warfare by agents of the state was first outlawed in the 1863 Lieber Code, adopted by the Union side in the American Civil War.[139] This legal prohibition was subsequently codified in international law in the 1907 Hague Regulations on Land Warfare, which required all military parties to wear uniforms and carry arms openly.[140]

Of course, there are some military actors—insurgents, tribal and ethnic groups, transnational terrorists and bandits—who do not adhere to professional military norms.[141] Precisely because they organize and act in ways contrary to norms of conventional warfare, they also happen to breach rules of international law. Such actors reject the Western military model both as a script for technical efficiency and as a moral code. Substate warrior collectives—be they ideological, ethnic, tribal, or criminal—may engage in unconventional operations as a means of asymmetric warfare.[142] In asymmetric warfare, the underdog seeks to neutralize the quantitative and/or technological superiority of opponents by fighting in unfamiliar ways and unexpected places and times.[143] State-imposed legal restraints on war not only hinder effective military options for substate actors, they are often just plain irrelevant to warrior collectives that thrive off disordered societies and terrorized civilians.[144] Far from undermining norms of conventional warfare, warrior collectives reproduce international legal rules in the very act of breaching them (more on this in Chapter 5). Mercenaries also operate on modern battlefields. But, here too, norms of conventional warfare are reinforced, both directly in the military training provided by privately employed military professionals, and indirectly in the rules that prohibit mercenaries from carrying or operating weaponry in war.[145]

The norm of civilian supremacy primarily expresses a moral code. To be sure, some officers do oppose military intervention in politics on technical grounds—because it does not produce effective government and/or it distracts the military from its core war-fighting task. But, for the most part, obedience of civilian leadership depends on a common civil-military value system that delegitimates possibilities for military disobedience. Where civilian government exists, this value system is encoded in law, embodied in policy and practice, and possibly expressed in political discourse (particularly where there has been a recent history of military interference in government). In short, the military stay out of government because that is the right place for them to be—and they know it.

In this chapter, I have demonstrated the logic of appropriateness in operation, in showing how transnational norms shape national patterns of military organization and civil-military relations. Generally speaking, instrumental calculations can and do, of course, affect the development and diffusion of transnational norms. The logic of consequences also matters. As Cortell and

Davis note, "international norms are more likely to become salient if they are perceived to support domestic material interests, whether economic or security."[146] While norms create interests, it is reasonable to expect that international norms will be better received where they recreate existing national and/or domestic interests. This is why norm transplantation is so easy in cases of cultural match.

Coercion and inducements have played a significant role in the diffusion of the transnational military norms. Many postcolonial states, like India, inherited conventional armies from departing imperial masters. India had its own rich military tradition. The Western model of military organization was forced upon some parts of India during imperial rule, and, over time, the Indian military elite became socialized into accepting norms of conventional warfare. When Britain left, an Indian version of the British Army stayed behind.[147]

There are also obvious inducements for adhering to transnational military norms. As we noted earlier, some non-European states choose to adopt European military structures and technology in attempting to resist the worldwide expansion of European power; equally, we noted the mixed success in these efforts at norm transplantation. Communities aspiring to statehood have an additional inducement to adopting norms of conventional warfare. This was illustrated when the Kosovo Liberation Army attempted to create a conventional army, which would have been more vulnerable than a guerrilla force to attack from Serbia, but which nevertheless would legitimate Kosovo's bid for statehood.[148] Observing the norm of civilian supremacy may also enable some states to enter advantageous alliances with powerful and rich democracies. The defining example is the requirement for postcommunist states to institutionalize norms of civilian supremacy as a prerequisite for entry into the North Atlantic Treaty Organization (NATO). There is no doubt that the promise of NATO membership has driven many postcommunist states to explicitly change their militaries in order to meet NATO standards (on interoperability as well as civil-military relations).[149]

This chapter has deliberately examined a case where norm transplantation was not driven by external imposition or inducement. This is because I want to illustrate the causal autonomy and deep effect of transnational military norms, by demonstrating that such norms are more than the expression of preexisting material interests (i.e., "roadmaps" or binding rules for self-interested action). The concrete benefits of observing transnational military norms are not at all evident in the case of early-twentieth-century Ireland. Irish statehood was legitimated by the treaty with Britain in 1921 and through membership of the League of Nations, and so a conventional army was not needed for this purpose.[150] It is equally difficult to see the material benefits for Ireland in observing norms of civilian supremacy. As a neutral state, Ireland had no interest in allying with anybody. Indeed, it refused to side with the Western democracies against fascist states in World War II.[151] Moreover, as I have shown, a conventional army did not suit Irish security needs, while submitting to civilian rule did not serve the army's interests. Ideas, not power and interest, shaped Irish military development.

Notes

1. Jeffrey T. Checkel, "The Constructivist Turn in International Relations Theory," *World Politics* 50, no. 2 (1998): 340–347.

2. Jeffrey T. Checkel, "International Norms and Domestic Politics: Bridging the Rationalist-Constructivist Divide," *European Journal of International Relations* 3, no. 4 (1997): 473–495; Jeffrey T. Checkel, "Norms, Institutions, and National Identity in Contemporary Europe," *International Studies Quarterly* 43, no. 1 (1999): 83–114; Andrew P. Cortell and James W. Davis Jr., "How Do International Institutions Matter?: The Domestic Impact of International Rules and Norms," *International Studies Quarterly* 40 (1996): 451–478; Andrew P. Cortell and James W. Davis Jr., "Understanding the Domestic Impact of International Norms: A Research Agenda," *International Studies Review* 2, no. 1 (2000): 65–90.

3. Jeffrey W. Legro, "Which Norms Matter? Revisiting the 'Failure' of Internationalism," *International Organization* 51, no. 1 (1997): 59.

4. On external balancing, see Stephen M. Walt, *The Origins of Alliances* (Ithaca, NY: Cornell University Press, 1987). On internal balancing, see Thomas J. Christensen, *Useful Adversaries* (Princeton, NJ: Princeton University Press, 1996).

5. Barry R. Posen, "Nationalism, the Mass Army and Military Power," *International Security* 18 (1993): 82.

6. Joào Resende-Santo, "Anarchy and Emulation of Military Systems: Military Organization and Technology in South America, 1870–1930," *Security Studies* 5, no. 3 (1996): 211.

7. Emily O. Goldman, "The Spread of Western Military Models to Ottoman Turkey and Meiji Japan," in Theo Farrell and Terry Terriff (eds.), *The Sources of Military Change: Culture, Politics, Technology* (Boulder, CO: Lynne Rienner, 2002), pp. 41–68.

8. The Irish Army also examined the US, French, and German military systems. General Staff, "Special Memo No. 3: Territorial Organisation of the Defence Forces," MJC Files, Irish Military Archives (IMA), p. 11.

9. John P. Duggan, *A History of the Irish Army* (Dublin: Gill and Macmillan, 1991), pp. 155–162; Peter Young, "Defence and the New Irish State, 1919–1939," *The Irish Sword* 19 (1993–1994): 6–7.

10. General Staff, "Estimate of the Situation That Would Arise in the Eventuality of a War Between Ireland and Great Britain," no. 1, October 1934, DP/00020, IMA; General Staff, "Fundamental Factors Affecting Saorstát Defence Problem," May 1936, G2/0057, IMA.

11. Army Chief of Staff, "Formation of Special Reserve," 12 November 1925, MA GS/0/2.

12. General Staff (G-1), "Memorandum No. 2: Observations on General Staff Estimate of the Situation No. 1," 1940, Emergency Defence Plans (EDP) 1, IMA.

13. General Staff (G-1), "Outline of General Defence Plan No. 2 (Final Draft)," 28 November 1940, EDP 1/2, IMA.

14. Ibid.

15. Major James Flynn, "Memo: General Defence Plan 2—Final Outline," 29 November 1940, EDP 1/2, IMA, pp. 1–2.

16. General Staff, "Report on Army Exercises," Parts I & II, January 1943, IMA.

17. Theo Farrell, "Figuring Out Fighting Organisations: The New Organisational Analysis in Strategic Studies," *Journal of Strategic Studies* 19, no. 1 (1996): 122–135.

18. Graham T. Allison, *The Essence of Decision* (Boston: Little, Brown, 1973); Morton H. Halperin, *Bureaucratic Politics and Foreign Policy* (Washington, DC: Brookings Institution, 1974).

19. Barry R. Posen, *The Sources of Military Doctrine* (Ithaca, NY: Cornell University Press, 1984), pp. 41–59.

20. The threat from Germany was also dismissed by Finance officials on the grounds that Britain could be expected to come to the rescue. Department of Finance, "Defence Estimates," 16 January 1939, MacEntee Papers, P67/196, UCD Archives (UCD).

21. Department of Finance, "Memorandum," 10 December 1923, D/Finance 747/148, Irish National Archives.

22. Posen, *The Sources.*

23. Theo Farrell, "The Model Army: Military Imitation and the Enfeeblement of the Army in Post-Revolutionary Ireland, 1922–42," *Irish Studies in International Affairs* 8 (1997): 78; Eunan O'Halpin, *Defending Ireland: The Irish State and Its Enemies Since 1922.* (Oxford: Oxford University Press, 1999), p. 92.

24. Kurt Weyland, "The American Bias in Organization Theory," *Governance* 8, no. 1 (1995): 113–124.

25. Deborah D. Avant, *Political Institutions and Military Change* (Ithaca, NY: Cornell University Press, 1994), p. 9.

26. S. E. Finer, *Man on Horseback* (London: Pall Mall, 1962); Eric Nordlinger, *Soldiers in Politics* (Englewood Cliffs, NJ: Prentice Hall, 1977); Samuel J. Fitch, *The Armed Forces and Democracy in Latin America* (Baltimore: Johns Hopkins University Press, 2000); Wendy Hunter, *State and Soldier in Latin America* (Washington, DC: US Institute for Peace, 1996). For a study combining insights from the organizational politics and civil-military relations literatures, see Risa Brooks, "Institutions at the Domestic/International Nexus: The Political-Military Origins of Strategic Integration, Military Effectiveness and War," Ph.D. dissertation, University of California, San Diego, 2000.

27. Eunan O'Halpin, "The Army and the Dáil," in Brian Farrell (ed.), *The Creation of the Dáil* (Dublin: Gill and Macmillan, 1994), p. 109.

28. Farrell, "The Model Army," pp. 112–115.

29. Ibid., pp. 116–118; Maryann Gialanella Valiulis, *Portrait of a Revolutionary: General Richard Mulcahy and the Founding of the Irish State* (Dublin: Irish Academic Press, 1992). Quote from O'Halpin, *Defending,* p. 37.

30. Rational choice institutionalism has a minimal concept of institutions, seeing them as material structures that impose constraints on self-interested behavior. Historical institutionalism is like sociological institutionalism in seeing institutions as having deeper, constitutive, effects—institutions also operate to shape actors' interests. Historical institutionalism differs from sociological institutionalism in having a broader conception of institutions, one that includes both material and ideational structures. Thus, historical instutionalists look at things like the structures of executive government, electoral systems, trade unions, and so forth. In contrast, sociological institutionalists focus on institutions as ideas. Peter A. Hall and Rosemary C. R. Taylor, "Political Science and the Three New Institutionalisms," *Political Studies* 44, no. 5

(1996): 936–957; Sven Steinmo, Kathleen Thelen, and Frank Longstreth (eds.), *Structuring Politics: Historical Institutionalism in Comparative Politics* (Cambridge: Cambridge University Press, 1992).

31. W. Richard Scott, *Organizations: Rational, Natural, and Open Systems*, 3rd ed. (Eaglewood Cliffs, NJ: Prentice Hall, 1992).

32. Paul J. DiMaggio and Walter W. Powell, "Introduction," in Walter W. Powell and Paul J. DiMaggio (eds.), *The New Institutionalism in Organizational Analysis* (Chicago: University of Chicago Press, 1991), p. 13.

33. John W. Meyer, John Boli, George M. Thomas, and Francisco O. Ramirez, "World Society and the Nation-State," *American Journal of Sociology* 193 (1997): 144–181; John Boli and George M. Thomas (eds.), *Constructing World Culture* (Stanford, CA: Stanford University Press, 1999).

34. Paul J. DiMaggio and Walter W. Powell, "The Iron Cage Revisited: Institutional Isomorphism and Collective Rationality in Organizational Fields," in Walter W. Powell and Paul J. DiMaggio (eds.), *The New Institutionalism in Organizational Analysis* (Chicago: University of Chicago Press, 1991), p. 64.

35. Ibid., pp. 70–74.

36. Royston Greenwood and C. R. Hinings, "Understanding Strategic Change: The Contribution of Archetypes," *Academy of Management Journal* 36, no. 5 (1993): 1052–1081.

37. Francisco O. Ramirez and John W. Meyer, "Comparative Education," *Annual Review of Sociology* 6 (1980): 369–399; John W. Meyer, Francisco O. Ramirez, and Yasemin Soysal, "World Expansion of Mass Education, 1870–1980," *Sociology of Education* 65, no. 2 (1992): 128–149; John W. Meyer, David Frank, Ann Hironaka, Evan Schofer, and Nancy B. Tuma, "The Structuring of a World Environmental Regime, 1870–1990," *International Organization* 51 (1992): 623–651; David Strang and Patricia Chang, "The International Labour Organization and the Welfare State: Institutional Effects on National Welfare Spending, 1960–1980," *International Organization* 47 (1993): 235–262.

38. Dana P. Eyre and Mark C. Suchman, "Status, Norms, and the Proliferation of Conventional Weapons," in Peter J. Katzenstein (ed.), *The Culture of National Security* (New York: Columbia University Press, 1996), pp. 79–113. See also Dana P. Eyre's Ph.D. dissertation, "The Very Model of the Major Modern Military: World System Influences on the Proliferation of Military Weapons, 1960–1990," Stanford University, 1997. Ann Hironaka also has produced some insightful (as yet unpublished) new institutionalist analysis on war. See Ann Hironaka, "Boundaries of War: Historical Change in Patterns of Warmaking, 1815–1980," Ph.D. dissertation, Stanford University, 1998; Ann Hironaka, "From Conflict to Consensus: The Decline of Wars of Colonial Independence, 1770–1985," unpublished manuscript, 2000.

39. These expressions and this argument are from Ann Swidler, "Culture in Action: Symbols and Strategies," *American Sociological Review* 51, no. 2 (1986): 273–286.

40. Bertrand Badie, *The Imported State: The Westernization of the Political Order* (Stanford, CA: Stanford University Press, 2000).

41. Amitav Acharya, "How Ideas Spread: Whose Norms Matter? Norm Localization and Institutional Change in Asian Regionalism," *International Organization* 58, no. 2 (2004): 239–275.

42. Martha Finnemore, "Norms, Culture, and World Politics: Insights from Sociology's Institutionalism," *International Organization* 50 (1996): 339.

43. Checkel, "Norms, Institutions, and National Identity," p. 85.

44. Eyre and Suchman, "Status"; Hironaka, "Boundaries of War"; Hironaka, "From Conflict to Consensus"; Janice Thomson, *Mercenaries, Pirates and Sovereigns* (Princeton, NJ: Princeton University Press, 1994).

45. The diffusion of such specific military knowledge is discussed in several chapters in Emily O. Goldman and Leslie C. Eliason (eds.), *The Diffusion of Military Technology and Ideas* (Stanford, CA: Stanford University Press, 2003).

46. There are 191 members of the United Nations, plus the Vatican (which has sovereign status) and Taiwan (which I am counting as a state).

47. The following states have no military expenditure: Andorra, Dominica, Gambia, Grenada, Iceland, Kiribati, Liechtenstein, Marshall Islands, Micronesia, Nauru, Palau, Panama, Saint Kitts and Nevis, Saint Lucia, Saint Vincent and Grenadines, Samoa, Solomon Islands, Timor-Leste, Tuvalu, and Vanuatu. The following states do have military expenditures (2003 figures indicated in parentheses in US$ millions) but not standing militaries: Bhutan (9.3), Comoros (6), Costa Rica (69), Gambia (1.2), Haiti (50), Maldives (34.5), Mauritius (9.7), Panama (128), San Marino (0.7), Sao Tome and Principe (0.4), Swaziland (20), and Tonga (23.7). Data from 2003 CIA World Factbook, available from http://www.cia.gov/cia/download2003.htm.

48. Moldova does not have a navy either, even though it does have access to the Black Sea.

49. Data from International Institute for Strategic Studies (IISS), *The Military Balance, 2003–2004* (Oxford: Oxford University Press for the IISS, 2003).

50. Alexander Wendt and Michael Barnett, "Dependent State Formation and Third World Militarization," *Review of International Studies* 19, no. 4 (1993): 328.

51. Data on gross national income (world ranking) is from World Bank, *World Development Indicators 2004,* chap. 1: World View, 15–16, at http://www.worldbank.org/data/wdi2004/index.htm.

52. Information on ECOWAS is available from http://www.sec.ecowas.int/. The importance of ECOWAS for security in West Africa is discussed in Barry Buzan and Ole Waever, *Regions and Powers: The Structure of International Security* (Cambridge: Cambridge University Press, 2003), pp. 238–241.

53. I focus on armies (and so exclude navies and air forces). Major weapon systems include main battle tanks, other armored fighting vehicles and personnel carriers, and artillery systems (excluding mortars). None of the African states listed have reserve forces, and so I have excluded reserve forces for the European powers I examine.

54. This figure reflects the higher cost of the European weapon systems, though this will be offset slightly by the higher cost of each European soldier.

55. Obviously there is some variation among these African states. Burkina Faso, Mauritania, and Senegal have relatively high personnel to weapons ratios. Against this, the Central African Republic and Gabon have almost as many major weapon systems per soldier as the European powers, and Guinea and Mali have half as many.

56. Wendt and Barnett, "Dependent State Formation," p. 325.

57. Giving it, upon mobilization, a personnel to weapons ratio of 100/1. International Institute for Strategic Studies, *The Military Balance,* p. 81. The Swiss government is considering scrapping its militia force posture. Jean Lalande, "La Suisse Change Son Fusil d'Epaule," *Le Point,* 19 August 2004, p. 32.

58. Ivan Arreguín-Toft, "How the Weak Win Wars: A Theory of Asymmetric Conflict," *International Security* 26, no. 1 (2001): 93–128.

59. The importance of light infantry operations in counterinsurgency is well illustrated in Avant, *Political Institutions.*

60. Indeed, conventional offensives formed the mainstay of communist strategy in 1965–1966. See James J. Wirtz, *The Tet Offensive* (Ithaca, NY: Cornell University Press, 1991), pp. 17–50.

61. Jacques van Doorn, *The Soldier and Social Change: Comparative Studies in the History and Sociology of the Military* (Beverly Hills, CA: Sage, 1975), pp. 29–46.

62. Geoffrey Parker, *The Military Revolution: Military Innovation and the Rise of the West, 1500–1800,* 2nd ed. (Cambridge: Cambridge University Press, 1996), pp. 16–24; William McNeill, *The Pursuit of Power: Technology, Armed Force, and Society Since AD 1000* (Chicago: University of Chicago Press, 1982), pp. 128–143.

63. M. D. Feld, "Middle-Class Society and the Rise of Military Professionalism," *Armed Forces and Society* 1 (1975): 419–442; Michael Howard, *War in European History* (Oxford: Oxford University Press, 1979), p. 57.

64. Charles Tilly, "Reflections on the History of European State-making," in Charles Tilly (ed.), *The Formation of Nation States in Western Europe* (Princeton, NJ: Princeton University Press, 1975), p. 42.

65. Barton C. Hacker, "Engineering a New Order: Military Institutions, Technical Education, and the Rise of the Industrial State," *Technology and Culture* 34 (1993): 1–27.

66. McNeill, *The Pursuit of Power,* pp. 158–159; Samuel P. Huntington, *The Soldier and the State* (Cambridge, MA: Harvard University Press, 1957), pp. 50–53.

67. Stephen Peter Rosen, *Societies and Military Power: India and Its Armies* (Ithaca, NY: Cornell University Press, 1996).

68. David B. Ralston, *Importing the European Army: The Introduction of Military Techniques and Institutions into the Extra-European World, 1600–1914* (Chicago: University of Chicago Press, 1990); Philip D. Curtin, *The World and the West: The European Challenge and the Overseas Response in the Age of Empire* (Cambridge: Cambridge University Press, 2002); Christon I. Archer et al., *World History of Warfare* (Lincoln: University of Nebraska Press, 2002), pp. 440–482.

69. G. Teitler, *The Genesis of the Professional Officers' Corps* (Beverly Hills, CA: Sage, 1977), pp. 34–37; Huntington, *The Soldier and the State,* pp. 19–58.

70. This is highlighted in Eyre and Suchman, "Status."

71. John A. Cope, *International Military Education and Training: An Assessment,* McNair Paper no. 44 (Washington, DC: National Defense University, Institute for National Strategic Studies, 1995), pp. 11–12.

72. Chris Demchak, "Maladaptions to Complexity," unpublished manuscript, 2000. An edited version of this paper was published as Chris Demchak, "Complexity and Theory of Networked Militaries," in Farrell and Terriff (eds.), *The Sources of Military Change: Culture, Politics, Technology* (Boulder, CO: Lynne Rienner, 2002), pp. 221–264.

73. While my definition of political intervention differs from Samuel Finer's, this discussion is based on his "modes and methods of intervention." Finer, *Man on Horseback,* pp. 140–163.

74. Huntington, The *Soldier and the State,* pp. 7–18, 80–97.

75. Nordlinger, *Soldiers in Politics,* p. 47; Fitch, *The Armed Forces,* p. 3.

76. Finer, *Man on Horseback,* pp. 24–30; Nordlinger, *Soldiers in Politics,* pp. 49–53; Fitch, *The Armed Forces,* p. 3.

77. Samuel P. Huntington, *Political Order in Changing Societies* (New Haven, CT: Yale University Press, 1968), p. 194.

78. Fitch, *The Armed Forces,* p. 62.

79. Brian Taylor, "Russia's Passive Army: Rethinking Military Coups," *Comparative Political Studies* 34, no. 8 (2001): 932.

80. Even Finer recognized this possibility. Finer, *Man on Horseback,* p. 23.

81. Avant, *Political Institutions,* pp. 21–48; Huntington, *The Soldier and the State,* pp. 163–237.

82. Samuel P. Huntington, "Reforming Civil-Military Relations," in Larry Diamond and Mark F. Plattner (eds.), *Civil-Military Relations and Democracy* (Baltimore: Johns Hopkins University Press, 1996), p. 7.

83. Deborah D. Avant, "From Mercenaries to Citizen Armies: Explaining Change in the Practice of War," *International Organization* 54, no. 1 (2000): 51–52. On natural selection versus cultural selection, see Alexander Wendt, *Social Theory of International Politics* (Cambridge: Cambridge University Press, 1999), pp. 318–320.

84. This echoes a similar finding with regard to the application of human rights norms. See Thomas Risse and Kathryn Sikkink, "The Socialization of International Human Rights Norms into Domestic Practices: Introduction," in Thomas Risse, Stephen C. Ropp, and Kathryn Sikkink (eds.), *The Power of Human Rights* (Cambridge: Cambridge University Press, 1999), pp. 19–22.

85. Chris C. Demchak, "Creating the Enemy: Structuration, Adaptation and Autopoesis in the International Military Community," unpublished manuscript; John Wilson Lewis and Xue Litai, "China's Search for a Modern Air Force," *International Security* 24, no. 1 (1999): 64–94.

86. Cortell and Davis, "Understanding," pp. 69–70.

87. Checkel, "Norms," pp. 86–87.

88. Colin S. Gray, *Nuclear Strategy and National Style* (Lanham, MD: Hamilton Press, 1986).

89. Meyer, Boli, Thomas, and Ramirez, "World Society," p. 164.

90. Constantine P. Danopoulos (ed.), *From Military to Civilian Rule* (London: Routledge, 1992); Taylor, "Russia's Passive Army."

91. Finer, *Man on Horseback,* p. 87.

92. Checkel, "Norms," pp. 86–87.

93. Richard M. Price, "Reversing the Gun Sights: Transnational Civil Society Targets Land Mines," *International Organization* 52, no. 3 (1998): 627–631.

94. Acharya, "How Ideas Spread," p. 251.

95. M. D. Feld, "Military Professionalism and the Mass Army," *Armed Forces and Society* 1 (1975): 193; Teitler, *The Genesis,* p. 187.

96. Goldman, "The Spread of Western Military Models," pp. 47–61. This westernization was reversed in the 1920s, as the Japanese military and society in general returned to traditional martial values. Leonard A. Humphreys, *The Way of the Heavenly Sword: The Japanese Army in the 1920s* (Stanford, CA: Stanford University Press, 1995).

97. Checkel, "Norms," p. 88; Checkel, "International Norms and Domestic Politics," pp. 476–477.

98. Ian Hurd, "Legitimacy and Authority in International Politics," *International Organization* 53, no. 2 (1999): 389.

99. G. John Ikenberry and Charles A. Kupchan, "Socialization and Hegemonic Power," *International Organization* 44, no. 3 (1990): 283–315.

100. Martha Finnemore and Kathryn Sikkink, "International Norm Dynamics and Political Change," *International Organization* 52, no. 4 (1998): 887–917.

101. Risse and Sikkink, "The Socialization," pp. 17–35.

102. Cortell and Davis, "Understanding," p. 74, emphasis added.

103. Tom Garvin, *1922: The Birth of Irish Democracy* (Dublin: Gill and Macmillan, 1996), pp. 37–41; M. L. R. Smith, *Fighting for Ireland* (London: Routledge, 1997), pp. 10–23.

104. Peter Hart, "The Social Structure of the Irish Republican Army, 1916–1923," *Historical Journal* 42 (1999): 207–231.

105. Charles Townshend, "The Irish Republican Army and the Development of Guerrilla Warfare, 1916–1921," *English Historical Review* 94 (1987): 327–329.

106. Arthur Mitchell, *Revolutionary Government in Ireland* (Dublin: Gill and Macmillan, 1995), pp. 65–79.

107. David Fitzpatrick, "The Geography of Irish Nationalism, 1910–1921," *Past and Present* 78 (1978): 113–144.

108. Peter Hart, *The IRA and Its Enemies* (Oxford: Oxford University Press, 1998), p. 269.

109. General Headquarters (GHQ), *An Introduction to Volunteer Training*, IRA, 1920, Mulcahy Papers, P7a/22, UCDA.

110. Mulcahy's own account of his formative military experiences is recorded in Risteárd Mulcahy, *Richard Mulcahy (1886–1971): A Family Memoir* (Dublin: Aurelian Press, 1999), pp. 25–56.

111. Ibid., pp. 57–68.

112. See, for example, General Headquarters, *Training Manual*, IRA, 1921, Mulcahy Papers, P7a/22, UCDA.

113. For one such fooled scholar, see Tom Bowden, "The Irish Underground and the War of Independence, 1919–1921," *Journal of Contemporary History* 8 (1973): 3–23.

114. Joost Augusteijn, *From Public Defiance to Guerrilla Warfare* (Dublin: Irish Academic Press, 1996); Hart, *The IRA;* Charles Townshend, *Political Violence in Ireland* (Oxford: Oxford University Press, 1983), pp. 336–338.

115. Brian Farrell, *The Foundation of Dáil Éireann* (Dublin: Gill and Macmillan, 1971); Garvin, *1922,* pp. 123–155. The existence and reassertion of a constitutional tradition in Irish political culture does not, in itself, explain why an organization that had previously thought of itself as sovereign should pay much heed to civilians. The IRA thought little of Irish voters and their representatives, a fact revealed in the IRA rebellion against the democratically elected Free State. The question then becomes, how was the Irish Army different from the IRA? External shock, personnel change, and effective entrepreneurial leadership help us to explain these differences and how they came about.

116. Farrell, "The Model Army," pp. 114–115; O'Halpin, *Defending,* pp. 86–88.

117. General Richard Mulcahy, "General Memo 3: Control of Army Expenditure," 18 July 1922, Mulcahy Papers P7a/56, UCDA; General Eoin O'Duffy, "Memo to the Executive Council," 18 March 1924, Blythe Papers, P24/154, UCDA.

118. O'Halpin, *Defending,* pp. 46–53; John Regan, *The Counter-Revolution* (Dublin: Gill and Macmillan, 1999), pp. 163–197.

119. Valiulis, *Portrait,* p. 216.

120. Department of Defence, "Memo to Executive Council Re: Defence Policy," 1925, Blythe Papers, P24/107, UCDA.

121. Colonel Dan Bryan, "Small Wars and Guerrilla Wars in Ireland," Lecture to Irish General Staff, unpublished manuscript, 1928, IMA.

122. Captain R. Boyd, "Memorandum on 'Present Commitments and Future Policy and Programme' Period About 1937," 9 February 1945, Bryan Papers, P71/27, UCDA, p. 9.

123. Major B. C. Dening, "Problems of Guerrilla Warfare," *An t-Óglách* (October 1927): 45–50; Colonel J. J. O'Connell, "Guerrilla Warfare as Standard Form," *An t-Óglách* (April 1930): 50–52. *An t-Óglách* was originally the journal of the revolu-

tionary IRA. It was revived in 1927 as the professional journal of the Irish Army, and published monthly until 1933.

124. G-2 Branch, "Anti-Tank Measures: Spanish Civil War," Intelligence Note No. 22, n.d.; "Anti-Tank Measures in the Polish Campaign," Intelligence Note No. 23, 25 July 1940; "Anti-Tank Measures: Russo-Finish War," Intelligence Note No. 21, 2 August 1940; "Lessons to Be Learned from the Success of the German Army in France," Intelligence Note No. 48, 18 November 1940; all of these can be found in Byran Papers, P71/38-41, UCDA.

125. General Headquarters, *General Staff Training Memo No. 1: Syllabus for One Month's Progressive Training for an Infantry Company* (Dublin: Stationery Office, 1923), Mulcahy Papers, P7a/71, UCDA.

126. Irish Free State, Department of Defence, *Defence Force Regulations: Annual Training* (Dublin: Stationery Office, 1926).

127. General Staff (G-1), "Instructions for the Training of Infantry Units of the Class B Reserve," 19 March 1931, IMA MB3; General Staff (G-1), "General Staff Training Memoranda," 1940, IMA MB5/27.

128. Chief of Staff to Minister of Defence, 22 September 1932, IMA, files of the assistant chief of staff (ACS) 2/72.

129. General Staff, "Comments on the Estimates 1933–1934: Prepared by the General Staff on the Basis of the 'Notes' Prepared by the Secretariat," March/April 1933, MA ACS 2/72, p. 1.

130. For more detailed discussion, see Theo Farrell, "Professionalization and Suicidal Defence Planning by the Irish Army, 1921–1941," *Journal of Strategic Studies* 21, no. 3 (1998): 77–78.

131. General Staff, "Estimate," p. 55.

132. Colonel Michael J. Costello, "Report to Chairman of Army Inquiry Committee," 22 April 1924, MJC 5, IMA, pp. 10–12.

133. Valiulis, *Portrait,* pp. 73–75, 160–161.

134. Ibid., pp. 227–230. For Mulcahy's own view on the IRB's influence in the Army, see Mulcahy, *Richard Mulcahy,* pp. 74–75.

135. Colonel Michael J. Costello, "Preparation for War: Draft for War Plans Division," 1928, MJC 9, IMA.

136. Colonel Michael J. Costello, "Outline of a Suggested Organisation for the Defence Forces," January 1938, MJC 13, IMA.

137. Demchak, "Complexity," pp. 221–264. Even the US Army has underappreciated how difficult it is to integrate new technology in its force structure. See Chris Demchak, *Military Organizations, Complex Machines: Modernization and the US Armed Services* (Ithaca, NY: Cornell University Press, 1991).

138. Thomson, *Mercenaries.*

139. Richard S. Hartigan, *Lieber's Code and the Law of War* (Chicago: Precedent, 1983).

140. Geoffrey Best, *Humanity in Warfare* (London: Weidenfeld and Nicolson, 1980), pp. 190–200.

141. Mary Kaldor, *New and Old Wars: Organized Violence in a Global Era* (Cambridge: Polity, 1999); Ralph Peters, "The Culture of Future Conflict," *Parameters* (Winter 1995–1996): 18–27.

142. Vincent J. Goulding Jr., "Back to the Future with Asymmetric Warfare," *Parameters* (Winter 2000–2001): 21–30.

143. Andrew Mack, "Why Big Countries Lose Small Wars: The Politics of Asymmetric Conflict," *World Politics* 26, no. 1 (1975): 175–200.

144. Ralph Peters, "The New Warrior Class," *Parameters* (Summer 1994): 16–26.

145. P. W. Singer, "Corporate Warriors: The Rise of the Privatized Military Industry and Its Ramifications for International Security," *International Security* 26, no. 3 (2001–2002): 186–220.

146. Cortell and Davis, "Understanding," p. 77.

147. Rosen, *Societies and Military Power;* Stephen P. Cohen, *The Indian Army: Its Contribution to the Development of a Nation* (Oxford: Oxford University Press, 1990).

148. Chris Bird, "KLA to Give Birth to Kosovo's New Army," *The Guardian,* 3 September 1999, p. 19. For a discussion of the interests underlying the transformation of militia forces into conventional armies, see Marie-Joelle Zahar, "Fanatics, Mercenaries, Brigands and Politicians: Militia Decision-Making and Civil Conflict Resolution," Ph.D. dissertation, McGill University, 1999.

149. Jeffrey Simon, *Central European Civil-Military Relations and NATO Expansion* (Washington DC: National Defense University Press, 1995); Frank E. Fields and Jack J. Jensen, "Military Professionalism in Post-Communist Hungary and Poland," *European Security* 7, no. 1 (1998): 117–156.

150. Michael Kennedy, *Ireland and the League of Nations, 1923–1946* (Dublin: Irish Academic Press, 1996).

151. Robert Fisk, *In Time of War* (Dublin: Gill and Macmillan, 1983).

3

Mass Industrialized War

Memory and imagination are essential ingredients of war. Memories of past injustice and past military service give cause and intensity to war. The purpose and process of war are also shaped by images of the "self" and the "other," and by images of future warfare. But when it comes to war, whose memory matters? And whose imagination imprints battle? This chapter considers these questions in the context of the two great mass industrial wars of the twentieth century—the two world wars. It looks at two sets of cultural beliefs that shape the conduct of mass industrialized war by Western states in these wars—norms of military mobilization and norms of machine warfare. This chapter does not look at norm causation but rather how norms constitute modern warfare. In other words, it explores how the above norms gave meaning to, and thereby made possible, mass industrialized war. This chapter is also especially concerned with norm creation. Following social historians of war, I concentrate on two things. First, on the role of collective memory and imagination in generating and sustaining norms of mass industrialized war. Second, on the role of state-society relations in shaping collective memory of wars past and imagination of future warfare.

Norms of military mobilization are moral codes that give meaning to the act of social organization for war. Such norms give people reason to fight and kill. They provide collective narratives telling civilians why they should leave their jobs, homes, and families and march off to battle. Norms of military mobilization also make it possible for people to participate in socially sanctioned mass homicide, and even commit acts of shocking savagery. Self-image and "other image," especially national identity, are central elements of these mobilization narratives; so is the image of war as a heroic endeavor, an image that is rooted in and nurtured through collective memories of glorious past wars. Norms of machine warfare are technical scripts about the efficiency of technology in war. Often the aspired efficiency of military machines has exceeded actual operational performance. Nevertheless, as the twentieth century rolled on, modern war was increasingly defined in terms of the machines that waged it. Such machines do not materially appear out of the blue, but rather their form and function come from human imagination.

Transnational trends and discourse suggest that these norms evolved in generic form across and beyond Europe in the mid-nineteenth century to mid-twentieth century. For example, as we shall see, pre–World War I norms of military mobilization were shaped by the militarization of young men through entertainment and education, which occurred in a number of European states from the late nineteenth century on. Equally, as also shown later, the imagined impact of the plane on warfare was debated transnationally, in popular magazines and by military professionals in the early twentieth century. However, we may expect norms of military mobilization and machine warfare to have taken specific form in national contexts, as a result of local cultural dynamics. Norms of military mobilization will be informed by nationally constructed collective memories of past wars. Equally, norms of machine warfare will be mediated by the military preferences encoded in preexisting organizational culture, and the experiences of military organizations.

State-society relations are central to these local cultural dynamics. And this is where there is a major difference in approach between social scientists and social historians of war. For social scientists, it does not really matter what the broader society thinks (i.e., remembers and imagines) when it comes to war. International Relations (IR) scholars have focused on military and elite beliefs when tracking the impact of culture on war. Equally, when it comes to the social construction of military technology, sociologists have concentrated on military policy–scientist networks. Social historians take the opposite view: that artists, performers, businesses, educators, the media, and society at large are all involved in the production and reproduction of memories and images of war. Indeed, as discussed later, social historians often emphasize the contest between the military and policy elites (what I term "primary agents") and cultural, commercial, and public groups (my "secondary agents") over collective memories of wars past. In this chapter, I also argue that secondary agents matter, but I emphasize their importance in terms of contributing to elite efforts to shape collective memory and public imagination about war.

Chapter Outline

I have opted for a constitutive approach given the scale and complexity of my canvass in this chapter—which spans a number of societies and a century. This chapter also differs in methodology from the rest the book, which deductively analyzes case studies using the theory outlined in Chapter 1. In this chapter the analysis is inductive. Given avoidance of causal theory by social historians, and the inattention of social scientists to wider state-society relations in the social construction of war, there is no body of literature from which to derive contingent generalizations about cultural agency. I suggest some inductively derived generalizations in the conclusion of the chapter.

The first section of this chapter considers how collective memory of war is constructed, contested, and contributes to social mobilization for war, focusing on the opportunities as well as obstacles that society presents for state control of collective memory. As shown in the case studies, imagination also contributes to norms of military mobilization—by enabling communities to construct "self" and "other" identities that make the brutality of war possible. The second section looks at the relationship between imagination and machine warfare. Again, I emphasize the importance of public imagination. I also explore the role of cultural and commercial elites in contributing to the work of state agents. The third and fourth sections examine two case studies of how memory and imagination shape the landscape of mass industrialized war. Respectively, these are Germany's Eastern front during both world wars and the US war in the Pacific during World War II. These cases enable me to explore how generic norms of mass industrialized war take specific form through local cultural dynamics, and especially the role of state-society relations.

First, however, I review the social science literatures on strategic culture and on the social construction of military technology. I conclude this introductory section by briefly commenting on the concept of "total war," and explain why I prefer the term "mass industrialized war."

The Social Science of Strategic Culture

In their studies on culture and war, social scientists have tended to prioritize elite beliefs about use of force.[1] But when it comes to the broader study of political beliefs, social scientists pay more heed to the ordinary voice. Here, we need to note that the sizable literature on strategic culture is matched by an even larger and more established literature on political culture.[2] In *Nuclear Strategy and National Style,* Colin Gray claims that "the concept of strategic culture is a direct descendant of the concept of political culture."[3] Indeed, one might expect this. However, in this seminal work on strategic culture, Gray does not actually draw on the political culture literature in developing his approach. Equally, political culture is only briefly discussed in Alastair Iain Johnston's more recent study of Chinese strategic culture.[4] Overall, the evidence appears to support John Duffield's conclusion that the concept of strategic culture "has in fact been developed independently, with little or no reference to the literature on political culture."[5] The only exception here is Thomas Berger, whose book on Japanese and German strategic culture does explicitly draw on the political culture literature.[6]

The concept of political culture was developed to explain patterns of political participation and political development through an examination of how people thought and felt about politics.[7] The dominant approach has been one of psychological reductionism, using sample survey techniques to build national profiles of public as well as elite opinion.[8] In contrast, social scientists in strategic studies have concentrated on national beliefs about the use of force in statecraft as expressed and practiced by political, policy, and military elites only. Early work on strategic culture was policy directed and theoretically unsophisticated, driven as it was by the concerns and circumstances of the Cold War.[9] More recently, social scientists have drawn on sociology and anthropology in their theorizing about strategic culture. This later, more theoretically informed work looks at how beliefs, expressed and codified in symbolic systems, shape the preferences and practices of communities of actors.[10] But note: the beliefs are elite ones; the communities in question are political institutions, policy groups, and military organizations. With the exception of Berger, no attention has been given to public beliefs.[11]

Constructivist scholars in IR differ to the extent to which they factor in societal and public beliefs in their theories. Understandably, heroic individuals, pressure groups, and public opinion figure prominently in constructivist accounts of the rise and spread of human rights norms.[12] However, constructivists working on force in world politics are far less inclined to take heed of nonstate agents.[13] Richard Price is an exception here, in that he does look at the role of "transnational civil society" in shaping a normative prohibition against antipersonnel mines. Such an approach is understandable given that the story is all about how pressure groups successfully framed the issue as a *human rights* one.[14]

So while popular beliefs and opinion polling are obviously relevant to explaining political participation, their relevance is not so obvious to many social scientists when it comes to explaining strategic behavior. For culturalists in strategic studies and most constructivists, the unstated assumption appears to be that popular beliefs are unimportant to explaining state preferences and military practice in war. Thus, even Duffield, who seeks to import the political culture literature into strategic studies, focuses on elite beliefs and values. He does this because, in his view, elite political culture is easier to measure, is more elaborate and detailed, and "is likely to have a much more immediate bearing on national security" than public beliefs.[15]

However, there is something nonsensical about this last point, particularly when it comes to the big wars of the last century—World Wars I and II. These wars are often referred to as "total wars" precisely because of the extent to which they involved whole societies. Such wars were total because entire populations were mobilized to fuel them, and because the distinction between the battle front and home front collapsed, as civilians and cities became legitimate targets for attack. They were also total because they were pursued to the bitter end; victory had to be total—likewise defeat.[16] When it comes to total war, what the public believes does matter. At the most basic level, they must believe in a cause to want to fund it and, critically, fight for it. To be sure, political elites have sought to manipulate memory of past wars and images of coming war in order to motivate and control their populaces. However, they have not been alone in this memory and imagination work. Recent studies on the social and cultural history of warfare (much of it focused on World Wars I and II) reveal a range of agents constructing beliefs about war. Cultural elites sought to memorialize wars past and represent future wars in literary, pictorial, and other artistic forms. Business elites did likewise, albeit for commercial rather than aesthetic reasons. At the junction of culture and business, media elites expressed memories and images of war. And ordinary people in the trenches and the towns—to varying degrees influenced by the views of cultural, commercial, and political elites—acted out their own ideas about what happened and what was about to happen in war.[17]

Underlying the social science bias toward political, policy, and military beliefs is a methodological issue. Many social scientists want to be able to *measure* what they observe. This is necessary in order to move beyond correlation—showing the coexistence of belief and behavior—and prove causation—showing that a particular belief explains the observed behavior. Since they are not shackled by this social science concern with causal theorizing, historians are happy to take a wider look at cultural beliefs about war.[18] At the same time, underlying this is also a methodological issue for those historians that are uneasy about typologies that seek to distinguish "elite culture" from "popular culture."[19] In short, in focusing on rigor, social scientists lose some essential richness in their accounts of how culture shapes war.[20]

The Sociology of Military Technology

When it comes to the study of human imagination and military technology, there are similarities and differences between social history and social science. The key social science literature here is the sociology of technology (which examines the social construction of civilian as well as military technology). The sociology of technology challenges the dominant causal account of technological development, that of technological determinism. Sociologists note that there is more than one way to design an artifact. Designs are chosen and artifacts built not through a process of natural selection whereby weak designs are supplanted by superior ones; rather, social networks develop around rival designs, each functioning to mobilize resources and build consensus for its own preference. Often it is this social process, whereby debate is closed down and consensus is built around a dominant design, and not design efficiency that shapes technological development.[21]

Where sociologists and social historians differ is in levels of analysis. Sociologists tend to concentrate on those social groups that directly fund, design, build, and use military technologies. In other words, the focus is on social networks that encompass policymakers, scientists and engineers, and military officers, and through which ideas are transmitted and fought over, and material support is mobilized.[22] Social historians are also interested in these social networks that immediately surround and sustain military technologies. But in addition to this, social historians examine the broader cultural milieu of military technology. This includes how technological development is imagined in popular culture, and how technological performance in war is represented in the media and received by the public. A particular concern of social historians, such as Michael Sherry and Craig Cameron, is the increasing technocracy and devastation of twentieth-century war, and the interaction of imagination and technology in shaping this trend.[23]

What social scientists and social historians share is a reluctance to identify lines of causation between imagination and technology. Beyond this main critique of technological determinism, the sociology of technology is cautious about making theoretical generalizations. Indeed, the dominant methodology in this literature, which involves induction from detailed single case studies, does not lend itself to theory development.[24] The picture that does emerge from these case studies is an immensely complex one. Technology and society are shown to be mutually constitutive: social forces shape technology, which in turn shape social relations. Identifying causation is difficult to say the least, given this complex picture. As the introductory chapter to one major collection of essays notes, "the social shaping of technology is, in almost all the cases we know of, a process in which there is no single dominant force."[25] If generalizing about causation between social network formation and technological development is difficult, then doing so for technological development and broader social currents is doubly difficult. Not surprisingly then, social historians also eschew identifying direct causal links between imagination and technology, and they also tend to see the relationship as a mutually constitutive one. Imagination is conceptualized as a shaper of technological development: for example, visionaries have to dream up warplanes before people can build them and start bombing each other. At the same time, technology shapes human imagination of war: so the horrors of bombing cities to the ground becomes possible because technology creates physical and emotional distance between those who plan, organize, and carry out the bombing, and the consequences of their acts.[26]

From Total to Mass Industrialized War

Historians have recently issued warnings about use and abuse of the term "total war." To begin with, total war contains inherent contradictions that militate against its realization. First, total mobilization on one side will trigger likewise on the other, thereby hindering total victory. Second, states cannot exert total control over national resources if they are to achieve total mobilization; rather they must collaborate with civil society in a collective effort of mobilization. For these reasons, Stig Forster suggests that "total war" is best thought of as an "ideal type," a standard against which to measure wars.[27] Roger Chickering raises, in my view, more fundamental concerns. For him, "total war" is a master narrative that has been employed by historians to explain "progressive heightening of warfare's intensity since the end of the eighteenth century."[28] This master narrative suggests certain patterns that are not based in historical fact. One is that wars of the past did not last as long, nor were they as devastating, as the total wars of the twentieth century. Yet, by both measures, the Thirty Years War and the Seven Years War were as bad, if not worse.[29] Another erroneous pattern is the notion that, as wars became more modern, so they became more total.[30] In fact, the European fronts in World Wars I and II reveal strikingly different levels of modernization across space and time. In overall terms, muscle power was more in evidence, and machine power far less so, on the Eastern than the Western front during both wars.[31] And yet war in the East was more total, both in the level of intensity and mobilization. Indeed, the German Army experienced a "profound demodernization" on the Eastern front during World War II as a consequence of the attrition of its resource base and force structure. This resulted in a more extreme, "total" style of German warfare, as the Nazis sought to use indoctrination to make up for the loss of their technological edge on the battlefield.[32]

Without looking for specific trends across the sweep of history, one can still say that mass mobilization and industrialization are central features of the big wars of the past two centuries. Following Napoleon's *levee en mass,* governments came to accept the logic of unlimited warfare—both in terms of the ends and means of war. As the American Civil War of 1861–1865 showed, given large enough stakes, entire societies would now mobilize behind a total war effort. And as economies industrialized in the nineteenth century, so did warfare. The major effect of this has been the mechanization of warfare—while such "progress" has not been steady nor uniform, greater mechanization is generally in evidence from the Franco-Prussian War of 1870–1871, through to the two world wars and beyond.[33] Accordingly, I use the term "mass industrialized war" in place of "total war," when referring to the dominant features of conventional warfare in the twentieth century.

Collective Memory and Mobilization for War

The first part of this section examines the social construction of collective memory. Drawing on the social history of warfare literature, it considers how obstacles and opportunities for elite manipulation of collective memory are generated by the interaction of two things: the psychology of remembering and the role of civil society in memory work. These obstacles and opportunities are then explored in part two through a discussion of collective memory formation following World War I. This period is the focus of much attention in the social history of warfare because the Great War is widely seen as having had a transformative effect on public beliefs about the nature of war.

Constructed Memory, Contested Memory

The struggle for memory is the struggle for political identity. Political and military elites usually seek to frame collective memories of national glory, determination, and heroism; memories that give purpose to war and the state.[34] The social history of warfare literature suggests that when it comes to manufacturing collective memories, elites must contend with the way communities remember traumatic events, and with the numerous agents in civil society involved in reproducing the past.

Naturally, wars are public events of such immense importance that memory of them is not simply a personal matter. Rather, as Jay Winter and Emmanuel Sivan observe, "warfare is no doubt a time of dramatic, unique experiences, which leave dense memory traces, individual and social."[35] Private memories are not only shaped by collective experiences of war, they are also nurtured and shared in social frameworks—ceremonies, rituals, monuments, literature, film, and art. Collective memories of war are the product, therefore, of psychological and social processes.

How individuals remember has significant bearing on the formation, preservation, and recovery of collective war memories.[36] Cognitive psychology reveals some fascinating insights in this regard. To begin with, memory is selective and rarely accurate. New memories are layered upon old ones, so that we remember in "schemata" as we reconstruct events in our mind in light of our own experience and knowledge. Over time, memory becomes simplified—details become blurred and basic story lines emerge and harden as we shift from a process of memory reconstruction to one of memory reproduction.[37] This literature also tells us that three other things shape memory construction and recall. First is the dramatic nature of the experience, which can increase the "density" or weight of memory. Obviously, war is a time of high drama. Second is the role of "rehearsal" through social rituals (story-telling, ceremonies, parades, etc.) in preserving and recalling memories.[38] Third is the importance of "trauma" in providing triggers for memory recovery, though there is some debate as to whether traumatic memories are any more fixed and accurate than everyday memories.[39]

Individual memories are molded into collective frameworks through social processes. Collective memory takes shape and gains some longevity through external expression in literary, pictorial and monument forms. These provide schemata for memory and foci for memory reproduction. But such "memory artifacts" are merely "aids" to memory, not memory itself. Monuments eventually lose their meaning, particularly as the original wartime generation dies off, and with that memory fades.[40] Critical then is the role of social rituals in keeping collective memories alive, and in activating latent memories.

This whole discussion has obvious implications for the role of agency in the social construction of war memory. As we shall see, political elites often try to shape and structure public memory, both during and after the event in question, in order to advance particular policy interests and ideas. Possibilities for such elite manipulation will be constrained by the inherent density and associated trauma of war memories. But such possibilities will also be expanded through state sponsorship of memory artifacts and social rituals. Through these means, for instance, the Soviet state was able to manufacture collective memory of the 60 million Russians killed in the first half of the twentieth century. Catherine Merridale has shown how memorials to the Great Patriotic War against Germany recorded the official war narrative, that of the "young, handsome, innocent soldier, the victim who fell in battle repelling the Nazi invader." Suppressed were memories of the many more Russian deaths at Russian hands, through Civil War, state repression, and starvation.[41]

While states are major memory agents, we must also recognize the role of civil society—of cultural, commercial, and community groups—in recovering and reproducing memories in physical, visual, and literary monuments to war.[42] Civil society can provide sites of resistance to official memory work, as artists, educators, businesses, and ordinary people remember and portray the horror and moral uncertainties of war. But equally, sometimes official pictures of the past are supported by memory work done by cultural and commercial elites, and community groups. Finally, we should not be tempted to place higher moral value on memory agents located in civil society, even when political elites seek to control collective memory in order to bring their states to war.[43] Sometimes such wars may be morally reprehensible (e.g., Nazi Germany's invasion of Western Europe), but equally sometimes there may be a moral necessity for mobilizing popular will for war (e.g., the US entry into World War II).

Collective Memory and the Great War

A major theme in the social history of warfare is that of collective memory as the site and product of contestation within and between state institutions and civil society. Individuals and groups seek for personal, artistic, and commercial reasons to recall, understand, explain, and represent the experience of war. This theme is central to Jay Winter's acclaimed study on the Great War in European cultural history, *Sites of Memory, Sites of Mourning*. In this book, Winter explores the ways in which modernists challenged many of the "patriotic certainties" expressed in traditional romantic and religious images of war, and how "they stretched, explored, and reconfigured [these images] in ways that alarmed conventional artists, writers, and the public at large."[44] Paul Fussell goes further in *The Great War and Modern Memory,* an earlier also acclaimed book, arguing that World War I caused a neat rupture between traditional and modernist representations of war. For Fussell, the scale of death and destruction experienced on the battlefields of Europe, and the horrific scale of loss suffered on the home fronts, led cultural elites to reject the certainty of romantic war imagery for harsher, more aggressive modernist expressions of war.[45] Fussell bases his argument on a study of British literature: work by cultural elites intended for educated elitist audiences. Winter discovers a different dynamic at play when it comes to war memorials, that is, cultural artifacts produced for the masses. These, Winter finds, combine romantic and modernist, literal and abstract, reassuring and shocking representations of war. A more balanced assessment, then, might be to say that while the Great War did not kill off romanticism, it did certainly generate wider acceptance of modernism. As one art critic declared in *The Observer* in 1917:

> It is fairly obvious that the ordinary representational manner of painting is wholly inadequate for the interpretation of this tremendous conflict in which all the forces of nature have to be conquered and pressed into service against the opposing enemy. A more synthetic method is needed to express the essential character of this cataclysmic war, in which the very earth is disembowelled and rocky mountain summits are blown sky-high to bury all life under the falling debris.[46]

With wider critical and common acceptance of modernism comes greater appreciation of the moral uncertainties and mortal danger of war. Politically speaking, war becomes a harder product to sell to the public.

The same cannot be said of it in purely commercial terms. Well before World War I, war had become an entertainment industry in its own right. Michael Paris shows how from 1850 onward, "war became deeply embedded in [British] popular culture, particularly in the cultural artefacts that are created for the youth of the nation"—namely, boys magazines and fiction, and from early 1900s, mass produced war toys and the new medium of cinema.[47] The image that was represented was of war as an exciting adventure, if not a righteous one. The glamour of war was also used to sell all manner of household products to the public. No doubt this contributed to the popular move to war in 1914, when almost two and a half million Britons volunteered to fight in France. What these young men actually experienced was death, dirt, exhaustion, and gnawing fear on the frontline—a far cry from the traditional imagery propagated in popular war culture.[48]

The marketability of war can also clearly be seen in the rising popularity of battlefield tourism following the Great War. In promoting their product, tourist companies broke down the barrier between tourist and pilgrim, and invited people to recall and appreciate the scale of sacrifice and suffering, death and destruction. One of Michelin's 1917 guides to World War I battlefields recommended that "such a visit should be a pilgrimage, not merely a journey across the ravaged. Seeing is not enough, one must understand; a ruin is more moving when one knows what has caused it." The net effect of this commercial activity was to include those who had no direct experience of the battlefield in the preservation and recollection of collective memory about the war. In this war tourism provides another illustration of how memory work occurs from below as well as above. As David Lloyd argues, "the active role of individuals in the construction of memory also explains why remembrance was not just a tool which was manipulated by the elites. In Great Britain in the 1920s and 1930s the memory of the war was pervaded by a deeply felt individual desire to remember and mourn the dead."[49]

Often the state can benefit from the complicity of civil society in maintaining traditional patriotic memories of war. Heroism and glory are easier to report, record, represent, and ultimately stomach than stories of suffering and images of horror. Patriotic narratives of war not only serve an important function in binding nations together; they also give comfort and meaning to the experiences of combatants and victims.[50] One such example is the myth of the "Great and Glorious War of 1870–1871" against France, a central component of Germany's founding story. Decades after the war, almost all Germans could "remember" the war, even though 97 percent of them had not actually fought in it.[51] The glorious war myth was kept alive in war monuments in every town, in school textbooks, popular illustrated histories, plays, novels, poetry, as well as in the ordinary objects of everyday life—postcards, place mats, sweet wrappers, and the like.

Alfred Kelly argues that this myth was a "privileged narrative." Poorly educated, and with only a "worms eye" view of the action, the average soldier "had to integrate his narrow experience into the larger narrative constructed by his leaders." Kelly also notes that war reporters, with limited sight of the battlefield, depended on German military authorities to interpret what happened. Accordingly, reporters reproduced stories and pictures of heroism rather than horror, and soldiers and public alike accepted this patriotic imagery, because they wanted to.[52] Veterans, in particular, needed the myth of a glorious war with France in order to "live comfortably with [their] terrible experience"; moreover, they "had little interest in challenging the myth, for to do so would have undercut their own self-esteem." In short, widespread acceptance of selective, glorious, memories of war, particularly by those who experienced it, rather than effective government manipulation, made the myth possible.[53]

Arguably, this myth is a specific manifestation of a more general Europe-wide Myth of War Experience, which George Mosse argues existed from Napoleonic times, when Europe witnessed the first mass conscript wars of the modern age. Mosse notes that this generic myth also operated to sanctify the experience and sacrifice of mass war. He finds that this Myth of War Experience did not survive the change in social attitudes to war that accompanied World War II.[54] This echoes the argument above about modernist representations of war reflecting greater artistic and public appreciation of the hazards of war. It also suggests European civil societies were more likely to be supportive of national mobilization for war before 1945 than after. The absence of major European wars after 1945 certainly correlates with this shift away from norms of military mobilization; one may infer a causal relationship between declining levels of social support and the declining practice of major war in Europe.[55]

The process of collective memory construction is thus a complex, context specific, and highly contingent one. Collective memory of war is often contested terrain, one which numerous agents, both state and in civil society, have tried to define for emotional, aesthetic, commercial, and political reasons. Political elites have sought to romantically frame collective memories of war in the mass industrial age, to give purpose to past, present, and future sacrifice. Elite success in this endeavor within particular temporal and national contexts is dependent on control of social rituals and memory artifacts. At the same time, there are macrosocial events that may affect the ability of elites across a number of states to mobilize their societies for war: World War I is one such event. Prior to World War I, former combatants were receptive to such framing, lacking the perspective and incentive to undermine their own wartime achievements. The romantic frame began to wear thin following the scale and apparent fruitlessness of the slaughter in World War I and in the face of modernist representations of war.[56] Accordingly, norms of military mobilization have lost some prescriptive affect in the Western world. State framing of collective war memories continues after World War II and, as we see below, sometimes civil society collaborates in this enterprise. But generally speaking, Western states have a harder time selling war to their societies in the postwar period.

Imagination and Machine Warfare

Visions of future war—often flights of pure imagination—flowed from a central narrative of modern war, that of technological progress. This section examines future war imagery and the development of machine warfare, focusing, in particular, on the development of the tank and the bomber.

The mechanization of warfare in the twentieth century unleashed terrible images of future war, images not drawn from past experience. It so happens that the horrendous slaughter of World War I was presaged by the mass industrialized American Civil War. Both the Union and Confederacy fully mobilized their respective societies in a long war of attrition. The major technological advances were in firepower and logistics, making battlefields more deadly and offensive maneuver much more difficult. Mass mobilization and total war aims also eroded the battle and home fronts, and drew civilian populations into the war. This was all characteristic of the future of warfare in the industrial age.[57]

The implications of this for the nature of future wars were not realized by all. As David Trask argues, Americans "failed to grasp the significance of the Civil War as a military portent—as a technical foretaste of a new kind of warfare."[58] John Whiteclay Chambers II agrees that the Civil War "was not seen as a harbinger of the nature of the future of modern war." He suggests that "pitting Americans against Americans, it seemed an aberration." To be clear, the Civil War did provide a reference point for discussion in popular magazines about the tactics and technologies of future warfare. Debate centered on the question of whether greater firepower would be matched by increased casualties. Some military contributors argued that the new technologies would make battles more lethal and therefore wars shorter, and so result in fewer casualties in the long run. In focusing on the detail of future land warfare, such commentators missed the big lesson of the Civil War, that industrialization not only made mechanized war possible, it also made long, drawn-out, mass war probable.[59] In contrast, as discussed in the next section, the German military elite accurately predicted that mass industrialized wars would be lengthy, draining affairs for European states.

Also missed by Americans and Europeans alike was the likely impact of mass industrialized war on the minds of those that experienced it. Industrialization made war more destructive and mechanization made it more furious (in pace and intensity) than ever before. Within months of the outbreak of World War I, the British Army found itself having to deal with an epidemic of men apparently suffering postcombat mental breakdown. By the end of the war it had incurred about 200,000 psychological casualties (the French and German armies took similar losses). Widespread "mind wounds" had been experienced in the American Civil War.[60] One Union Army physician observed the bravest of soldiers becoming "as hysterical as the veriest woman." Nonetheless, medical opinion took a dim view of those who exhibited such symptoms. The *American Journal of Medical Science* reported in 1864 that "The great majority of malingerers consist rather of men who exaggerate real maladies of trifling character, or who feign disease outright."[61] Ironically that same decade saw neurology rapidly establishing itself as one of the first specialisms in medicine.[62] In the latter half of the nineteenth century the Victorian "stiff upper lip" steadily eroded as men began to display nervous disorders previously associated with the "weaker sex." Industrialization and mechanization made modern living more stressful as humans sought to harness the vigor and power of the machine. Work-related traumatic neuroses became so widespread that allowance was made for them in welfare provision schemes and employers' liability insurance (both of which emerged in late-nineteenth- and early-twentieth-century

Britain).[63] Notwithstanding the growth of nervous disorders in civilian society in the decades leading up to World War I, the British Army was caught completely unprepared. In 1913 there were still no specialist neurologists or psychiatrists in the Royal Army Medical Corps.[64] This is not so surprising however, and not only because the lessons of the American Civil War were dismissed by the US medical profession. Many Europeans who volunteered for war did so in the hope of escaping the pressures of modern civilian life—pressures generated by industrialization and mechanization.[65] Thus in failing to anticipate that such pressures would be more intense in war, expert opinion was in line with popular opinion.

Ironically, the reverse was true of air war: its form was accurately predicted despite the lack of precedent. Indeed, Michael Sherry maintains that "more than any other modern weapon, the bomber was imagined before it was invented."[66] Much has been made in the academic literature of the role of cultural and military elites in producing and realizing visions of air war.[67] Particularly noted in this regard, is H. G. Wells's *The War in the Air* published in 1908, in which the author predicted the great powers sending fleets of airships and aircraft to bomb each others' homelands in a terrible global war. Remarkably, the prophets of air war were unanimous in their vision of what it would look like—that is, strategic bombing to terrorize enemy populations. As Basil Liddell Hart reasoned, "aircraft enable us to jump over the army which shields the enemy government, industry and people, and so strike direct and immediately at the seat of the opposing will and policy."[68] While the most vocal and impatient proponents of air power were military mavericks—Hart, J. F. C. Fuller, Giulio Douhet, and Billy Mitchell—it was mainstream military leaders, particularly in the Royal Air Force and US Army Air Force, who fostered the technology and created the force structures to wage war from the air.[69]

Air power took off not only in elite minds but also in public imagination. In the early twentieth century, people marveled at the possibility of air travel: tens of thousands regularly turned out to watch air displays. Even in World War I, the public was as much fascinated as frightened by air attacks. In Germany, people rushed onto the streets to look at the approaching enemy bombers instead of hurrying to air raid shelters. In one German town, city council records reveal officials discussing how "to give the population an opportunity to observe the air battles in safety."[70] In the lead-up to World War II, public views of air power were informed by reassuring expert opinion. Air power enthusiasts like Alexander de Seversky—war hero, fighter ace, and aircraft designer—preached directly to the people: 20 million Americans knew of Seversky and his message in the early 1940s.[71] To be sure, interwar publics in the United States and Europe recognized the airplane as a fearful instrument of destruction, but they also identified it as a symbol of industrial creativity.[72] This mirrored a more general view shared by cultural elites, about the industrialization and mechanization of war in the late nineteenth and early twentieth centuries alluding to both creative and destructive forces in modern society.[73] Wells's original terrible vision of airpower was finally realized in the massive bombing campaigns of World War II. Military organization and technology had finally caught up with flights of human imagination.

When it came to the tank, imagination and technology also combined to shape machine warfare on the ground. Once again, Wells predicted what was to come in a science fiction story called "The Land Ironclads" published in the *Strand* magazine in 1903.[74] However, Wells was the not the first to come up with the idea of mechanized armored vehicles; indeed, such an idea had been patented in Britain as early as 1855. The impetus to realize this idea came from the Western front of World War I, specifically the need to develop offensive technologies that would increase forward mobility on the battlefield. State and society joined forces in Britain to produce the first tanks. The technology was developed by amateur civilian inventors, promoted by visionary military officers, and supported by key individuals in the political establishment. Among them was Winston Churchill, who as first Lord of the Admiralty became chief sponsor of "landships." Right from the beginning, imagination shaped the tank. Its very name was dreamt up to keep the new weapon secret while it was being tested in Britain. Locals who stumbled across prototype landships were told that they were in fact "mobile water tanks." The name stuck, and as they were run through their paces on English country estates, tanks captured the imagination of visiting dignitaries. Fans included the Chief of the Imperial Defense Staff and Churchill's replacement at the Admiralty, A. J. Balfour.

Tanks made a disappointing first public appearance at the Battle of the Somme, on 15 September 1916. Of the 49 tanks deployed, only 32 made it into action—the rest got bogged down or simply broke down. Many soldiers, on both sides, collapsed in laughter at first sight of these machines as they awkwardly made their way across the battlefield. Press reports from the front painted a very different picture—that of a juggernaut terrifying Germans as it smashed through their lines. In part, such exaggerated reporting was caused by strict censorship. The first images of the tank were not released until mid-November, and in the intervening 2 months reporters came up with their own exaggerated imagery to hint at what the tank looked like and could do. Wildly over the top reporting fueled a cult of the tank in Britain. The British public looked to technology to break the military stalemate and shorten the war, and all too readily believed that the tank would do the trick.[75]

In fact, World War I tanks were not the wonder weapons they were made out to be. They were clumsy machines, only capable of overtaking infantry when going downhill, and unable to operate for more than 8 hours. Tank crews were subjected to deafening noise, petrol fumes, and seasickness. Further limitations included that tanks tended to sink in muddy ground and were vulnerable to armor-piercing bullets. Proponents of armored warfare claimed that tanks failed to achieve the great breakthrough because they were used incorrectly. British generals tended to parcel them out in small packages across a wide front, instead of massing tanks to attack a narrow frontage. In short, tanks could have made a real difference to the war had they been deployed in force.[76] The Battle of Cambrai in November 1917 seemed to validate this view, when 378 tanks advancing along 12,000 yards of front easily overran enemy trenches. However, these tanks still lacked the range and stamina to push in any depth through German lines.[77] Armored warfare advocates came up with even more ambitious plans to build on Cambrai. Colonel Fuller, intellectual father of the Tank Corps, proposed (in his famous fantastical "Plan 1919") an attack by 2,000 tanks along a 90 mile front. The head of the War Office Tank Directorate, Major General Sir John Capper, came up with an even more ambitious plan involving over 8,000 tanks. In fact, both plans were based on a completely unrealistic hope that Britain would be able to produce huge numbers of new "cruiser" tanks. They also ignored the main reasons for success at Cambrai—namely, new British artillery techniques combined with surprisingly weak German defenses at the point of attack.[78]

The problem with the tank in World War I was that military (and public) imagination exceeded the technological capabilities of the day. The leadership of the British Army was far more supportive of the new weapon than commonly assumed—after all, it did establish the first Tank Corps in the world. It continued to support the development of tank tactics in the interwar period. But technical problems persisted with the machines themselves. The tank was failing the British Army, not the other way around.[79] In World War II, the tank did finally realize its full potential to return mobility to the battlefield, when range and reliability of tanks had increased, communications technology had improved, and tank enthusiasts had come to accept the need for combined arms warfare.[80] In fantasy, perhaps, tanks could win wars by themselves, but in reality they had to fight alongside infantry, artillery, and aircraft.

Imagination is central to how communities wage war. Human imagination furnishes the machinery of warfare in the mass industrial age. Norms of machine warfare are evident in the blind faith placed in military machines by political and military elites, and press and public opinion. Only those on the firing line were able to judge where faith exceeded fact.

German Purpose and the Two World Wars

In addition to men and material, memories and images were mobilized when Germany went to war in 1914 and 1939. In the late nineteenth century, militarism was actively promoted by the German government, in order to reduce internal social divisions and unite the people against external enemies. However, German militarism soon developed a dynamic of its own, and the government found itself under increasing popular pressure to be more adventurous in trying to elevate Germany to world power.[81]

This growing tide of popular militarism may be observed in the radicalization of the ex-servicemen's association—which played a particularly important role in mobilizing German society for World War I. From 1890 onward, the social makeup of this movement changed, with local veterans' associations also admitting reservists. Veterans' associations thus changed from being memorials to war experiences to being forums for celebrating the German Army, and this resulted in a change of ideological orientation, away from commemorating past military service to glorifying war in general. Drills and displays organized by the veterans' and reservists' associations fed the public's appreciation of militarism. Particularly important was the relationship between war veterans and new recruits. Thomas Rohkramer argues that "because the members of the older generation presented themselves as heroes after their participation in the wars of unification, the members of the younger generation, who had never participated in war, felt inferior." This spurred on the young reservists to prove their worth. "Thus, they turned the backward-looking glorification of the Franco-Prussian War into a forward-looking militarism that touted German expansion and future war in which these 'would-be heroes' could prove themselves to be 'true heroes' like their fathers."[82]

The imagination of the German military elite also contributed to the outbreak of World War I. There are two basic views on this. One is that a combination of widespread German paranoia, social Darwinism, and worst-case planning typical of military professionals produced fatalism in the German General Staff. German generals recognized that war was incredibly risky and yet, at the same time, they considered it necessary. Experience of the Franco-Prussian War seemed to rule out a quick victory in the next war. Popular French resistance following defeat of the regular French Army showed that nations could no longer be beaten into submission on the battlefield. In this context, German military leaders expected the next war against France and Russia to last years, and they had no idea how to win it. In his last speech to the Reichstag, in May 1890, former chief of the General Staff Helmuth von Moltke warned, "the age of cabinet war is over—all we have now is people's war . . . if this war breaks out, then its duration and its end will be unforeseeable."[83] Viewed thus, General Alfred von Schlieffen's (the new chief of the General Staff) evolving plan for the coming war was not a "foolproof receipt for a short war," but rather "a desperate operational plan for the opening campaign of a long war." German military leaders still took their country to war. For starters, they felt that war was unavoidable—here the General Staff shared "the paranoia of encirclement" that was widespread in Germany at the time. The conservative military leadership also felt that war was even desirable, both to prove Germans' worth in a Darwinian struggle for international survival, and in order to purify a nation corrupted by the social development accompanying industrialization.[84]

An alternative view, based on a different reading of German military imagination, is that military leaders were reasonably optimistic about the prospect of war. Here we may see the Schlieffen Plan as the most visible manifestation of the General Staff's faith in detailed preparation, whereby the war could be won provided everything worked as planned. In short, the army was not marching "fully conscious into catastrophe" but rather "into high risk."[85] Historians all agree that, properly speaking, Germany entered World War I without a strategy.[86] The General Staff's war plan turned out to be merely a timetable for mobilizing and moving troops, a guide for starting the war but hardly a blueprint for victory.[87] German officers mistook this for strategy because they thought of modern war in terms of the mechanics of mobilization.[88]

Popular feelings were mixed in Germany when war did finally come to Europe.[89] The war was most favored by young, middle-class city dwellers. However, it generated anxiety and fear among older and poorer Germans, and those living in the countryside. Moreover, many people had mixed emotions: feelings of excitement, exhilaration, trepidation, and concern. Nevertheless, a myth of universal war enthusiasm rapidly established itself in German political culture. In his study of this myth—called "the spirit of 1914"—Jeffrey Verhey provides an instructive case of how collective memories are manipulated and mobilized for war. Here cultural and political leaders collectively constructed the "spirit of 1914": the myth was promoted not only in government propaganda, but also by a compliant conservative press and in popular literature and theater. This myth was further able to take root in political discourse because liberal opposition groups also tried to co-opt and take advantage of the "spirit of 1914" narrative instead of debunking it.[90]

Collective memory of defeat was also manufactured by military and conservative political elites, with disastrous consequences. According to the "spirit of 1914" myth, Germany would be victorious provided its people exercised the will to win. Even when the balance of material forces began to favor the Allies, Germans were told that with "grim determination" they could still win the war. If willpower was the key to victory, then it was also central to defeat. German military leaders argued that the decline in public morale, rather than the increase in the enemy's material superiority, had lost the war. In short, the civilian population, under the influence of left-wing and enemy propaganda, had "stabbed the army in the back." The "stab-in-the-back" legend was ridiculed by the left, nevertheless it was believed by the public because "people wanted to believe in it." Germans concluded from this that the way to undo the defeat of World War I was to increase one's own will. The appeal of this mythological epistemology was given political force in the 1930s under the Nazis. Where fatalism took Germany to war in 1914, fanatical will did so in 1939.[91]

Memory and imagination also shaped the character of German warfare, particularly the intensely savage war pursued by German forces on the Eastern front during World War II. Where Omer Bartov explains German barbarism in the context of the brutalizing influence of appalling battlefield conditions and Nazi racial ideology, Vejas Gabriel Liulevicius locates German Army action in the collective memory of Germany's previous invasion of Russia. In 1914, the East was totally alien territory to invading Germans, who had no idea what to expect. As they pushed into the Russian Empire, German soldiers encountered a land left barren by retreating Russian forces. Germans associated conditions created by war—dirt, disease, disorder, and human misery—with the normal character of the region. In response, the German Army sought to structure and bring *Kultur* to the East by building a monolithic military state, named *Ober Ost*. The scale of the project was impressive: *Ober Ost* covered over 100,000 square kilometers (roughly half the size of the United Kingdom today) and contained around 3 million inhabitants. However, "vaunting, overreaching ambition led to constant conflict between the utopian ends and brutal means of the state's policies, which sped towards immobilization." Even though Germany defeated Russia in 1917, *Ober Ost* failed a year later because "instead of successfully manipulating native peoples, yoking them to the program of German work, the regime called forth a desperate native resistance, as subject peoples articulated national identities in a struggle for survival."[92]

A variant of the "stab-in-the-back" legend was employed to explain this failure: namely, that German soldiers who had mutinied in the November 1918 revolution were influenced by natives (especially Jews) and infected with Bolshevik ideas. The collapse of *Ober Ost* led Germans to reject all they had learned about the East. Previous recognition of it as a region of "lands and peoples" to be ordered and cultivated gave way to a new concept of it as containing "races and spaces" to be exterminated and exploited. Liulevicius notes that "the imperative of the future had to be: leave out the people and take the spaces." When the Nazis unleashed war in the East, the purpose was not to defeat the Russians but "clearing and cleaning the space for a new order and settlement." The Nazis' General Plan for the East envisaged removing and murdering 31 million people, and using the remaining 14 million natives as slave labor for German settlers. Luilevicius concludes that "the line of continuity between the military utopia and Nazi plans can be traced in the way in which *Ober Ost*'s practices and assumptions were radicalized and then put into action in a renewed war in the East." In this way, manipulated memory of the past combined with terrible vision for the future to produce German barbarism on the Eastern front in World War II.[93]

On both occasions when Germany invaded the East, elite plans captured the public's imagination. From the late nineteenth century onward, proponents of German imperialism promoted the new science of geopolitics in public consciousness. When World War I broke out, public enthusiasm for geography peaked, and "war geography" became the popular script for explaining the cause and consequences of the conflict. In the context of this territorial imagination, a clear imperative for eastward expansion was constructed. Throughout the 1920s and 1930s, cultural elites continued to feed the public a steady diet of *Wehr-Geopolitik,* producing a "geographic hysteria, a mass claustrophobia in the Weimar Republic." Geopoliticians also provided Nazi leaders with the concepts around which to construct a program of eastward expansion. So when the Nazis came to sell this program to the public, from 1933 on, through an official campaign of propaganda and education, they found a ready-made audience. Once again, Germans were prepared to go eastward at all costs.[94]

The German case illustrates how imagination and memory combine, and primary and secondary cultural agents interact, in the origins and operation of norms of military mobilization. Military elites imagined the coming World War I either as an unavoidable rite of Darwinian purification or a risky play for German expansion. Political elites constructed a myth of war enthusiasm—the spirit of 1914—to bolster public support for the war. The spirit of 1914 myth provided the narrative to explain Germany's defeat in World War I: failure of popular will. Nazi ideologues seized this collective memory in constructing a new terrible image of eastward German expansion. Secondary agents also had important roles in shaping norms of military mobilization. German militarism rose as a popular movement, nurtured in ex-servicemen's associations, performance arts, and the conservative press. German militarism gained popular expression in the memory of the glorious Franco-Prussian War, in public ownership of the spirit of 1914, and, following World War I, in public imagination of German expansion as legitimated by geopolitics.

US Power and the Pacific War

The US war in the Pacific in 1941–1945 occurred in the context of the rise of the US military and the global expansion of US trade and capital. Interests and imagination combined to generate the great navy of the United States. In 1890, the United States committed itself to acquiring a blue-water fleet that within a few decades would be second only to Britain's.[95] That same year, US naval officer and historian Alfred Thayer Mahan gave academic credence to the navalists' cause, with the publication of his famous *The Influence of Seapower upon History, 1660–1783.* Previously, US naval ambitions had been modest, so much so that the navy was allowed to slip into technological and material obsolescence in 1865–1883.[96]

There were domestic political incentives for naval expansion: Republican Party leaders sought to stimulate industrial growth in the hard-pressed Northwest, and to neutralize agrarian discontent in the trans-Mississippi West.[97]

However, political and popular imagination also played a part in the creation of US naval power. According to Mark Shulman, "the navalists were part of a larger movement in late-nineteenth-century American political culture—an elite rebellion against the long-standing commercial and agrarian national ethos."[98] Essentially, progressive thinkers sought to replace the Jeffersonian image of a minimalist, agrarian-commercial democracy with the Hamiltonian vision of a stronger, more interventionist republic. Social Darwinism played a role here, just as it did in Germany, leading the US political elite to see virtue in state expansion and international struggle, and informing Mahan's theories of US sea power.[99]

There were also broader social forces at play, specifically the need to construct a new US national identity in the late nineteenth century that would lock in the newly integrated (post–Civil War) South, and respond to the increasing irrelevance of the "frontier" image in the face of industrialization. This too required the construction of a muscular outward-looking identity to replace that of a modest inward-looking nation: the "self" would be defined by encountering the "other" (foreigners). In addition, commercial pressures, in terms of the expansion of US trade, were important in the reconstruction of national identity. This new vision of national greatness fueled the pronavy lobby: as a great nation, the United States needed a great navy to protect its trade interests. The logic of this argument enabled the pronavy lobby to attach their cause to the rise of US greatness, and thereby build domestic support for naval expansion.[100]

Imagination not only shaped the rise of US military power, but also how that power was used in the war against Japan. Graphic racial imagery played a central role in shaping the war for Americans. In official propaganda and popular publications, the Japanese were invariably given animal form—simians, rats, snakes, cockroaches, and other kinds of vermin. Such images were perpetuated by big business, in advertising campaigns designed to tie products— from fridges to fly-spray—to the great patriotic cause. US soldiers, sailors, and airmen took this imagery with them into battle, and it provided the narrative for their actions: fighting Japanese was often compared to wiping out "nests" of vipers or rats; bombing the enemy was likened to quashing insects; and operations became "hunts" for "monkey-meat" (as one US admiral put it).[101]

Racist brutality toward the enemy was reinforced by the discomfort of jungle conditions and Japanese fanaticism and treachery. On the Pacific island of Guadalcanal, only 1.2 percent of the Japanese garrison were captured alive by US forces. On occasion, surrendering Japanese attempted suicidal attacks when US troops lowered their guard. The reality and rumors of this led many US units to take no prisoners. As one marine told a reporter, "you've probably heard about their using white surrender flags to suck us into traps. We're onto that one now."[102] His superiors agreed. A US naval conference in 1943 concluded, "the only way to beat the Japs is to kill them all. They will not sur-

render and our troops are taking no chances and are killing them anyway."[103]
As it happened, the Japanese also considered their Western foe to be racially
inferior (though not by dehumanizing Westerners, but by elevating the Japanese race). Accordingly, as John Dower argues, "war words and race words
came together in a manner which did not just reflect the savagery of the war,
but contributed to it by reinforcing the impression of a truly Manichaean
struggle between completely incompatible antagonists. The natural response
to such a vision was an obsession with extermination on both sides—a war
without mercy."[104]

In the end, Japan was bombed into submission with an air campaign that
destroyed most of its urban centers and killed somewhere between 400,000
and 900,000 civilians. This level of destruction was caused mostly by firebombing. Cities were literally burnt to the ground along with their inhabitants.
Racism and revenge (for Pearl Harbor and treatment of Allied POWs) certainly facilitated US warfare on such a savage scale. However, for Sherry, the
US military were ultimately able to realize terrible visions of air war because
"leaders and technicians of the American air force were driven by technological fanaticism—a pursuit of destructive ends expressed, sanctioned, and dis-
guised by the organization and application of technological means."[105] The
military were supported in this by civilian scientists and industry, which produced and actively promoted the technology for, and methods of, incendiary
bombing.[106] To be sure, there were strategic imperatives for firebombing
Japan's cities, chiefly, the need to reduce bomber losses (firebombing could
be conducted at night) and the need to end the war as quickly as possible. The
point is, however, that technology made the apocalyptic air war against Japan
possible, both literally and psychologically. It offered an attractive and easy
way to exercise military power and, at the same time, the technical demands
of bombing (for planners and pilots alike) created emotional distance between
airmen and their victims. Thus one observer found airmen "not to be concerned with killing and . . . hardly aware of an enemy," but rather preoccupied
"with the proper handling of their complicated machine along the lines laid
down in meticulously organized plans."[107]

In his history of the US Marine Corps campaign in the Pacific, Craig
Cameron finds that racism and technological fanaticism also interacted to produce the most brutal form of warfare on the ground. For this division (as for
Allied forces in general) popular racist imagery, reinforced by sanctioned
ruthless tactics, led marines to view their enemies as "termites" to be wiped-
out. But brutality on the battlefield was also shaped by a tough "elite warrior"
self-image, carefully cultivated by the Marine Corps in public relations and
recruitment campaigns, represented in popular media and film, and inculcated
in military training. This elitist self-image had a discernible impact on military action in the Pacific in that it produced a gung-ho, go-it-alone style of operations, which inhibited effective cooperation between the marines and the

army. The marines believed that the army's style of warfare, which emphasized massing force and indirect attack, was too slow and deliberative for the
Pacific island-hopping campaign. This was because island invasions required
naval amphibious task forces to stay in vulnerable offshore anchorages. Thus,
the Marine Corps were prepared to sacrifice their own troops in quick assaults
in order to preserve navy ships. Many marines also felt that army soldiers
lacked sufficient aggressiveness and fighting spirit for the job. One marine
general complained of army soldiers, "They're yellow. They are not aggressive. They've just held up battle and caused my Marines casualties." This
view was undoubtedly reinforced by the army's willingness to surrender positions in order to preserve units; marines never gave up territory except when
under annihilating enemy fire. For these reasons, marines preferred to work
alone rather than rely on army units for support.[108]

In the closing months of the Pacific campaign, the Marine Corps achieved
a sufficient level of technological domination to realize the extremist logic of
their style of warfare. Three marine and four army divisions, 180,000 troops in
all, were deployed to seize Okinawa, an island 60 miles long and up to 18
across. Operationally speaking, the army's style of warfare dominated at this
stage, as the United States was able to bring overwhelming firepower to bear on
the enemy. US tanks, artillery, and aircraft blasted Japanese defenses, but the
key new technology that marines brought into the battlefield was the
flamethrower. These were particularly effective in killing Japanese dug in cave
positions—the occupations were suppressed with flame, and explosives were
then used to seal cave entrances: a technique marines called "blowtorch and
corkscrew." Cameron argues that identity and technology thus operated in synergy. "In land warfare the marines on Okinawa established a close reciprocal relationship whereby they harnessed their warrior image to the military machine,
and in return that technology empowered their own specific exterminationist
ideology." Where Germany's wars were fueled by ideological fanaticism, those
of the United States expressed the "triumph of technological fanaticism."[109]

The US case illustrates the origins and operation of norms of military mobilization and norms of machine warfare. Collective memory of the attack on
Pearl Harbor undeniably played an important role in mobilizing Americans to
fight, and fight savagely, against the Japanese. But in this case study I have
focused on how imagination shaped both moral codes and technical scripts for
US military action. Images of self—of the United States as a great power—
fueled the rise of US naval power at the turn of the twentieth century. This
self-image gained expression in norms of machine warfare—specifically in
the powerful naval task forces that the United States relied upon to defeat
Japan in the Pacific. Racist images of the other—of the enemy as subhuman—
made it possible for the Marine Corps to prosecute a brutal ground war against
Japanese forces, and for the US Army Air Force to conduct a horrific air war
against Japanese cities. The US ground and air wars in the Pacific were also

shaped by norms of machine warfare; norms that were rooted in an image of war as a technical exercise in the application of technological solutions to military problems. To be sure, political and military elites set out to create and sustain these images of the self, other, and technology. But secondary agents—commercial and cultural elites, and public opinion—also played important roles in producing and promoting these images of the United States as great, the Japanese as despicable, and technology as the answer.

Conclusion

This chapter has broadened our perspective on the culture of modern warfare in two respects. First, it has explored two of the essential building blocks of norms of war—collective memory and imagination. Second, it has examined the role of primary and secondary agents in remembering and imagining war.

The Cultural Building Blocks of War

Collective memory is particularly important in defining the moral purpose of a war. As we saw in the case of Germany, collective memory of the failed attempt to colonize the East in World War I spurred an even more extreme plan to dominate the region in World War II. Imagination also played a role. The geographic consciousness of ordinary Germans—legitimated by the pseudo-science of geopolitics and commercialized in popular media—fed a public will and desire for eastward expansion. The German case also illustrates how manufactured memory of defeat can shape the security policy of a state. The German military blamed defeat on a failure of public morale—the lesson drawn from this was the need for the public to have complete faith in order to persevere in war. From this, the Nazis successfully generated the fanatical will for their aggressive grand strategy.

We also saw how imagination can define the instruments of mass industrialized war. Bombers and tanks had to be imagined, before they could be designed and built. Imagination also defines how these instruments are used, and their perceived effects. The prophets of air war uniformly imagined it in terms of strategic bombing of urban-industrial centers. This prophecy came true in World War II. The advocates of the tank imagined that it would make future wars more mobile. This, it eventually did, after some initial technological hiccups. Planes were first greeted by curious crowds, even when they were delivering bombs! Tanks were greeted as wonder weapons by weary populaces at home. Cultural and commercial elites played their part in promoting these new war toys. Public enchantment with these new technologies also reflected the modernist spirit of the age, with its fetishism of the machine and the celebration of action, speed, and vigor.[110]

Images of the self and the other can determine the intensity of machine warfare. Against opponents deemed to be barbarians, or otherwise lesser beings, anything goes—the gloves are off. Whereas, against other civilized opponents, certain restraints are often observed in war.[111] For instance, while the German General Staff had long opposed the introduction of machine guns in Europe, it approved their use against natives in Africa in the late nineteenth century.[112] The case of the US war against Japan reveals how racial imagery informs unrestrained machine warfare.[113]

Equally important is the interaction of imagination and technology on warfare (regardless of the enemy). The mechanization of war creates distance between those operating modern weapon systems and their human targets—distance in the physical sense, but also in the emotional sense as weapons operators become occupied by the technical demands of what they are doing and lose sight of the human consequences. In the US case, we saw how this dynamic operated within US military organizations to create a technological fanaticism in the conduct of the US air and ground war against Japan in World War II.

Cultural Agency and Modern War

A key contribution of the social history of warfare is to highlight the broad array of agents involved in constructing, contesting, and reconstructing norms of war. These include cultural and commercial elites as well as community groups and professional associations. This diversity of memory agents complicates the state's task in using collective memory and imagination to mobilize and prepare their populaces for war. Obviously, such popular mobilization became much more important with the development of mass industrial war. Ironically, at the same time, popular mobilization becomes more difficult as the intensity of modern warfare challenges romantic memories of war and gives greater force to stark, modernist war imagery.

Critical to the construction and recall of collective memories are memory artifacts and social rituals. Primary agents can be sponsors of memory artifacts, such as war memorials but also war movies. For example, the US Marine Corps supported a number of Hollywood movies in the interwar period as part of an elaborate public relations campaign to promote the elite martial image of the Corps.[114] However, states are unlikely to be the sole (or even main) producers of memory artifacts. As we saw, given the commercialization of war from the late nineteenth century on, artifacts that embody war images and experiences have taken all manner of forms, including pulp fiction, celebratory china, and even candy wrappers. State agency also relies on the sponsorship of social rituals—indeed, such rituals can become an important means for attaching meaning (and thereby memories) to artifacts. Thus, the Nazis intentionally recalled the "spirit of 1914" in their spectacular celebration to mark the appointment of Adolf Hitler as chancellor in January 1933.[115] As we noted, this myth was then used by the Nazis to promote national unity and public will as central to the success of German expansion.

The German and US cases generally illustrate the role played by secondary agents in *supporting* the norm work of primary agents. State-sponsored militarism was nurtured in ex-servicemen's associations, the arts, and the press, developing an aggressive dynamic of its own in late-nineteenth-century Germany. As we also saw, the German government's campaign to shape collective memory in terms of a mythical "spirit of 1914" was supported by the German cultural elites. Equally, geopolitics captured the imagination of the German public, providing the central narratives for two invasions of Russia because it was widely promoted in the press and popular literature. In the case of the United States, big business helped to shape a permissive public imagination of the Pacific war. Government propaganda designed to dehumanize the Japanese was echoed in patriotic advertisements for commercial products. Strategic bombing was also promoted by corporations, both in terms of the direct benefit to the US war effort and in terms of domestic appliances for the patriotic household.

Some may argue that the support of secondary agents in mobilizing public imagination and collective memory of war is less important with the decline of mass industrialized war in the West. Certainly, since the end of the Cold War, the wars fought by Western states have been "wars of choice" rather than "wars of necessity."[116] These wars are fought using limited means, to limited intensity, and for limited ends. Those fighting are trained volunteers rather than conscripts, and the action tends to take place in far-off battlefields. The net effect is to make war more distant in all senses for Western publics.[117] However, it would be a mistake to infer from this that publics are no longer involved when their states go to war. Public beliefs matter even when it comes to small humanitarian wars: public outrage can push states to use force (the so-called CNN effect) and public sensitivity to mounting casualties (the "body-bags" effect) can pull states out of these wars. Recent scholarship does point to the importance of political unity and policy certainty in controlling the CNN effect: when political and policy elites are in agreement on a foreign policy matter, then they can resist and even erode public calls for action.[118] The body-bags effect is widely considered to be pronounced in the United States, resulting in a "casualty phobia" among US political and military leaders.[119] But empirical analysis of polling data suggests that, in fact, the US public have a higher tolerance of casualties than previously assumed.[120] These qualifiers on the CNN and body bags effects do not, however, negate the importance of public opinion in "wars of choice." Indeed precisely because the stakes are much lower in limited wars, so is the public's willingness to pay for the war (in blood and currency). Not surprisingly then, political and military elites are eager as ever to shape images and memories of war. And in reporting and representing such wars of choice, cultural elites in the media and arts often draw on images and memories of the great wars of the past (especially World War II).[121] The West may have stopped waging mass industrialized war, but it lives on in Western imagination and memory.[122]

Notes

1. There are two exceptions here, namely, social science work on ethnic conflict and on peace movements. However, social scientists working on these subjects do not relate their approach or findings to the strategic culture literature. On the former, see Stuart J. Kaufman, *Modern Hatreds: The Symbolic Politics of Ethnic War* (Ithaca, NY: Cornell University Press, 2001). On the latter, see Matthew A. Evangelista, *Unarmed Forces: The Transnational Movement to End the Cold War* (Ithaca, NY: Cornell University Press, 1999); Jeffrey W. Knopf, *Domestic Society and International Cooperation: The Impact of Protest on US Arms Control Policy* (Cambridge: Cambridge University Press, 1998).

2. For literature reviews, see Walter A. Rosenbaum, *Political Culture* (London: Nelson, 1975); Dennis Kavanagh, *Political Culture* (London: Macmillan, 1972). Critical discussion is provided in Stephen Welch, *The Concept of Political Culture* (Basingstoke: Macmillan, 1993).

3. Colin S. Gray, *Nuclear Strategy and National Style* (Lanham, MD: Hamilton, 1986), p. 34.

4. Alastair Iain Johnston, *Cultural Realism: Strategic Culture and Grand Strategy in Chinese History* (Princeton, NJ: Princeton University Press, 1995), pp. 34–35.

5. John S. Duffield, *World Power Forsaken: Political Culture, International Institutions, and German Security Policy After Unification* (Stanford, CA: Stanford University Press, 1998), p. 24.

6. Thomas U. Berger, *Cultures of Antimilitarism: National Security in Germany and Japan* (Baltimore: Johns Hopkins University Press, 1998). Indeed, Berger's book is based on a Ph.D. dissertation that was cosupervised by Lucian Pye, a leading scholar on political culture (see note 7, below).

7. Gabriel A. Almond and Sidney Verba, *The Civic Culture: Political Attitudes and Democracy in Five Nations* (Princeton, NJ: Princeton University Press, 1963); Lucian W. Pye and Sidney Verba (eds.), *Political Culture and Political Development* (Princeton, NJ: Princeton University Press, 1965).

8. Lowell Dittmer, "Political Culture and Political Symbolism: Toward a Theoretical Synthesis," *World Politics* 29, no. 4 (1977): 554–555. See, for example, Ronald Inglehart, *The Silent Revolution: Changing Values and Political Styles Among Western Publics* (Princeton, NJ: Princeton University Press, 1977); Ronald Inglehart, *Culture Shift in Advanced Industrial Societies* (Princeton, NJ: Princeton University Press, 1990).

9. For debate on this point, see Alastair Iain Johnston, "Thinking About Strategic Culture," *International Security* 19, no. 4 (1995): 36–39; Colin S. Gray, "Strategic Culture as Context: The First Generation of Theory Strikes Back," *Review of International Studies* 25, no. 1 (1999): 49–70.

10. Johnston, "Thinking About Strategic Culture," pp. 44–49; Peter J. Katzenstein, *Cultural Norms and National Security: Police and Military in Postwar Japan* (Ithaca, NY: Cornell University Press, 1996), pp. 18–22; Jeffrey W. Legro, *Cooperation Under Fire: Anglo-German Restraint During World War II* (Ithaca, NY: Cornell

University Press, 1995), pp. 17–29; Elizabeth Kier, *Imagining War: French and British Military Doctrine Between the Wars* (Princeton, NJ: Princeton University Press, 1997), pp. 31–32.

11. Peter Katzenstein also looks at public beliefs (via opinion polls) in his book on Japanese strategic culture, but the overwhelming emphasis in this book is on the beliefs of policy, police, and military elites. Peter J. Katzenstein, *Cultural Norms and National Security: Police and Military in Postwar Japan* (Ithaca, NY: Cornell University Press, 1996).

12. Thomas Risse, Stephen C. Ropp, and Kathryn Sikkink (eds.), *The Power of Human Rights: International Norms and Domestic Change* (Cambridge: Cambridge University Press, 1999); Ann Marie Clark, *Diplomacy of Conscience: Amnesty International and Changing Human Rights Norms* (Ithaca, NY: Cornell University Press, 2001); Jeffrey T. Checkel, "Norms, Institutions and National Identity in Contemporary Europe," *International Studies Quarterly* 43, no. 1 (1999): 83–114.

13. Alexander Wendt, *Social Theory of International Politics* (Cambridge: Cambridge University Press, 1999), pp. 8–9; Ward Thomas, *The Ethics of Destruction: Norms and Force in International Relations* (Ithaca, NY: Cornell University Press, 2001), pp. 19–20.

14. Richard M. Price, "Reversing the Gun Sights: Transnational Civil Society Targets Land Mines," *International Organization* 52, no. 3 (1998): 613–644. Another possible exception is Ted Hopf, who does look at the public sources (even including pulp fiction!) of foreign policy identity; see Ted Hopf, *Social Construction of International Politics: Identities and Foreign Policies, Moscow, 1955 and 1999* (Ithaca, NY: Cornell University Press, 2002).

15. Duffield, *World Power Forsaken*, pp. 33–34.

16. Stig Forster, "Introduction," in Roger Chickering and Stig Forster (eds.), *Great War, Total War: Combat and Mobilization on the Western Front, 1914–1918* (Cambridge: Cambridge University Press, 2000), p. 7.

17. Thus the socialization of civilians into military culture is rarely complete. It does not erase past civilian norms so much as template a new set of identities, scripts, and codes over existing ones. On this, see Tarak Barkawi, "Peoples, Homelands, and Wars? Ethnicity, the Military, and Battle Among British Imperial Forces in the War Against Japan," *Comparative Studies in Society and History* 46, no. 1 (2004): 132–163.

18. On this "disciplinary divide," see Colin Elman and Miriam Fendius Elman (eds.), *Bridges and Boundaries: Historians, Political Scientists and the Study of International Relations* (Cambridge, MA: MIT Press, 2001). In this same volume, Paul Schroeder argues that this disciplinary divide does tend to be overdrawn. See also Paul Schroeder, "History and International Relations Theory: Not Use or Abuse, but Fit or Misfit," *International Security* 22, no. 1 (1997): 64–74. I am grateful to one of the reviewers for drawing my attention to this point.

19. Simon Schama, *The Embarrassment of Riches: An Interpretation of Dutch Culture in the Golden Age* (London: Fontana, 1991), p. 4.

20. On this trade-off, see Jack Snyder, "Richness, Rigor and Relevance in the Study of Soviet Foreign Policy," *International Security* 9, no. 3 (1984–1985): 89–108.

21. Wiebe E. Bijker, Thomas P. Hughes, and Trevor J. Pinch (eds.), *The Social Construction of Technological Systems: New Directions in the Sociology and History of Technology* (Cambridge, MA: MIT Press, 1987); Merrit Roe Smith and Leo Marx (eds.), *Does Technology Drive History? The Dilemma of Technological Determinism* (Cambridge, MA: MIT Press, 1994). Also relevant is Jan Golinski, *Making Natural*

Knowledge: Constructivism and the History of Science (Cambridge: Cambridge University Press, 1998).

22. Donald MacKenzie, *Inventing Accuracy: A Historical Sociology of Nuclear Missile Guidance* (Cambridge, MA: MIT Press, 1990); Graham Spinardi, *From Polaris to Trident: The Development of US Fleet Ballistic Missile Technology* (Cambridge: Cambridge University Press, 1994).

23. Michael S. Sherry, *The Rise of American Air Power: The Creation of Armageddon* (New Haven, CT: Yale University Press, 1987); Craig M. Cameron, *American Samurai: Myth, Imagination and the Conduct of Battle in the First Marine Division, 1941–1951* (Cambridge: Cambridge University Press, 1994).

24. Typical on this score is Everett Meddelsohn, Merritt Roe Smith, and Peter Weingart (eds.), *Science, Technology and the Military* (Dordrecht: Kluwer, 1998).

25. Donald MacKenzie and Judy Wajcman, "Introductory Essay," in Donald MacKenzie and Judy Wajcman (eds.), *The Social Shaping of Technology*, 2nd ed. (Buckingham: Open University Press, 1999), p. 16.

26. This is examined later in the context of the US bombing of Japan during World War II.

27. Forster, "Introduction," p. 9.

28. Roger Chickering, "Total War: The Use and Abuse of a Concept," in Manfred F. Boemeke, Roger Chickering, and Stig Forster (eds.), *Anticipating Total War: The German and American Experiences, 1871–1914* (Cambridge: Cambridge University Press, 1999), p. 25.

29. Forster, "Introduction," p. 5.

30. Chickering, "Total War," p. 20.

31. Though the Eastern front did see some of the largest mechanized engagements of the war—especially the Battle of Kursk in 1943 for which each side employed more than 6,000 tanks. For a first-hand account of this battle, see Georgi K. Zhukov, *Marshall Zhukov's Greatest Battles* (London: Sphere, 1971), pp. 195–258.

32. Omer Bartov, *Hitler's Army: Soldiers, Nazis, and War in the Third Reich* (Oxford: Oxford University Press, 1992).

33. Stig Forster and Jorg Nagler (eds.), *On the Road to Total War: The American Civil War and the German Wars of Unification, 1861–1871* (Cambridge: Cambridge University Press, 1997).

34. This is explored in Jenny Edkins, *Trauma and the Memory of Politics* (Cambridge: Cambridge University Press, 2003). See also David Campbell, "Cultural Governance and Pictorial Resistance," in Bice Maiguashca, David Armstrong, and Theo Farrell (eds.), *Governance and Resistance in World Politics* (Cambridge: Cambridge University Press, 2003).

35. Jay Winter and Emmanuel Sivan, "Setting the Framework," in Jay Winter and Emmanuel Sivan (eds.), *War and Remembrance in the Twentieth Century* (Cambridge: Cambridge University Press, 2000), p. 9.

36. Omer Bartov, "Trauma and Absence: France and Germany, 1914–1945," in P. Addison and A. Calder (eds.), *Time to Kill: The Soldier's Experience of War in the West, 1939–1945* (London: Pimlico, 1997), p. 348.

37. This is discussed in Winter and Sivan, "Setting the Framework," pp. 10–19.

38. Michael Schudson (ed.), *Memory Distortion: How Minds, Brains and Societies Reconstruct the Past* (Cambridge, MA: Harvard University Press, 1995).

39. Eugene Winograd and Ulric Neisser (eds.), *Affect and Accuracy in Recall: Studies of Flashblub Memories* (Cambridge: Cambridge University Press, 1992).

40. Thomas Berger, "The Power of Memory and Memories of Power: The Cultural Parameters of German Foreign Policy-Making Since 1945," in Jan-Werner

Muller (ed.), *Memory and Power in Post-War Europe* (Cambridge: Cambridge University Press, 2002), pp. 76–99.

41. Catherine Merridale, "War, Death, and Remembrance in Soviet Russia," in Jay Winter and Emmanuel Sivan (eds.), *War and Remembrance in the Twentieth Century* (Cambridge: Cambridge University Press, 2000), quotes from pp. 62–63. See also Catherine Merridale, *Night of Stone: Death and Memory in Russia* (New York: Penguin, 2002).

42. T. G. Ashplant, Graham Dawson, and Michael Roper (eds.), *The Politics of War Memory and Commemoration* (London: Routledge, 2000).

43. Sue Harper, "Popular Film, Popular Memory: The Case of the Second World War," in Martin Evans and Ken Lunn (eds.), *War and Memory in the Twentieth Century* (Oxford: Berg, 1997), p. 164.

44. Jay Winter, *Sites of Memory, Sites of Mourning: The Great War in European Cultural History* (Cambridge: Cambridge University Press, 1995), p. 3.

45. Paul Fussell, *The Great War and Modern Memory* (Oxford: Oxford University Press, 1975).

46. Cited in Arthur Marwick, "Painting and Music During and After the Great War: The Art of Total War," in Roger Chickering and Stig Forster (eds.), *Great War, Total War* (Cambridge: Cambridge University Press, 2000), p. 513.

47. Michael Paris, *Warrior Nation: Images of War in British Popular Culture, 1850–2000* (London: Reaktion, 2000), p. 8.

48. Denis Winter, *Death's Men: Soldiers of the Great War* (London: Penguin, 1978).

49. David W. Lloyd, *Battlefield Tourism: Pilgrimage and the Commemoration of the Great War in Britain, Australia, and Canada, 1919–1939* (Oxford: Berg, 1998), pp. 28, 220.

50. See, for example, Ian Ousby, *The Road to Verdun: France, Nationalism and the First World War* (London: Jonathan Cape, 2002).

51. Alfred Kelly, "Whose War? Whose Nation? Tensions in the Memory of the Franco-German War of 1870–1871," in Manfred F. Boemeke, Roger Chickering, and Stig Forster (eds.), *Anticipating Total War* (Cambridge: Cambridge University Press, 1999), p. 281.

52. Likewise, British reporters at the front during World War I struggled to situate the horrors they witnessed in heroic and nationalist narratives of the war. Matthew Farish, "Modern Witnesses: Foreign Correspondents, Geopolitical Vision, and the First World War," *Transactions of the Institute of British Geographers* 26, no. 3 (2001): 273–287.

53. Kelly, "Whose War?" pp. 304–305.

54. George L. Mosse, *Fallen Soldiers: Reshaping the Memory of the World Wars* (Oxford: Oxford University Press, 1990).

55. John Mueller, *Retreat from Doomsday: The Obsolescence of Major War* (New York: Basic, 1989); Michael Mandelbaum, "Is Major War Obsolete?" *Survival* 40, no. 4 (1998–1999): 20–26.

56. John Mueller, "Changing Attitudes Towards War: The Impact of the First World War," *British Journal of Political Science* 21, no. 1 (1991): 1–28.

57. Edward Hagerman, *The American Civil War and the Origins of Modern Warfare* (Bloomington: Indiana University Press, 1988).

58. David F. Trask, "Military Imagination in the United States, 1815–1917," in Manfred F. Boemeke, Roger Chickering, and Stig Forster (eds.), *Anticipating Total War* (Cambridge: Cambridge University Press, 1999), p. 333.

59. Small wonder that Jean de Bloch's *The Future of War in Its Technical, Economic, and Political Relations*, which is famous for accurately predicting the "total" nature of mass industrialized war, received such little attention in the United States when it was published in 1899. John Whiteclay Chambers II, "American Debate over Modern War, 1871–1914," in Manfred F. Boemeke, Roger Chickering, and Stig Forster (eds.), *Anticipating Total War* (Cambridge: Cambridge University Press, 1999), p. 245.

60. Eric Dean Jr., *Shook over Hell: Post-Traumatic Stress, Vietnam and the Civil War* (Cambridge, MA: Harvard University Press, 1997).

61. Quotes from Wendy Holden, *Shell Shock* (London: Channel Four Books, 1998), p. 9.

62. Ben Shephard, *A War of Nerves: Soldiers and Psychiatrists, 1914–1994* (London: Pimlico, 2002), p. 7.

63. Peter Leese, *Shell Shock: Traumatic Neurosis and the British Soldiers of the First World War* (Basingstoke: Palgrave Macmillan, 2002), pp. 15–19.

64. Shephard, *A War of Nerves*, p. 17.

65. Eric J. Leed, *No Man's Land: Combat and Identity in World War One* (Cambridge: Cambridge University Press, 1981).

66. Sherry, *The Rise of American Air Power*, p. 1.

67. I. F. Clarke, *Voices Prophesying War: Future Wars, 1763–3749*, 2nd ed. (Oxford: Oxford University Press, 1992); Robert Wohl, *A Passion for Wings: Aviation and Western Imagination, 1908–1918* (New Haven, CT: Yale University Press, 1994). See also I. F. Clarke, "Future-War Fiction: The First Main Phase, 1871–1900," *Science Fiction Studies* 24, no. 3 (1997), http://www.depauw.edu/sfs/clarkeess.htm.

68. Sherry, *The Rise of American Air Power*, p. 1.

69. Stephen Peter Rosen, *Winning the Next War: Innovation and the Modern Military* (Ithaca, NY: Cornell University Press, 1989), pp. 148–182.

70. Christian Geintz, "The First Air War Against Noncombatants: Strategic Bombing of German Cities in World War I," in Roger Chickering and Stig Forster (eds.), *Great War, Total War* (Cambridge: Cambridge University Press, 2000), p. 22.

71. Phillip S. Meilinger, "Proselytiser and Prophet: Alexander P. de Seversky and American Airpower," *Journal of Strategic Studies* 18, no. 1 (1995): 7–35.

72. Sherry, *The Rise of American Air Power*, pp. 22–75.

73. Daniel Pick, *War Machine: The Rationalisation of Slaughter in the Modern Age* (New Haven, CT: Yale University Press, 1993).

74. "Land ironclads" was a reference to the armor-plated warships of the American Civil War.

75. My discussion on the origins and early appearance of tanks is based on Patrick Wright, *Tank: The Progress of a Monstrous War Machine* (London: Faber and Faber, 2000), pp. 23–80; J. P. Harris, *Men, Ideas and Tanks: British Military Thought and Armoured Forces, 1903–1939* (Manchester: Manchester University Press, 1995), pp. 1–78.

76. This counterfactual is explored in Tim Travers, "Could the Tanks of 1918 Have Been War-Winners for the British Expeditionary Force?" *Journal of Contemporary History* 27, no. 3 (1992): 389–406.

77. Paddy Griffith, *Battle Tactics of the Western Front: The British Army's Art of Attack, 1916–1918* (New Haven, CT: Yale University Press, 1994), pp. 161–168.

78. Harris, *Men, Ideas and Tanks*, pp. 159–194.

79. John Stone, "The British Army and the Tank," in Theo Farrell and Terry Terriff (eds.), *The Sources of Military Change: Culture, Politics, Technology* (Boulder, CO: Lynne Rienner, 2002), pp. 187–204.

80. On mechanized warfare in the Western front, see Michael D. Doubler, *Closing with the Enemy: How GIs Fought the War in Europe, 1944–1945* (Lawrence: University Press of Kansas, 1994); John Stone, *The Tank Debate: Armour and Anglo-American Military Tradition* (Amsterdam: Harwood, 2000), pp. 31–38. On the Eastern front, see John Erickson, *The Road to Stalingrad: Stalin's Road with Germany, Vol. 1* (London: Panther, 1975); John Erickson, *The Road to Berlin: Stalin's War with Germany, Vol. 2* (London: Grafton, 1983).

81. Jack Snyder, *Myths of Empire* (Ithaca, NY: Cornell University Press), pp. 66–111.

82. Thomas Rohkramer, "Heroes and Would-Be Heroes: Veterans' and Reservists' Associations in Imperial Germany," in Manfred F. Boemeke, Roger Chickering, and Stig Forster (eds.), *Anticipating Total War* (Cambridge: Cambridge University Press, 1999), pp. 191–192, 198–199.

83. Stig Forster, "Dreams and Nightmares: German Military Leadership and the Images of Future Warfare, 1871–1914," in Manfred F. Boemeke, Roger Chickering, and Stig Forster (eds.), *Anticipating Total War* (Cambridge: Cambridge University Press, 1999), p. 347.

84. Ibid., pp. 367, 375.

85. Dennis E. Showalter, "From Deterrence to Doomsday Machine: The German Way of War, 1890–1914," *Journal of Military History* 64 (July 2000): 679–710.

86. For a review of the literature, see Hew Strachan, "Germany in the First World War: The Problem of Strategy," *German History* 12, no. 2 (1994): 237–249. This problem persisted throughout the war, as the kaiser's incompetence combined with his constitutional position as supreme commander prevented the development of an effective strategy-making structure. See Wilhelm Deist, "Strategy and Unlimited Warfare in Germany: Moltke, Falkenhayn, and Ludendorff," in Roger Chickering and Stig Forster (eds.), *Great War, Total War* (Cambridge: Cambridge University Press, 2000), pp. 265–280.

87. Arden Bucholz (ed.), *Moltke, Schlieffen, and Prussian War Planning* (New York: Berg, 1990).

88. As Hew Strachan notes, "The travel plan created standard operating procedures, so making strategy the servant of technology." Hew Strachan, *The First World War: Vol. 1: To Arms* (Oxford and New York: Oxford University Press, 2001), p. 167.

89. This reflected a Europe-wide phenomenon. Strachan concludes that "the enthusiasm with which Europe went to war was therefore composed of a wide range of differing responses. The common denominator may more accurately be described as passive acceptance, a willingness to do one's duty." Strachan, *The First World War*, pp. 161–162.

90. Jeffrey Verhey, *The Spirit of 1914: Militarism, Myth and Mobilization in Germany* (Cambridge: Cambridge University Press, 2000).

91. Ibid., pp. 206–238.

92. Bartov, *Hitler's Army;* Vejas Gabriel Liulevicius, *War Land on the Eastern Front: Culture, National Identity and German Occupation in World War I* (Cambridge: Cambridge University Press, 2000), p. 9.

93. Liulevicius, *War Land*, pp. 252, 272.

94. Ibid., pp. 165–170, 254–257.

95. On the rise of the US Navy, see George W. Baer, *One Hundred Years of Sea Power: The U.S. Navy, 1890–1990* (Stanford, CA: Stanford University Press, 1994).

96. Lance C. Buhl, "Maintaining 'An American Navy,' 1865–1873," in Kenneth J. Hagan (ed.), *In Peace and War: Interpretations of American Naval History, 1775–1984* (Westport, CT: Greenwood, 1984), pp. 145–173.

97. Peter Trubowitz, "Geography and Strategy: The Politics of American Naval Expansion" in Peter Trubowitz, Emily O. Goldman, and Edward Rhodes (eds.), *The Politics of Strategic Adjustment: Ideas, Institutions and Interests* (New York: Columbia University Press, 1999), pp. 105–138.

98. Mark Shulman, "Institutionalizing a Political Idea: Navalism and the Emergence of American Sea Power," in Peter Trubowitz, Emily O. Goldman, and Edward Rhodes (eds.), *The Politics of Strategic Adjustment* (New York: Columbia University Press, 1999), pp. 79–104.

99. Imgard Steinisch, "Different Path to War: A Comparative Study of Militarism and Imperialism in the United States and Imperial Germany, 1871–1914," in Manfred F. Boemeke, Roger Chickering, and Stig Forster (eds.), *Anticipating Total War* (Cambridge: Cambridge University Press, 1999), pp. 41–42.

100. Edward Rhodes, "Constructing Power: Cultural Transformation and Strategic Adjustment in the 1890s," in Peter Trubowitz, Emily O. Goldman, and Edward Rhodes (eds.), *Politics of Strategic Adjustment,* pp. 29–78.

101. John W. Dower, *War Without Mercy: Race and Power in the Pacific War* (New York: Pantheon, 1986), pp. 77–93.

102. Cameron, *American Samurai,* p. 113.

103. Cited in Edmund Russell, *War and Nature: Fighting Humans and Insects with Chemicals from World War I to Silent Spring* (Cambridge: Cambridge University Press, 2001), p. 99.

104. Dower, *War Without Mercy,* p. 11.

105. Sherry, *The Rise of American Air Power,* pp. 251–252.

106. Russell, *War and Nature,* pp. 105–106, 139–144. For analysis of the "unholy alliance" between the US military and chemical industries, see Dominick Jenkins, *The Final Frontier: America, Science and Terror* (London: Verso, 2003).

107. Cited in Sherry, *The Rise of American Air Power,* p. 211. The role of technology in creating emotional distance in modern warfare is discussed in Jonathan Glover, *Humanity: A Moral History of the Twentieth Century* (London: Pimlico, 2001), pp. 69–88, 111–116.

108. Cameron, *American Samurai,* pp. 130–165.

109. Ibid., pp. 167, 178–180.

110. Azar Gat, *Fascist and Liberal Visions of War: Fuller, Liddell Hart, Douhet and Other Modernists* (Oxford: Oxford University Press, 1998).

111. Philip K. Lawrence, *Modernity and War: The Creed of Absolute Violence* (New York: St. Martin's, 1997), pp. 6–34.

112. Trutz von Trotha, "'The Fellows Can Just Starve': On Wars of 'Pacification' in the African Colonies of Imperial Germany and the Concept of 'Total War,'" in Manfred F. Boemeke, Roger Chickering, and Stig Forster (eds.), *Anticipating Total War* (Cambridge: Cambridge University Press, 1999), pp. 415–436.

113. The US Air Force adopted firebombing in its air campaign against Germany, suggesting that racism may not have had a determining influence on the degree (or lack) of restraint in air operations. Dower's and Cameron's work (discussed above) suggests otherwise: that race did clearly inform how US troops saw and acted towards their Japanese enemy. This is also mirrored in the case of Australian forces, for whom racism clearly did shape restraint in military operations during World War II. Mark Johnston shows how contempt for the Japanese led Australian troops to be merciless towards this enemy, whereas compassion was given to widely ridiculed Italian enemies, and respect was shown to admired German foe. Mark Johnston, *Fighting the Enemy: Australian Soldiers and Their Adversaries in World War II* (Cambridge: Cambridge University Press, 2000).

114. Cameron, *American Samurai*, p. 45.

115. Verhey, *The Spirit*, pp. 223–224.

116. Lawrence Freedman, *The Revolution in Strategic Affairs* (Oxford: Oxford University Press for the International Institute for Strategic Studies, 1998).

117. Colin McInnes, *Spectator-Sport War: The West and Contemporary Conflict* (Boulder, CO: Lynne Rienner, 2002).

118. Piers Robinson, *The CNN Effect: The Myth of News, Foreign Policy and Intervention* (London: Routledge, 2002).

119. Jeffrey Record, "Collapsed Countries, Casualty Dread, and the New American Way of War," *Parameters* (Summer 2002), http://carlisle-www.army.mil/usawc/parameters/.

120. Steven Kull and I. M. Destler, *Misreading the Public: The Myth of a New Isolationism* (Washington, DC: Brookings, 1999); James Burk, "Public Support for Peacekeeping in Lebanon and Somalia: Assessing the Casualties Hypothesis," *Political Science Quarterly* 114 (1999): 53–78.

121. This is nicely illustrated from the British perspective in the 1982 Falklands War, in Kevin Foster, *Fighting Fictions: War, Narrative and National Identity* (London: Pluto, 1999).

122. For a recent essay on this, see James Wolcott, "Color Me Khaki," *Vanity Fair*, September 2004, pp. 70–72.

4

Nuclear War

Cultural beliefs have played an especially important role in shaping the way states have prepared for nuclear war. Whereas states could test their assumptions about the effectiveness of particular conventional military techniques and technologies in battle, this has not been true of nuclear strategies and nuclear weapons. The destructive potential of atomic weapons quickly created the widespread assumption in the early Cold War period that the primary purpose of such weapons must be to deter war rather than fight it. As Bernard Brodie famously observed in *The Absolute Weapon* (1946), "Thus far the chief purpose of a military establishment has been to win wars. From now on its chief purpose must be to avert them."[1] This assumption was reinforced by the development of even more powerful hydrogen weapons in the 1950s, and by the growth in the superpowers' nuclear arsenals throughout the Cold War. Thus, it was widely expected (and indeed hoped) that ideas about nuclear war, regarding the possibility of limiting it, the possibilities of intrawar deterrence, the effectiveness of different forms of targeting, and so forth, would never be put to the test.

Nuclear weapons were themselves tested, and this way the nuclear powers did develop some technical knowledge about the capabilities of such weapons.[2] However, when it came to actually waging nuclear war, planners and policymakers had to rely on imagination rather than experience. As Colin Gray recently pointed out, "One needs to remember that nobody has *any* experience of the actual conduct of bilateral nuclear combat. . . . Expertise on virtual nuclear combat is virtual expertise only."[3] The implications of this were noted by Robert Jervis: "In this sort of world, the lack of objective answers to many crucial questions allows unusual scope for the power of ideas we develop and the concepts we employ."[4] This assumption is explored in the first part of this chapter through an examination of the practice of the world's first and most powerful nuclear state. In essence, I argue that the practice of nuclear deterrence in the United States has been shaped by, and in turn has

shaped, a stable set of commonly held beliefs about the appropriate use of nuclear weapons. This idea is not new. Indeed, back in 1984 Jervis argued that
"The paucity of evidence about the effect of alternative nuclear strategies
feeds the enlarged role of doctrines and beliefs. To a greater extent than in the
past, they now shape, rather than describe, reality."[5] But how norms shape the
practice of nuclear deterrence has been little explored. Some attention has
been given the nuclear taboo—a norm that explains the nonuse of nuclear
weapons by states (especially in circumstances where the nuclear power concerned has no reason to fear nuclear retaliation).[6] This chapter examines both
norms that define when nuclear weapons should be used (the nuclear taboo)
and how they should be used (a norm of countercity targeting).

The causal impact of these norms is illustrated in Table 4.1. The nuclear
taboo prohibits first-use of nuclear weapons. For it to take effect, the United
States should not use nuclear weapons in international crises. The norm of
countercity targeting prescribes the targeting of cities for nuclear attack. For
it to take effect, US nuclear war plans should give prominence, if not priority,
to this target set.

In the first section of this chapter, I examine the nuclear taboo situated in
US strategic culture. It is a belief shared and practiced by senior US policymakers since the Truman administration. I show how this norm originated in
the shocking devastation wrought by the atomic attacks on Japan in 1945, and
how President Harry Truman mobilized support in US government for a taboo
against first nuclear use. Evidence of the nuclear taboo may be found in the
discourse, policy, and legislation. Successive administrations made statements
revealing their awareness that there was some kind of taboo against nuclear
use. This was encoded in policy under Truman and later under President
Jimmy Carter, not to use nuclear weapons against nonnuclear opponents. The
nuclear taboo was also institutionalized in a law that handed nuclear weapons
over to civilian custody in the early Cold War years. Finally, the historical
record shows that the United States has not used nuclear weapons since 1945.
More revealing still is US nonuse of nuclear weapons when at war against
nonnuclear opponents: Korea, Vietnam, and Iraq. On these occasions, it was
the nuclear taboo and not fear of retaliation that restrained the United States.

Table 4.1   Causal Impacts of US Nuclear Norms

Independent Variable	Dependent Variable	Hypothesized Impact
Nuclear taboo	Role of nuclear weapons in international crises	Prohibits first-use of nuclear weapons
Norm of countercity targeting	Nuclear war planning	Prescribes targeting of cities for nuclear attack

Section two explores the norm of countercity targeting, which was situated in the organizational culture of Strategic Air Command (SAC), the US Air Force (USAF) organization charged with drawing up and executing the US nuclear war plan. I argue that this norm was derived from the US Army Air Force's (USAAF) experience of countercity bombing during World War II. The officers who carried out the bombing of German and Japanese cities came to staff SAC, and in this way the norm was learned by the new Cold War organization. Evidence of the countercity targeting norm may be found in SAC discourse and documentation, which show that SAC officers were convinced that annihilating the Soviet Union's main cities would bring a swift and sure victory. The historical record also clearly shows that this belief was institutionalized in successive nuclear war plans. Ignored by SAC was data suggesting that bombing cities would not automatically lead to a collapse in enemy morale. Likewise ignored were arguments for withholding countercity strikes in order to encourage the Soviets to do likewise. These ideas suggesting more moderate and discriminating nuclear targeting did not sit well with the organizational culture of SAC.

In the concluding section, I locate these norms in the overall social structure of US nuclear deterrence. I relate these norms to the main positions taken in the central debate in the Cold War United States about the nature of nuclear war. I also briefly explore the tension between the nuclear taboo and the US alliance strategy, and the tension between the countercity targeting norm and US obligations under international law.

The Nuclear Taboo

The concept of the nuclear taboo tells us that states are prevented from employing nuclear weapons by a "norm of moral revulsion at the thought of their use."[7] This practice of nonuse embodies the belief that nuclear weapons are intrinsically special and, as such, are weapons of very last resort. This belief in the specialness of nuclear weapons extends beyond their capacity for destruction, to exclude very powerful conventional weapons (such as, fuel-air explosives) and include nuclear weapons with very low explosive yields (such as mini- and micro-nukes).[8] In effect, very last resort rules out nuclear first-use. Eric Herring suggests that the nuclear taboo is reinforced by "an implicit expectation of punishment, either automatic or through human agency," but importantly "punishment for violating the nuclear taboo does not have to be in kind."[9] Thus, it is a moral prohibition reinforced by a general expectation that the consequences of nuclear employment would be disastrous, and not the specific fear of nuclear retaliation, that leads states to refrain from employing nuclear weapons.

According to Nina Tannenwald and Richard Price, the nuclear taboo is a norm shared by US policymakers and the public that emerged only gradually during the Cold War. They note that the US atomic bombing of Hiroshima and Nagasaki in 1945 enjoyed widespread popular support in the United States, and that "it was only later, when the development of [far more powerful] thermonuclear weapons [in 1952] appeared to clearly violate any previous existing conceptions of proportionate weapons, that a normative stigma against nuclear use emerged."[10] To my mind, Tannenwald and Price have got it wrong in terms of when and where the nuclear taboo appeared on the scene. They locate the nuclear taboo norm in a shift in US public and policy opinion, suggesting a post-Hiroshima acceptance of atomic weapons gave way to a rejection of hydrogen (i.e., thermonuclear) weapons. In a later article, Tannenwald suggests that the nuclear taboo predated the development of hydrogen weapons by a couple of years, in that it shaped US policy from the outset of the Korean War.[11] In fact, the picture is more complex: right from the beginning, the American public treated the atom bomb with a mixture of admiration and apprehension. Contrary to Tannenwald's portrayal, this love-hate relationship between the public and nuclear weapons continued throughout the Cold War. On the other hand, US civilian policymakers came to believe soon after World War II that there was a moral prohibition against nuclear use in circumstances short of retaliation for nuclear attack.

The nuclear taboo constituted a radical departure from the traditionally technocentric strategic culture of the United States.[12] Indeed, Chapter 3 found evidence of this cultural bias in the technological fanaticism that characterized the conduct of the US war against Japan during World War II. The notion that a powerful weapon was practically unusable for moral reasons was new to US policymakers. Consistent with the model outlined in Chapter 1, we see shock-induced change being championed by a powerful norm entrepreneur in the form of President Harry Truman. Secondary agents played a minor, if complex, role both in collaborating with and undermining efforts by those policy elites that sought to weaken the nuclear taboo. Notwithstanding various public relations campaigns designed to promote nuclear weapons, the persistent power of this norm is evident in US policy discourse and national practice throughout the Cold War and after.

The Bomb in Public Imagination

Tannenwald argues that "after the war, 80 percent of Americans surveyed supported use of the atomic bombs."[13] Initially, most Americans did indeed approve of the atomic bombing of Japan. As Paul Boyer notes, "the lack of visual evidence of the bomb's effects reinforced this initial response. US occupation authorities censored reports from the city and suppressed the more horrifying films and photographs of corpses and maimed survivors."[14] The official line was that not only did nuclear use hasten the end of the war; it also avoided the necessity of a US invasion of the main Japanese islands that would have cost up to 1 million US casualties. This message was promoted through an unofficial public relations campaign by senior policymakers, which included an article in *Harper's* magazine by Henry Stimson (the former secretary of war) on "The Decision to Use the Atomic Bomb." As so many times in the past, history was written by the victors and the victims were silenced.[15]

However, joy at the end of the war and awe at the atomic bomb were offset by fear for the future. The bomb was certainly both awesome and fearsome at the same time. *Life* magazine reported that Hiroshima had been "blown . . . off the face of the earth" when an atom bomb was dropped on it on 6 August 1945. Nagasaki followed suit 3 days later. These two bombs instantly killed 100,000 to 140,000 people.[16] The speed with which Japan surrendered following Nagasaki reinforced the image of the atomic bomb as the ultimate weapon.[17] US national pride at such a devastating demonstration of technological prowess, directed against a much-hated enemy, was tinged with anxiety for the nation's future in a nuclear world. In announcing the atomic bombing of Hiroshima, NBC radio boomed, "Anglo-Saxon science has developed a new explosive 2,000 times as destructive as any known before." NBC warned its listeners that "for all we know, we have created a Frankenstein! We must assume that with the passage of only a little time, an improved form of the new weapon we use today can be turned against us." In the utter destruction of Hiroshima and Nagasaki, Americans foresaw their own doom. This creeping doubt undermined public confidence in the atom bomb. Between 1945 and 1947, Gallup recorded the percentage of Americans considering the bomb to be a "good thing" dropping from 69 percent to 55 percent, while those rating it a "bad thing" jumped from 17 percent to 38 percent.[18]

The US government tried to reassure the public about nuclear war. Scientists, educators, and industry were roped into this public relations campaign. Typical on this score was the publication of an official Los Alamos study on *The Effects of Atomic Weapons* (1950):

> It is the purpose of this book to state the facts concerning the atomic bomb, and to make an objective, scientific analysis of these facts. It is hoped that as a result, although it may not be feasible completely to allay fear, it will at least be possible to avoid panic.[19]

So-called scientific analysis was marshaled for the purpose of convincing Americans that protecting them in nuclear war would not be that troublesome. Through a series of films, television shows, and pamphlets, the public were told how to survive atomic attack. In a government film for primary school kids, "Bert the Turtle" demonstrated the "Duck and Cover" drill. The suggestion was that hiding under school desks (or some other item of furniture) would somehow make a difference. This rather unsound advice was repeated in 20 million cartoon booklets and 55 million wallet-sized instruction cards.[20]

Civil society and the commercial world cooperated with the government in promoting the bomb. Teachers sought to remove anxiety about atomic war through education. As Spencer Weart notes in his history of nuclear imagery, "from state education organizations to local advisors of high school Atomic Energy Clubs, everybody wanted students to face the future not only with knowledge but with good cheer." Industry also got in on the act: "General Electric helped too, distributing millions of copies of its comic book 'Inside the Atom,' and reaching about two million students a year with its animated color film *A Is for Atom*." Of course, "A" is also for "Apocalypse," but this was left unmentioned. Censorship was used to keep the more unruly elements of civil society in line. Thus, when *Scientific American* began printing an article in 1950 about hydrogen bombs using nonclassified information, the government forced the magazine to halt production of that issue and to destroy the 3,000 copies that had already come off the press.[21] The Federal Civil Defense Administration was the lead government agency working with schools and the media to normalize and "domesticate the bomb" for ordinary Americans.[22]

The public arrival of hydrogen bombs changed all this. The hydrogen device tested by the United States in 1952 produced a 10-megaton explosion (roughly 500 Hiroshimas), wiping a small Pacific atoll off the map in the process. The "Mike" test created a fireball 3 miles in diameter, a cloud 30 miles high and 27 miles across, and a shock-wave that could be felt 2,000 miles away. It left behind a mile-wide crater, 200 feet deep.[23] The US government did not even try to persuade the populace that they could be protected against such weapons. Instead, it prepared for mass evacuation of US cities in the event of nuclear war. As one Federal Civil Defense official explained, the focus shifted "from 'Duck and Cover' to 'Run Like Hell.'"[24] Once again, the public felt threatened by the bomb.

But it would be a mistake to suggest, as do Tannenwald and Price, that this produced a permanent sea change in public support for nuclear weapons. Indeed, according to Michael Mandelbaum, public concern about the nuclear peril actually climaxed later, in a brief period from the late 1950s to early 1960s, and subsequently subsided. This crisis in public opinion began with the launch of the Soviet *Sputnik*—a dramatic demonstration that Soviets could fire satellites into space and, therefore, warheads onto US soil—and ended with the peaceful resolution of the 1962 Cuban Missile Crisis and the signing of the Limited Test Ban Treaty the following year.[25] Writing in 1981, Mandelbaum argued that:

Almost no one appears particularly upset about the bomb. Americans seem to have abdicated responsibility for nuclear war and peace to their leaders, especially to the President, and to regard the nuclear threat as something to be passively endured, not actively resisted.[26]

As it happened, later that year the Reagan administration issued a new declaratory policy on nuclear strategy that was to trigger fierce public opposition. Under Jimmy Carter, the declared policy was for the United States to be able to fight a protracted nuclear war; under Reagan, the United States had to be able to *prevail* in such a war. Senior administration figures readily admitted that "prevail" meant "win." The notion that victory was possible offended many Americans who feared that this might so embolden their political leaders as to make nuclear war more likely. The result was a massive demonstration in New York and a series of resolutions and referenda across the United States on a Nuclear Freeze. Essentially, Reagan's vision of victory in nuclear war stirred up latent nightmares of the "Duck and Drill" generation.[27] The Cold War of the early 1980s was not only a period of renewed concern for US policymakers, it was also a time of reawakened fears for the general populace.

In a bible of the Nuclear Freeze Movement, Jonathan Schell's best-selling *The Fate of the Earth,* the nightmare is portrayed in brutal detail. Schell notes:

> When one pictures a full-scale attack on the United States, or on any other country . . . the picture of a single city being flattened by a single bomb—an image firmly engraved in the public imagination, probably because of the bombings of Hiroshima and Nagasaki—must give way to a picture of substantial sections of the country being turned by a sort of nuclear carpet-bombing into immense infernal regions, literally tens of thousands of square miles in area, from which escape in impossible.[28]

Weart points out that "Schell's *Fate of the Earth* troubled people because it was the first widely read work to show clearly what would happen if *all* the available bombs were dropped."[29] However, in a masterstroke of public relations, President Ronald Reagan announced the Strategic Defense Initiative (SDI) in March 1983. SDI promised to remove the nuclear threat by providing a shield against missile attack. In effect, Reagan was saying to the Nuclear Freeze Movement, "I share your concern, and here is my solution." Critics derided the fantastical technologies involved in SDI, quickly dubbing it "Star Wars." But, as Boyer notes, "as debate shifted to the merits of Reagan's proposal (and as the stalled arms-control talks resumed), the freeze movement faded."[30]

Public opinion never turned against the bomb, once and for all. Rather, as Boyer observes, there were "shifting cycles of activism and quiescence in America's decades-long encounter with the nuclear threat." This view is shared by Mandelbaum who noted in 1984 that "Americans have normally ignored the nuclear peril. Each episode of public anxiety about the bomb has given way to longer periods in which nuclear weapons issues were the preoccupation of the nuclear specialists alone."[31]

The Origins of the Nuclear Taboo

Unlike the public, US policymakers have been much more consistent in their beliefs about the bomb as a peculiarly immoral weapon. Right from the earliest days of the Cold War, they recognized a normative prohibition on nuclear use. Indeed, there is evidence of immediate recognition by US civilian policymakers that even the first atomic weapons were especially horrific. However, it took an external shock, in the form of the unexpected scale of destruction caused by the atomic bombing of Hiroshima and Nagasaki, for the nuclear taboo to rapidly take hold in the US political establishment.

Shortly after he received news of the first tests of the atomic bomb in July 1945, President Truman described it in his diary as "the most horrible bomb in the world." This did not stop the president authorizing the military to use nuclear weapons "as made ready." Almost everybody in the know believed that there was no alternative to using the bomb against Japan. Demonstrations—by dropping an atomic bomb on a deserted island or evacuated city—were considered impractical. The Scientific Panel advising on the bomb reported that "we can propose no technical demonstration likely to bring an end to the war; we can see no acceptable alternative to direct military use." The chosen target was automatically assumed to be an urban-industrial center yet, following some bizarre logic, the Target Committee concluded that civilian targets would not be hit. War industry and war workers were to be targeted, but this would supposedly exclude civilians. This artificial distinction was also maintained by Truman, who noted in his diary that "I have told the Sec. Of War, Mr. Stimson, to use it so that military objectives and soldiers and sailors are the target and not women and children. . . . He and I are in accord. The target will be a purely military one." This was after Truman had approved a target list that included Hiroshima and Nagasaki![32]

Sure enough, the first atomic bombs were dropped on their targets as soon as they were built. Leading bomb historian Barton Bernstein notes that the president was so "appalled by the mass carnage at Hiroshima and Nagasaki" that he "secretly specified on August 10 that additional atomic bombs could be used *only* upon his explicit order." This was 3 days before Japan surrendered. Nevertheless, the president could no longer delude himself about the nature of the targets and scale of civilian suffering.[33] To be sure, the first bomb killed many more than expected. Robert Oppenheimer, scientist in charge of the project to build the atomic bomb, estimated that the death toll would be 20,000. In the event, it was *five* to *seven* times that number.[34] A few months later, Truman told his budget director that he was not sure that the atomic bomb could ever be used again.[35] Truman's view of nuclear weapons as being intrinsically special is clear in his comment to senior policymakers: "You've got to understand that this isn't a military weapon. . . . It is used to wipe out women and children and unarmed people, and not for military uses. So we have got to treat it differently from rifles and cannon and ordinary things like that."[36]

There was surprisingly little moral reservation on the part of the civilian leadership involved in planning nuclear use in 1945. Exceptions here are John McCloy and Ralph Bard, senior officials in the War and Navy Departments respectively, who both briefly advocated warning Japan in advance so as to permit the targeted cities to be evacuated. Equally, senior military leaders were generally supportive of nuclear use. Again, an exception was the army chief of staff, General George C. Marshall, who was morally opposed to the atomic bombing of Japanese cities. The devastation of Hiroshima and Nagasaki shocked those responsible into reconsidering the wisdom of their action. Indeed, when the ash had cleared, two of the most senior US military leaders— Admiral William Leahy and General Dwight Eisenhower—both published regrets over what had happened.[37] However, Truman is the key figure in constructing the postwar taboo on nuclear use. Whether or not the United States really had to use atomic weapons to force Japan to surrender has been much debated by historians.[38] What is clear is that afterward, the president considered nuclear weapons to be usable only in dire need when all else failed. Furthermore, as president, Truman was in a unique position to frame policy debate on this issue, as well as to push a policy line.

No detailed policy was produced under the Truman administration as to when nuclear weapons would be used. The only policy on this subject, approved in September 1948 (NSC 30), simply states that "the decision as to the employment of atomic weapons in the event of war is to be made by the Chief Executive when he considers such [a] decision to be required."[39] In short, nuclear use was left at the discretion of the president. Truman used this discretion to impose his concept of nukes as special weapons of last resort on US policy. Thus, when presented by the Joint Chiefs of Staff (JCS) with their first nuclear war plan in 1948, he ordered them to replace it with a conventional war plan. He also categorically ruled out preemptive nuclear strikes by the United States.[40]

Institutionalizing the Nuclear Taboo

Truman also played an important part in institutionalizing the nuclear taboo. The belief in the specialness of atomic weapons was embodied in, and reinforced by, the Atomic Energy Act of 1946, and the civilian Atomic Energy Commission (AEC) that was created by it. This act was formulated by the chairman of the Senate's Special Committee on Atomic Energy, Senator Brien McMahon, in response to prompting from Truman about the need for civilian control of nuclear weapons. It gave the AEC sole responsibility for the production and custody of all US atomic weapons.[41]

The military saw things differently and resisted handing over peacetime control of atomic weapons (which up to then had been in the hands of the army's covert wartime atomic weapons development organization, the Manhattan Engineer District). However, popular and congressional distrust of the military operated to support Truman's view that nuclear weapons should be under civilian control. The president did not want "some dashing lieutenant colonel to decide when would be the proper time to drop one."[42] Accordingly, not only were the military denied direct access to atomic bombs, the military were also kept in the dark as to how many were available, and what they could do to their targets.

Civilian control over nuclear weapons was temporarily relaxed in the 1950s under President Dwight Eisenhower. This was followed by the election of a new president who was more suspicious of the military, John F. Kennedy, and a resurgence of congressional concern about the custody of US nuclear weapons, which led to the further institutionalization of civilian control through the development of Permissive Action Links (PALs). PALs enable nuclear weapons to be locked out until the activating codes are released by civilian policymakers.[43]

The Nuclear Taboo in US Practice

The nuclear taboo is most clearly evident in US practice in its refusal to launch nuclear attacks against nonnuclear opponents. In such cases, fear of nuclear retaliation cannot have held back the United States, suggesting that the taboo did.

Truman's refusal to contemplate using nuclear weapons to protect the US nuclear monopoly is the first possible example of the taboo in action. In the late 1940s, influential figures among the US policy, political, and cultural elite called for the United States to destroy the Soviet Union with nuclear weapons while it still could use the bomb with impunity. By the early 1950s, this idea had become orthodoxy in the Air War College, and was shared by those air force officers in charge of US nuclear bomber fleets. However, when the commanding officer of the Air War College, General Orvil Anderson, publicly advocated preventative war—"Give me the order to do it and I can break up Russia's five A-bomb nests in a week," he was quoted as saying—he was fired by Truman. When the air force secretary tried to push the Anderson line, Truman dismissed the arguments as "drivel" and "bunk."[44] These arguments were to resurface nonetheless, over a decade later, when the Kennedy administration faced the prospect of communist China becoming a nuclear power. As before, a military proposal (this time from the Joint Chiefs) to consider US nuclear attacks as an option to retard China's bomb program was rejected out of hand by civilian policymakers.[45]

Moreover, as Tannenwald shows, in Korea, Vietnam, and the Gulf, policy-makers ruled out nuclear use even when the going got tough for the United States in time of war. Tannenwald usefully points out that the nuclear taboo norm was adhered to by policymakers for both normative and instrumental reasons. Some presidents in some wars, such as Truman in Korea, Lyndon Johnson in Vietnam, and George H. W. Bush in the Persian Gulf, were not prepared to contemplate nuclear use because they believed it to be morally wrong. In other cases, such as Eisenhower in Korea and Nixon in Vietnam, presidents were prevented from seriously considering nuclear use by the belief that US public and world opinion would not bear it. However, in the United States at least, as discussed above, public opposition to the bomb was not as certain nor consistent as presidents believed it to be it. But equally, public support was uncertain and inconsistent—not enough to give much encouragement to political leaders contemplating nuclear use.[46] The two logics of consequences and appropriateness also shaped the behavior of other policymakers. Instrumental reasons prevailed in Korea: State Department officials worried that nuking North Korea would look bad on the world stage and cause the United States serious diplomatic problems. Whereas, Secretary of Defense Robert McNamara and Secretary of State Dean Rusk (as Rusk put it) "never seriously considered using nuclear weapons in Vietnam" because both found the idea abhorrent. Indeed, in his memoirs, McNamara makes repeated references to the "moral issues raised by nuclear strikes" in discussing his strong opposition to any such proposal.[47]

The nuclear taboo worked by both regulating and constituting the US way of war. Thus, it regulated US strategy under the Eisenhower administration. Personally, Ike had no problems using nukes—which were "simply another weapon in our arsenal"[48]—he just thought it would be bad public relations. As John Lewis Gaddis notes, "the records are full of statements by Eisenhower about the need to erase the distinction between nuclear and conventional weapons."[49] Equally, Secretary of State John Foster Dulles declared that since "in the present state of world opinion we could not use an A-bomb, we should make every effort now to dissipate this feeling, especially since we are spending such vast sums on the production of weapons we cannot use."[50] This view gained expression in the policy of Massive Retaliation, which promised to respond to Soviet-led communist aggression with US nuclear attack. But in practice, Eisenhower was all talk and no action. In three cases of perceived communist aggression in the early 1950s—in Korea, Indochina, and the Taiwan Straits—the Eisenhower administration found military, political, and, significantly, moral obstacles to the use of nuclear weapons.[51] Essentially, Eisenhower and Dulles discovered that contrary to their own personal beliefs, in social reality nuclear weapons were indeed special and could only be used in last resort.[52]

In the case of the 1990–1991 Gulf War, Tannenwald argues that "the [nuclear] taboo had clear constraining effects. But deeper, constitutive effects were also evident in arguments that using nuclear weapons would violate America's concept of itself as a moral, civilized nation." She cites White House Chief of Staff John Sununu's reply when asked about the possible use of tactical nuclear weapons: "we don't do things like that."[53] In what Secretary of State James Baker called a policy of "calculated ambiguity," the United States did hint at nuclear retaliation for Iraqi chemical or biological attacks. One senior official declared that under such circumstances, the United States would "obliterate Iraq"; Bush's letter to Saddam Hussein warned that "your country will pay a terrible price if you order unconscionable actions of this sort." However, in reality, no actual thought was given to using nukes. Discussing the Camp David strategy meeting on 24 December 1990, Bush and National Security Adviser Brent Scrowcroft noted in their joint memoirs:

> No one advanced the notion of using nuclear weapons, and the President rejected it even in retaliation for chemical and biological attacks. We deliberately avoided spoken or unspoken threats to use them on the grounds that it is bad practice to threaten something you have no intention of carrying out. Publicly, we left the matter ambiguous. There was no point in undermining the deterrence it might be offering.[54]

In short, for policymakers nuclear use was unacceptable and "uncivilized." The United States could not even get away with threatening nuclear use—not even in retaliation for chemical or biological attack. Indeed, such a belief was encoded in the United States' 1978 pledge (the "Negative Security Assurance") not to use nuclear weapons against nonnuclear states and states in nonnuclear alliances.

Undermining the Nuclear Taboo

The life span of the nuclear taboo is hard to predict, however. The primary security concern of the United States has shifted away from superpower competition to the spread of weapons of mass destruction to so-called "rogue regimes" and transnational terrorists. This new security environment has created strategic imperatives for more permissive policy on nuclear use. This may be seen in the blunt nuclear threat issued to Libya by the United States in 1996. Defense Secretary William Perry warned that the United States would consider employing its full range of weapons in order to stop Libya building an underground chemical weapons plant (that had been detected by US intelligence). In a departure from the policy of calculated ambiguity, one senior Defense official told reporters that a newly developed bunker-busting nuclear bomb would be the "weapon of choice" for this mission. Note also that what was threatened was *preventative* nuclear use, and not *retaliatory* nuclear use (as would have been the case in 1990 had this threat been made).[55]

This shift toward first nuclear use is further reflected in the latest presidential guidance on nuclear weapons employment—National Security Presidential Directive (NSPD 17). Arising from the 2002 Nuclear Posture Review (NPR), NSPD 17 instructs Strategic Command (STRATCOM) to draw up plans for nuclear use against several "rogue states"—including Iraq, Iran, Libya, North Korea, and Syria—as well as to develop plans for nuclear retaliation against chemical and biological attacks, and other unspecified "surprising military developments."[56] Underlying this development in the NPR, the undersecretary of state for arms control, John Bolton, publicly announced in February 2002 that the United States would no longer be bound by the Negative Security Assurance.[57] One year later, the threat of first nuclear use was again made by US officials in the lead-up to the 2003 war against Iraq. Consistent with NSPD 17, STRATCOM produced a "Theater Nuclear Planning Document" identifying targets for nuclear attack in Iraq. At the same time, US officials refused to rule out nuclear use in the war. When asked in February 2003 if the United States might use nuclear weapons in the upcoming war, the White House spokesman told the press that "I'm not going to put anything on the table or off the table."[58] That same month, Defense Secretary Donald Rumsfeld declared in open testimony before Congress that "our policy historically has been generally that we will not foreclose the possible use of nuclear weapons if attacked."[59]

The NPR also contains two other policy initiatives that could possibly undermine the nuclear taboo. First is the integration of nonnuclear and nuclear weapons into a unified strategic strike force. In testimony before the Senate Armed Services Committee (SASC), the undersecretary of defense responsible for the NPR argued that this would "not blur the line between nuclear and nonnuclear weapons."[60] The commander in chief of STRATCOM told the SASC that it would, in fact, "raise the nuclear threshold by providing the President with strategic options in a crisis or conflict that do not rely solely on nuclear weapons."[61] But critics argue otherwise; that by lumping conventional and nuclear weapons together, the line between conventional and nuclear use may be crossed more easily than in the past.[62]

Second, the NPR calls for the development of low-yield nuclear weapons (i.e., mini-nukes) capable of destroying Hard and Deeply Buried Targets (HDBTs) while minimizing collateral damage. In 1993 Congress passed legislation banning research and development into mini-nukes—nuclear warheads with yields of below 5 kilotons—precisely because such "low-yield nuclear weapons blur the distinction between nuclear and conventional war."[63] In consequence, the US government developed a variety of conventional earth-penetrating weapons. In 1997 it also deployed the B61-11, an existing medium-yield gravity bomb, retrofitted to give it some limited earth-penetrating capabilities. In the 2001 Defense Authorization Act, Congress instructed the administration to report on US anti-HDBT capabilities. The joint Department of

Defense (DoD)–Department of Energy (DoE) report detailed various new conventional weapons and noted that "there is no current program to design a new or modified HDBT Defeat nuclear weapon."[64] However, with the renewed emphasis on defeating HDBT in the NPR, the administration's 2003 Energy budget request included funds for a new 5-kiloton weapon called the Robust Nuclear Earth Penetrator (RNEP)—funds which it received from Congress. The administration also sought funding for a study on mini-nukes but this was blocked by the Senate.[65]

As might be expected, civil society has played a role in the technical debate over the RNEP and mini-nukes. Scientists, academics, and antinuclear campaigners have critiqued the administration's case for such weapons— which is that they are needed to penetrate deeply buried facilities and have the added benefit of being able to destroy any biological and chemical agents contained within such facilities. The basic problem, critics point out, is that nuclear weapons are too fragile to penetrate to a depth sufficient to prevent surface contamination by radioactive fallout, lethal over several kilometers per kiloton of yield. Such a weapon used against an HDBT in Baghdad, for instance, would have killed tens of thousands of civilians. An added problem is that the nuclear warhead must detonate close to any biological and chemical agents in order to destroy them, and it is most unlikely to be able to penetrate to sufficient depth to do this either. Indeed, it is more likely to simply disperse such agents into the surface environment by the force of the blast. Critics also point out that, in any case, the DoD has developed a range of precision conventional munitions capable of sealing and disabling HDBTs, with far less risk of collateral damage.[66] Finally, in order to develop these new nuclear weapons, the United States may have to resume nuclear testing in contravention of the Comprehensive Test-Ban Treaty (the United States has not ratified the CTBT but a sufficient number of states have ratified it for it to come into legal force)—something that is explicitly allowed for in the NPR.[67]

In its 2004 budget submission to Congress, the DoD once again asked for funds to permit research into mini-nukes. Repealing the 1993 ban, Congress provided $15 million for this purpose in the 2004 Defense bill. Rumsfeld declared that the DoD and DoE just wanted to study mini-nukes, "not to develop, not to deploy, not to use them." However, opponents in Congress are not convinced. One Democrat senator responded, "I don't believe it's just a study. I believe it's an announced intent to begin to generate a new generation of nuclear weapons."[68]

The overall thrust of current US policy—threatening nuclear first-use, combining conventional and nuclear strike forces, and developing mini-nukes—is designed to reduce normative barriers to nuclear use. The additional threatened resumption of nuclear testing, in breach of international legal rules, adds to the impression of a government seeking to erode normative constraints on strategic policy options. Whether or not the United States violates the nuclear taboo in some future action remains to be seen. It is equally possible that George W. Bush, like Eisenhower before him, may find the normative prohibition on actual nuclear use too powerful to overcome.

Causing the Nuclear Taboo

In origins and operation, the nuclear taboo follows the model of culture change outlined in Chapter 1. Some political and military leaders had moral misgivings about atomic weapons, but it took the shocking destruction of Hiroshima and Nagasaki to mobilize civilian leaders into viewing nukes as special weapons of last resort. Truman's role was crucial, as an effective norm entrepreneur at the heart of the decisionmaking process. Truman was able to frame debate, promote policy, and create institutions in such a fashion as to encode the nuclear taboo in the US polity.

All three causal mechanisms for norm following were at play here. Support for the norm was mobilized by Truman using both coercion and persuasion. As the central norm entrepreneur, Truman would have been able to exert some coercive authority by virtue of being president. This included, as we saw, sacking one air force general who publicly advocated preemptive nuclear use by the United States. Truman also had the power to determine US practice under his presidency since nuclear use was at his discretion. At the same time, it is commonly recognized that the president has considerable problems in exercising his authority over the vast and complex organization that is US government. Presidents simply lack the time, knowledge, and political capital to impose their will on all areas of government activity. The separation of powers, particularly along the executive-legislative axis, also complicates things, as bureaucracies and military services can (and often do) appeal to Congress should the president threaten a favored policy or program. For all these reasons, presidents must often rely on persuasion to get things done—coercion alone rarely works.[69] We saw this dynamic in this case when Truman persuaded Congress to limit military powers through the Atomic Energy Act. Truman's promotion of the nuclear taboo took the form of rhetorical action and not truth-seeking argument. As we saw, following the atomic bombing of Japan, Truman was uncompromising in his view that the United States must never again use nuclear weapons except in retaliation for nuclear attack.[70] Hence, David Alan Rosenberg notes "Truman's unwillingness, or inability, to conceive of the atomic bomb as anything other than an apocalyptic terror weapon, a weapon of last resort."[71]

Coercion and persuasion under Truman then gave way to social learning under subsequent administrations. Political leaders accepted that nuclear first-use was impossible, either because they personally believed it to be immoral, or because they anticipated international and national moral outrage at nuclear use. Policymakers in the latter category sought to weaken the nuclear taboo, in order to increase strategic policy options. To this end, successive administrations in the early Cold War period sponsored public relations campaigns, supported by elements in civil society and the commercial world, to reassure the public about the prospects of nuclear war. However, public opinion about the bomb followed endless cycles of admiration and apprehension throughout the Cold War. In other words, the government was unable to stabilize public support sufficiently to create the political space for nuclear use. Thus US political leaders were unable to overcome the nuclear taboo during this period. One can only hope that Bush will not succeed where Eisenhower failed.

Nuking Cities

Unlike Truman, the military saw nothing inherently special about nuclear weapons; the JCS regarded the atomic bomb as simply a more powerful conventional weapon.[72] Nonetheless, the military's approach to nuclear war was shaped by cultural beliefs; specifically, the belief that nuclear weapons could be legitimately and efficiently used against population centers. This norm was rooted in US bombing operations of World War II. The operating mechanism was one of social learning, as US airmen took the knowledge they had acquired about conventional bombing and applied it to nuclear weapons. Central to this process was a social network through which wartime experience and technical knowledge was transmitted and institutionalized in US nuclear war plans.

The Roots of Countercity Targeting

Pre–World War I writers like H. G. Wells imagined strategic air war in terms of bombing cities to undermine enemy morale, as did the prophets of air war in the interwar period, Giulio Douhet, Basil Liddell Hart, J. F. C. Fuller, and Billy Mitchell.[73] This view of air war became orthodoxy in the young Royal Air Force (RAF) under the leadership of Sir Hugh Trenchard, chief of the Air Staff from 1919–1929. For Trenchard, the primary aim of bombing was to undermine the enemy's will to fight; undermining the enemy's capacity to fight was secondary to this. Unlike Douhet, who thought that the best way to do this was by targeting civilians directly, Trenchard believed that civilian morale would more effectively be undermined by destroying the industries and infrastructure that made modern civilian life possible. In both cases, however, heavily populated cities were to be the main targets.[74]

Since Trenchard founded the Air Force Staff College, and all subsequent chiefs of the Air Staff were his protégés, the Trenchard Doctrine of blanket countercity bombing became institutionalized within the RAF, and its Bomber Command established in 1936. Throughout the 1920s and 1930s, the Air Corps Tactical School developed a similar doctrine for the USAAF. But unlike the

Trenchard Doctrine in the RAF, countercity doctrine was never institutionalized in the USAAF. Instead, the USAAF's Air War Plan 1, drawn up by the Air Corps Staff in 1941, concentrated on the precise targeting of German war-supporting industry.[75] In theory, then, the RAF and USAAF sought to defeat Germany in very different ways, with the RAF believing that victory was best achieved through blanket countercity targeting to destroy enemy morale, and USAAF believing that more precise countereconomy targeting to destroy the enemy's war economy was more effective. In practice, given wartime pressures and the technical difficulties of precision bombing, the USAAF was not all that more precise than the RAF. Moreover, the effect was the same, that is, wholescale destruction of German urban-industrial centers. As discussed in Chapter 3, from March 1945 onward the USAAF explicitly adopted blanket countercity targeting in its firebombing campaign against Japan.[76]

The process whereby these beliefs were translated into targeting norms and encoded in nuclear war plans centered on the continuity of personnel between the wartime leadership of the US Army Air Force and leadership of the postwar USAF. As David Alan Rosenberg notes, the war planners in SAC, the air force command set up in 1946 and charged with preparing and executing US nuclear war plans, "were all veterans of the bombing campaigns against Germany and Japan." In other words, beliefs about strategic bombing traveled with these people into SAC, and thereby were sustained within a continuing social network. A key figure in this regard was air force general Curtis LeMay, who had led the firebombing campaign against Japan and who, as its commander from 1948 to 1957, turned SAC into "the nation's most elite military unit."[77]

For SAC planners, the norm of countercity targeting defined the efficiency of using nuclear weapons to destroy cities. This norm even blinded SAC to the conclusions of the US Strategic Bombing Survey of World War II, which suggested that German and Japanese industries and civilian morale were far more robust in the face of bombing than previously believed.[78] It is not surprising then, that when the Joint Intelligence Staff turned its attention in late 1945 to how atomic weapons might be used against the Soviet Union, they selected 20 Soviet cities for nuclear attack. Admittedly, these early war planners also concentrated on large urban-industrial centers because Soviet territory was "vast and unknown" to them—they could just about find cities using old Tsarist maps. However, this consideration cannot account for continuation of a city-centric strategy into the 1950s, as a massive SAC photo-reconnaissance effort had by then greatly increased the range of possible targets.[79] Cities were chosen for destruction not because they were easy to spot, but because SAC believed this would most hurt the enemy. SAC's view was that:

In the foreseeable future [the atomic bomb] will be primarily a strategic weapon of destruction against concentrated industrial areas vital to the war effort of an enemy nation. In addition, it may be employed against centers of population with a view to forcing an enemy state to yield through terror and disintegration of national morale.[80]

This emphasis was reversed by the time SAC drew up its first Emergency War Plan in 1949 (EWP 1-49), which envisaged dropping 133 atomic bombs on 70 Soviet cities. Under EWP 1-49, targets were "selected with the primary objective of the annihilation of population, with industrial targets incidental." But for air force planners, targeting industry and population amounted to the same thing: as one planner already noted in 1947 "what was a city besides a collection of industry?"[81]

Destruction on this scale was to be achieved by hitting everything all at once. EWP 1-49 established the goal of increasing SAC capability "to such an extent that it would be possible to deliver the entire stockpile of atomic bombs, if made available, in a single massive attack." This vision of a fast and furious nuclear assault reflected LeMay's belief, expressed in 1948, that "the next war will be primarily a strategic air war and the atomic attack should be laid down in a matter of hours."[82] As one military liaison officer who received the SAC war plan briefing in 1954 put it, the basic idea was to leave the Soviet Union "a smoking, radiating ruin at the end of two hours."[83]

The politics, which attended the creation of an independent air force in 1947, and centralization of nuclear war planning in the USAF-controlled SAC provided the context within which norms of countercity targeting were able to take root and flourish within the US polity. The USAF gained its independence at a time of fierce rivalry between it, the army, and navy over the new unified and declining postwar defense budget.[84] Air force leaders were very effective in mobilizing support among Republicans in Congress who opposed the Truman administration's plan to bolster national defense on the cheap by introducing Universal Military Training.[85] Some senior administration officials were also broadly sympathetic to the air force's program for a 70-group bomber force as a means to forestall a postwar slump in the aircraft industry.[86] In addition, air force leaders were successful in discrediting proposals for strategic defense, by undermining the character of those advocating air defenses rather than questioning the technological feasibility.[87] Thus, debate closed around strategic airpower as the most cost-effective and politically acceptable way of defending against an exaggerated Soviet threat.[88]

Challenges to Countercity Targeting

Countercity targeting was challenged by some military leaders in the early Cold War period. In 1949, a JCS panel chaired by air force general Hubert Harmon questioned the effectiveness of EWP 1-49. Harmon's panel estimated that the atomic bombing of 70 Soviet cities would kill around 3 million people, cause an additional 4 million casualties, and (in a remarkable example of military understatement) make life "vastly complicated" for the remaining 28 million inhabitants. Nevertheless, the Harmon Report concluded that such devastation would not *"per se,* bring about capitulation"; indeed it was more likely to "unify" the Soviet people rather than turn them against their own government.[89] Following this, the Joint Strategic Plans Committee produced an alternative counterforce plan, which spared Soviet cities, called *Dropshot.* However, significantly, *Dropshot* was never formally approved by the JCS.[90]

Navy leaders also opposed countercity targeting on moral and strategic grounds. In the "Revolt of the Admirals" in late 1949, senior navy leaders publicly denounced nuclear attacks on cities as barbaric and strategically ineffective. In testimony before the House Armed Services Committee of the US Congress, the chief of naval operations (the most senior admiral in the US Navy) mentioned the Harmon Report in his broadside against SAC strategy. However, because it was highly secret, the actual contents of the report could not be cited to support the navy's case. Without proof, Congress and everybody else dismissed navy criticisms as self-interested interservice backstabbing.[91] The idea that the navy truly had moral objections to countercity targeting is, in hindsight, even less persuasive. Particularly given that a decade later, naval chiefs strongly advocated the targeting of Soviet cities because the navy was acquiring a highly inaccurate submarine-launched nuclear missile that could hit little else.[92]

From 1950 onward, countercity targeting lost favor with civilian policymakers who at first began to question the efficiency, and later the legitimacy, of targeting population centers. This occurred in the context of civilian criticism of SAC's all-or-nothing strategy. While the nuclear war plan was a closely guarded secret, civilian analysts were able to guess the general thrust of it. For instance, a panel of consultants appointed by the State Department to look into nuclear disarmament in the early 1950s noted, "it is at present probable that the atomic tactics of the United States in any major war would involve an immediate and overpowering strategic blow designed to put as many atomic bombs as possible on strategic targets within the homeland of the enemy country."[93] Those analysts who did get sight of SAC's operational plan were not at all impressed. Brodie, then a professor at Yale, was asked by the air force chief of staff to review SAC strategy in 1950. He found that SAC had failed to actually calculate the damage its war plan would inflict on the enemy. Instead, planners "simply expected the Soviet Union 'to collapse' as a result of the bombing campaign. . . . People kept talking about the 'Sunday punch.'"[94] Civilian analysts in the USAF's Research and Development think-tank argued that rather than trying to wipe out the whole Soviet Union, deterrence would be strengthened by attacking Soviet military targets first and holding their cities in reserve.[95] Brodie, who was fascinated with Freud, used a sexual metaphor to illustrate the options. He likened the no-cities/withhold strategy to "withdrawal before ejaculation, while the SAC war plan was like going all the way." This metaphor was picked up by Brodie's outspoken and colorful colleague, Herman Kahn, who told a high-level group of SAC officers, "Gentlemen, you don't have a war plan, you have a war orgasm."[96] Eventually, the "no-cities" strategy was adopted by the Kennedy administration in 1962. It was designed not only to enhance deterrence, but also to discourage early Soviet nuclear attacks on US cities. Counterforce was followed by a variety of civilian-inspired nuclear strategies in the following decades, including counterrecovery, counterindustrial, countermilitary, and counterleadership targeting.[97]

The Persistence of Countercity Targeting

However, shifts in declaratory policy made no real difference to SAC's actual nuclear war planning beyond justifying an expansion of the target list. (Accordingly, the number of nuclear targets grew from 4,100 in 1960 to an all-time high of 50,000 in 1982.[98]) Throughout the 1950s, SAC dominated nuclear war planning, with little interference even from the Joint Chiefs.[99] This situation was institutionalized when Eisenhower gave SAC command of the newly created Joint Strategic Target Planning Staff (JSTPS), which was tasked with drawing up the first Single Integrated Operational Plan (SIOP) for nuclear war. Naturally, SAC ensured that the SIOP codified its existing plan to destroy the entire Soviet target base—cities and all—in a single massive preemptive strike.[100]

By the early 1970s, civilian policymakers and Congress no longer accepted the legitimacy of a war plan based (as one senior defense official put it) on "the mass killing of hostages."[101] This led to "population *per se*" being removed as a target category from the SIOP in 1974. However, as Terry Terriff notes in his authoritative account of this review of the SIOP, this was "distinction without a difference, for the United States would continue to target economic and industrial assets located in cities and so hold enemy civilians hostage."[102] US planners still intended to obliterate hundreds of cities, killing many millions of civilian inhabitants. Sure enough, in 1978 Defense Secretary Harold Brown reported to Congress that the United States needed to be able to "inflict an unacceptable level of damage on the Soviet Union, including the destruction of a minimum of 200 major Soviet cities."[103] According to one official estimate, the removal of "population" as a target category from the US nuclear war plan would result in 20–30 million fewer civilian deaths, but 50–100 million people would still have been killed had the SIOP been executed.[104]

In any case, civilian concerns about countercity targeting had little impact on the SIOP. Since nuclear war planning was a highly complex technical business, civilian policymakers were unable to produce meaningful guidance for the JSTPS, and so SAC could interpret civilian policy on avoiding cities, and other limited nuclear options, any way it liked. Civilian oversight of nuclear war planning was further hampered by the need for absolute secrecy; all information on the war plan was subject to its own special classification code, SIOP-ESI (i.e., "extremely sensitive information"). In short, for much of the Cold War, the SIOP was "virtually etched in stone," leaving civilian policymakers "bound by the contours of the war plan rather than the other way around."[105]

Things improved in Washington from the late 1980s onward. Under pressure from then secretary of defense, Caspar Weinberger, the JSTPS co-operated with policymakers in drafting civilian guidance on nuclear targeting and operations. This enabled civilians to finally shift SAC away from its "Sunday punch" and build a variety of limited attack options into the SIOP.[106] A 1991 study by the US General Accounting Office found that this practice of getting SAC planners to help write meaningful guidance from the secretary of defense continued under Weinberger's successors. Moreover, the JSTPS began briefing civilians on the nuclear target list prior to submitting the SIOP for civilian approval.[107]

However, for those on the receiving end of US nuclear warheads, surprisingly little changed with the end of the Cold War. Under a 1994 agreement, US and Russian ballistic missiles are now aimed at the Arctic Ocean. But each side retains their Cold War targets in computer memory, and is able to retarget their missiles in seconds. The USAF no longer practices large-scale conventional bombing of urban centers—both because of normative prohibitions and because it has the technology to cause the desired pattern of damage through precision strikes.[108] However, the United States has retained urban-industrial targets on its Nuclear Strategic Target Data Base. Enemy cities were assigned a far lower priority in US war plans following a review of presidential guidance of nuclear weapons employment in 1997.[109] But nuclear war simulations by the Natural Resources Defense Council estimated that "precision" strikes against Russian nuclear forces would still kill 8–12 million people, while major attack against the full range of war-supporting targets would kill or injure up to 50 million Russians.[110]

Social Learning and Countercity Targeting

During World War II, US airmen gradually developed a belief in the efficiency of targeting population centers for destruction. Initially, they favored the precise targeting of war-supporting economy. However, under pressure from wartime imperatives and the demands of precision bombing, the USAAF gravitated toward the British practice of blanket countercity bombing. The USAAF perfected this form of operations in a merciless campaign against Japan. Nuclear weapons offered a new way to practice a tried and tested form of air war. Wartime experience was preserved, recovered, and transmitted through a common social network that spanned the leaders of the US World War II bombing campaigns and the authors of early US nuclear war plans. These advocates of countercity targeting were able to consolidate the centrality of strategic airpower in US Cold War grand strategy, institutionalize their policy position in the newly created SAC, and encode their targeting preferences in successive nuclear war plans. The highly technical nature of nuclear targeting frustrated civilian efforts to revise targeting options and remove cities from the list of targets scheduled for immediate destruction. It also meant that, unlike the nuclear taboo, secondary agents played no part in reproducing or revising nuclear targeting norms.

The Social Structure of Nuclear Deterrence

There is far more to the social structure of US nuclear deterrence than norms of nuclear nonuse and nuclear targeting. In this final section of the chapter, I want to expand our horizon to examine more broadly the cultural terrain of US nuclear deterrence. I will navigate us through this immensely complex subject by following a central debate about nuclear war. The nonuse and targeting norms will be located in relation to the two main positions adopted in this debate, and in terms of clashing technical requirements for Cold War deterrence and moral impediments to military action.

Contested Cultural Terrain

The cultural landscape of nuclear deterrence has been fundamentally shaped by irresolvable tensions "created by the conflicts between the destructive power of [nuclear] weapons, which makes them unusable, and the need to make them serve political goals." Greatest of all, according to Jervis, is the tension between strengthening deterrence by raising the costs of nuclear war and limiting the damage of nuclear war should deterrence fail.[111]

This central tension has produced two irreconcilable visions of nuclear war and related beliefs about how nuclear deterrence operates. The first vision is of nuclear apocalypse, where each side obliterates the other. Deterrence is straightforward here, and is achieved by the simple, terrible promise of "mutual assured destruction" (MAD). The second vision is of nuclear war as a strategic exercise, much like any other war, where each side deploys forces to best advantage in pursuit of war aims. Deterrence is a more complicated matter here, and requires the manifest ability to fight (if not "win") a nuclear war. Each vision of nuclear war came with its own prescription as to how such wars ought to be planned for and fought. Hence, nuclear warfighters demanded a force structure that was larger, more varied and complex than the enemy's, while the MAD lot called for more modest nuclear forces, just enough to blow up the Soviet Union once (instead of many times over!). The MAD versus nuclear warfighting debate has been a central feature of the cultural terrain of US nuclear deterrence, with each defining the other and the cultural landscape in much the same way as mountains and valleys.[112]

Notions of nuclear warfighting originated in a civilian-led critique of the military's viewed of a sudden, all-out, "atomic blitz." Chief among the critics was Brodie, who has we have seen, called for enemy cities to be held in reserve, in order to limit the scale of nuclear war and provide for intrawar deterrence. This "golden age" of US strategic studies in the 1950–1960s produced a variety of civilian-inspired nuclear strategies. Each was designed to manipulate risk by proving to the enemy that any nuclear exchange would ultimately work to the advantage of the United States, no matter what.[113] The logical conclusion of this way of thinking was Kahn's *On Thermonuclear War*. Applying systems analysis—a method of using statistical data to study social phenomena—Kahn set out to *prove* that nuclear weapons could be employed to advantage in a superpower war. Driving Kahn's analysis was the assumption that if fought intelligently, the United States could not only survive a nuclear war, but that the majority of survivors could return to "normal and happy lives."[114]

Such visions of fighting nuclear war were understandably greeted by derision by those who believed that nuclear war equaled mutual annihilation. Ironically, one such skeptic was Brodie, who defected to the MAD camp in the mid-1960s. Brodie took issue in particular with Kahn's idea that nuclear war could be fought to national ends. For Brodie, "Kahn [had] undoubtedly underestimated the problems of recovery" from general nuclear war. Destruction was likely to be on such massive scale, Brodie concluded, that nuclear war would violate the "simple Clausewitizian premise" that military operations must match and serve political ends.[115] In the 1950s Brodie had tried to escape the logic of MAD, a decade later he surrendered to it.[116]

This debate between MAD theorists and nuclear warfighters rumbled on into the 1980s, gathering renewed momentum as the Cold War heated up under Reagan. In the leading US journal *International Security,* Gray presented "The Case for a Theory of Victory" in nuclear war. Gray argued that MAD thinking "virtually ensures self-deterrence and denies us the freedom of strategic-nuclear action that is a premise of NATO's strategy of flexible response." Gray was launching a broad critique against MAD theorists who (intentionally) failed to come up with a plan for nuclear war and instead "tended to think of the superpowers as though they were two missile farms."[117] For Gray, growing warheads would not in itself produce an effective nuclear deterrent. This cut little ice with the MAD crowd, who thought that any belief that a nuclear war could be won was insane. In a response to Gray's article, Oxford don Michael Howard fired back that "a nuclear exchange on any scale would cause damage of a kind that would make a mockery of the whole concept of 'victory.'" Claiming to speak for the "intelligent European," Howard declared, "few of us believe that there would be much left of our highly urbanized, economically tightly integrated and desperately vulnerable societies after even the most controlled and limited strategic nuclear exchange."[118] A major disagreement then, between MAD and nuclear warfighting positions, was over the shape of the post–nuclear war world, with the likes of Kahn and Gray being much more optimistic than Brodie and Howard.

Gray's article also pointed quite precisely to a central problem with the MAD approach and major preoccupation of US policymakers: the United States had to be able to threaten nuclear use in order to underwrite its security guarantees to its European allies. The North Atlantic Treaty Organization (NATO) rested on the United States extending its nuclear deterrent to Europe. This was especially important as the Soviet Army was widely believed to be far larger than NATO's; a Soviet attack was expected to sweep aside conventional Western defenses. As the Soviet Union began to build up its own strategic nuclear forces, it became clear that the United States could only credibly extend its nuclear deterrent if it had a plan to fight and win a general nuclear war. The United States also had to produce a lot more besides—and a series of initiatives were pursued to "couple" Western Europe's fate with the US strategic nuclear arsenal. Most of these involved deploying shorter-range US nuclear weapons in Europe, which would have to be used should the Soviet Union invade Western Europe.[119] Thus, a Soviet invasion would "trigger" US nuclear retaliation. The purpose was to convince the Soviets that, come what may, the United States would sacrifice Boston for Berlin. This attempt to improve US deterrence by increasing the risk of escalation from conventional war in Europe to a global nuclear war greatly worried MAD theorists. At the heart of MAD theory was the fear of uncontrollable escalation.[120] MAD theorists believed once the nukes went flying, all bets were off as to when the war would stop. Any notion that such a war could be controlled (a necessary condition for victory at minimum cost) was wishful thinking.[121] As Howard warned, "to attempt to use strategic nuclear weapons for 'warfighting' would be to enter the realm of the unknown and unknowable, and what little we do know about it is appalling."[122]

MAD and nuclear warfighting doctrine do not amount to norms as such. Both are discrete sets of beliefs about the nature of nuclear war and requirements for deterrence. However, neither provided a coherent prescription for action that became embodied in US behavior. As we saw above, US nuclear targeting consistently incorporated elements of both MAD and nuclear warfighting throughout the Cold War. That is to say, SAC's basic plan for a sudden and all-out nuclear war (the "Sunday punch") mirrored the MAD vision of unlimited apocalypse but was intended to deliver nuclear victory.[123] Rather, MAD and nuclear warfighting doctrine are best thought of as rival metanarratives about nuclear war. They served to structure and frame debate about nuclear use, and thereby provided the context for particular norms about nuclear use.

Both nuclear norms explored in this chapter may be located in terms of the MAD side of the MAD–nuclear warfighting debate. MAD theory is sympathetic to the nuclear taboo; both operate on the assumption that nuclear use is too awful to contemplate except in the direst of situations. Nuclear warfighters are unlikely to have much time for the nuclear taboo—even if they accept that it exists—because it places limits on options for nuclear use. As Gray recently put it, "although there is a very widespread taboo that stigmatizes nuclear weapons—possession, threat, and use—that normative proscription cannot handle arguments and assertions of security necessity." For Gray, the nuclear taboo "helps disarm us psychologically, politically and militarily" in the face of threats from weapons of mass destruction.[124] Countercity targeting is also more consistent with MAD than nuclear warfighting. As noted already, nuclear warfighting doctrine originated in civilian critiques of countercity targeting in US war plans. However, for MAD theorists, targeting cities is actually welcome when it raises awareness of the true consequences of nuclear use and thereby makes nuclear war less likely.

Moral Codes and Technical Scripts for Nuclear Action

In contrast to the metanarratives of MAD and nuclear warfighting, nuclear norms are those specific beliefs that provided moral codes and technical scripts for US action. The nuclear taboo clearly proscribed particular action on moral grounds, in that personal qualms and/or public outrage prevented policymakers from contemplating nuclear use. Equally, the countercity targeting norm prescribed action on the grounds of technical efficiency. Drawing on personal and institutional experience of World War II, the US Air Force plainly believed that blasting enemy cities to smithereens and burning what was left to the ground was the quickest road to victory, and that nuclear weapons were the perfect tool for the job. However, the nuclear norms studied in this chapter do not reveal a clear divide between moral code and technical script. Rather, the moral code about nuclear nonuse clashed with important technical requirements for early nuclear use in defense of NATO, while the technical script about nuking cities breached a moral code prohibiting attacks on civilians.

As noted above, come a superpower war, NATO chiefs did not expect their conventional armies to be able to repulse the Soviet invader. Rather, NATO's conventional forces were to provide a "shield" to buy time for the alliance to unsheathe the "sword" of US (British and French) nuclear forces. By 1967 this concept of deterring Soviet attack by threatening nuclear escalation was encoded in NATO's "flexible response" strategy. The Allies differed on how escalation would actually occur, with Germany insisting that NATO would go nuclear first, and the United States being a bit more vague.[125] In any case, NATO had to be prepared to go nuclear first in order to make good on its promise that its nuclear "sword" would strike should its conventional "shield" collapse. Herein lay the problem with taboo norm, which prohibits nuclear use except in retaliation for nuclear attack. In the early 1980s, a group of former senior US policymakers produced a stinging critique of NATO's policy of threatening nuclear first-use in the pages of *Foreign Affairs*. Adopting a position consistent with MAD theory and the taboo norm, they argued that "given the appalling consequences of even the most limited use of nuclear weapons and the total impossibility for both sides of any guarantee against unlimited escalation, there must be the gravest doubt about the wisdom of a policy which asserts the effectiveness of any first use of nuclear weapons by either side."[126] Note that this is a critique on technical grounds: the argument is not so much that nuclear first-use would be immoral as that it would be imprudent. A response in the same journal by a group of German policymakers defended the first-use policy, again on technical grounds. They argued that "the coupling of conventional and nuclear weapons has rendered war between East and West unwageable and unwinnable up to now. It is the inescapable paradox of this strategy of war prevention that the will to conduct nuclear war must be demonstrated in order to prevent war at all."[127] Thus, the nuclear taboo norm impinged on a technical debate by the appropriateness of nuclear first-use as a method of defense for NATO.

Similarly, the technical norm of countercity targeting ran into trouble on moral grounds. More precisely, it violated a rule encoded in international humanitarian law that prohibits military attacks on civilians. This rule was first stated in the St. Petersburg Declaration of 1868, but it was only authoritatively codified in the 1949 Geneva Conventions (i.e., following the horrendous strategic bombing campaigns of both the Allied and Axis powers during World War II).[128] Its continued legal force and relevance was confirmed by the International Court of Justice, when it gave an opinion in 1996 on the legality of nuclear use. In a finding consistent with the nuclear taboo, the Court concluded that nuclear use was generally illegal except perhaps "in an extreme circumstance of self-defense, in which the very survival of the State would be at stake." However, the Court clearly stated that under no circumstances may nuclear weapons be used against civilians: "States must never make civilians the object of attack and must consequently never use weapons that are incapable of distinguishing between civilian and military targets." It is abundantly clear from this that SAC's plan to defeat the Soviet Union by causing mass civilian casualties was illegal. Arguably, so too is the practice of targeting war-supporting industries in cities, because such attacks would not distinguish between war-workers and "innocent" civilians. The judges were less decided on this latter point, as some recognized that unintentionally killing civilians may be justified on grounds of military necessity. However, no judge accepted that military necessity could extend to the killing of millions upon millions of noncombatants.[129] As noted earlier, US civilian policymakers did raise moral objections decades ago to the targeting of civilians with nuclear weapons. But such moral considerations, to say nothing of international legal obligation, appear to have made no impact of SAC's war plans.

Thus the nuclear taboo and countercity targeting norm both nested in a complex social structure, which also housed conflicting norms. Moral concerns made no dent on the norm prescribing targeting priorities. However, in the case of the technical requirement for nuclear first-use in defense of NATO, one may speculate that this could have neutralized any normative prohibition against nuclear use except in retaliation for nuclear attack. For instance, General David Jones (chairman of the US Joint Chiefs of Staff) offered the view in 1982 that "it is unreasonable to expect that promises [of no first-use] made with cool reason in peacetime will be kept in the heat of battle when a nation is threatened with military conquest."[130] In short, defense of Europe may well have pushed the United States to go nuclear first.

Conclusion

With up to a billion projected casualties, and possible complete destruction of the Earth's ecosystem, nuclear war must surely be the ultimate irrational human enterprise. And yet, people imagined the unimaginable, and experts thought the unthinkable. This chapter has focused on two specific beliefs about nuclear use—the nuclear taboo and the countercity targeting norm—and examined how they became institutionalized in US nuclear practice.

The US public approached the bomb with a mixture of awe and apprehension. However, policymakers quickly came to view nuclear weapons as inherently special, and usable only in last resort. This nuclear taboo is most evident in instances where the United States failed to deploy the absolute weapon when it got into military difficulty against nonnuclear opponents. The US military had no such qualms about using nuclear weapons. SAC devised a war plan that was terrifyingly simple: to drop the entire US nuclear arsenal on the Soviet enemy in one fell swoop. The chief targets for SAC were Soviet cities. Drawing on institutional memory of the bombing campaigns against Germany and Japan during World War II, SAC planners believed that the fastest route to victory was to terrorize the enemy's civilian population and, effectively, bomb them into submission.

Both nuclear norms may be located within a wider cultural system. Two rival metanarratives of nuclear war—MAD and nuclear warfighting—served to frame debate for civilian strategists and military men in the United States. Within this overall social structure of US nuclear deterrence were ideas and imperatives that happened to clash with the taboo and countercity targeting norms. The requirement to be able (and to be seen to be able) to deploy nuclear weapons first in defense of NATO ran counter to the nuclear taboo. Equally, a moral prohibition against targeting civilians, institutionalized in international law, cannot be squared with a norm prescribing just such action. Cultural systems are perfectly able to contain competing norms. As discussed in Chapter 1, where norms compete behavior may be shaped by the logic of argumentation rather than the logic of appropriateness. Actors must reason through what action to take in particular circumstances, rather than automatically apply a moral code or technical script.

Both norms were given institutional form and this helps account for their persistence. The nuclear taboo was institutionalized in early Truman administration policy that ruled out preemptive nuclear use, as well as in a law (1946 AEA) that gave civilians control over these terrifying new weapons. This norm was also reinforced in the 1978 policy of not threatening nonnuclear opponents with nuclear attack. Norms of countercity targeting were institutionalized in successive nuclear war plans (from EWP 1-49 through to the SIOP), as well as in a Nuclear Strategic Target Data Base. These institutions—presidential policy, law, war plans, and target database—were vital to the embedding of these norms in, respectively, US strategic culture and SAC organizational culture.

The future of both norms is difficult to predict, however. While the norm of countercity targeting has persisted into the post–Cold War period, it has less potency. US nuclear targeting priorities have shifted from causing massive damage to a peer competitor (i.e., the Soviet Union), to precise and discriminate destruction of WMD facilities in "rogue states." Obliterating cities must also have lost considerable appeal given the growing force of humanitarian law (as discussed in the next chapter). As the ICJ made clear, humanitarian law prohibits such indiscriminate use of nuclear weapons. Few would disagree that this is all for the good.

But equally, the future nuclear taboo is open to question. The indefinite extension of the Nuclear Non-Proliferation Treaty in 1995 and adoption of the 1996 CTBT point toward continued efforts at the world level to control the development and spread of these unusually dangerous weapons. Secondary agency has played a significant role here, through national and transnational activist networks, in identifying a moral imperative in abolishing nuclear weapons, and in mobilizing wider public and political support for this project.[131] Some segments of the scientific community have also played their part in educating politicians and policymakers on both sides of the Cold War divide about the dangers of nuclear war.[132] Recent actions by the United States, however, have undercut these international efforts to stigmatize nuclear weapons. The new strategic priority—forcible disarmament of "rogue states"—has renewed interest in creating a new generation of low-yield nuclear weapons. It has informed the restructuring of US strategic strike forces to integrate nuclear and conventional weapons. It has led the United States to revoke its pledge not to use nukes against nonnuclear opponents. The US effort to find ways to make nuclear weapons more usable is all the more worrying in the context of continued nuclear armament around the world. India and Pakistan have recently joined the nuclear club, North Korea and probably Iran are trying to build nuclear weapons, and the established nuclear powers (Britain, China, France, and Russia) all have nuclear modernization programs. Jonathan Schell gloomily concludes from this that "the bomb is back."[133] Of course, it may be that the nuclear taboo will survive the Bush years, just as it outlasted Eisenhower. Time will tell.

Notes

1. Bernard Brodie (ed.), *The Absolute Weapon: Atomic Power and World Order* (New York: Harcourt, Brace, 1946).

2. Though in the case of the United States at least, this was imperfect knowledge. For an excellent study on this, see Lynn Eden, *Whole World on Fire: Organizations, Knowledge and Nuclear Weapons Devastation* (Ithaca, NY: Cornell University Press, 2004).

3. Colin S. Gray, *Modern Strategy* (Oxford: Oxford University Press, 1999), pp. 333–334.

4. Robert Jervis, *The Meaning of the Nuclear Revolution: Statecraft and the Prospects for Armageddon* (Ithaca, NY: Cornell University Press, 1989), p. 183.

5. Robert Jervis, *The Illogic of American Nuclear Strategy* (Ithaca, NY: Cornell University Press, 1984), p. 38.

6. Eric Herring, "The Power of the Nuclear Taboo," paper presented at the British International Studies Association (BISA) annual conference, Swansea, December 1992; Eric Herring, "Nuclear Totem and Taboo," paper presented at the BISA annual conference, Leeds, December 1997; Richard Price and Nina Tannenwald, "Norms and Deterrence: The Nuclear and Chemical Weapons Taboo," in Peter J. Katzenstein (ed.), *The Culture of National Security: Norms and Identity in World Politics* (New York: Columbia University Press, 1996), pp. 114–152; Nina Tannenwald, "The Nuclear Taboo: The United States and the Normative Basis of Nuclear Non-use," *International Organization* 53, no. 3 (1999): 433–468; T. V. Paul, "Nuclear Taboo and War Initiation in Regional Conflicts," *Journal of Conflict Resolution* 39, no. 4 (1995): 696–717.

7. Herring, "Nuclear Totem," p. 16; Tannenwald, "The Nuclear Taboo."

8. Thus the judge advocate general of the US Air Force recently signed off on the legality of a fuel-air explosive munition with a yield of 18,000 pounds of explosive. Major General Thomas J. Fiscus, Judge Advocate General, "Requested Legal Review of the Massive Ordnance Air Blast Weapon," Department of the Air Force, HQ USAF, Washington, DC, 21 March 2003.

9. Herring, "Nuclear Totem," pp. 20–21.

10. Price and Tannenwald, "Norms and Deterrence," p. 120.

11. Tannenwald, "The Nuclear Taboo," pp. 442–447.

12. Colin S. Gray, *Weapons Don't Make War* (Lawrence: University of Kansas Press, 1993), p. 1.

13. Tannenwald, "The Nuclear Taboo," p. 443.

14. Paul Boyer, "Exotic Resonances: Hiroshima in American Memory," *Diplomatic History* 19, no. 2 (1995): 299.

15. Gar Alperovitz, *The Decision to Use the Atomic Bomb* (London: Fontana, 1996), pp. 437–497; Barton J. Bernstein, "Seizing the Contested Terrain of Early Nuclear

History: Stimson, Conant, and Their Allies Explain the Decision to Use the Atomic Bomb," *Diplomatic History* 17 (1993): 35–72.

16. According to official Japanese statistics, when those killed by radiation sickness are included, the final death toll of Hiroshima and Nagasaki is a staggering 300,000 to 350,000. John Dower, "The Bombed: Hiroshima and Nagasaki in Japanese Memory," *Diplomatic History* 19 (1995): 282, fn. 16.

17. This is noted in Lawrence Freedman, *The Evolution of Nuclear Strategy* (Basingstoke: Macmillan, 1981), p. 21.

18. Paul Boyer, *By the Bomb's Early Light: American Thought and Culture at the Dawn of the Atomic Age,* 2nd ed. (Chapel Hill: University of North Carolina Press, 1994), pp. 1–26.

19. The US Department of Defense and the US Atomic Energy Commission, *The Effects of Atomic Weapons* (New York: McGraw-Hill, 1950), p. 1.

20. John E. Pike, Bruce G. Blair, and Stephen I. Schwartz, "Defending Against the Bomb," in Stephen I. Schwartz (ed.), *Atomic Audit: The Costs and Consequences of US Nuclear Weapons Since 1945* (Washington, DC: Brookings Institution, 1998), pp. 312–313.

21. Spencer R. Weart, *Nuclear Fear: A History of Images* (Cambridge, MA: Harvard University Press, 1988), pp. 169, 180.

22. Laura McEnaney, *Civil Defense Begins at Home* (Princeton, NJ: Princeton University Press, 2000).

23. Richard Rhodes, *Dark Sun: The Making of the Hydrogen Bomb* (New York: Simon and Schuster, 1995), pp. 508–509.

24. Pike, Blair, and Schwartz, "Defending Against the Bomb," pp. 312–313.

25. Michael Mandelbaum, *The Nuclear Revolution: International Politics Before and After Hiroshima* (Cambridge: Cambridge University Press, 1981), pp. 218–219.

26. Ibid., p. 225.

27. Weart, *Nuclear Fear,* p. 378. The agenda for the Nuclear Freeze Movement is detailed in Senator Edward M. Kennedy and Senator Mark O. Hatfield, *Freeze! How You Can Help Prevent Nuclear War* (New York: Bantam, 1982).

28. Jonathan Schell, *The Fate of the Earth* (New York: Avon, 1982), pp. 56–57.

29. Weart, *Nuclear Fear,* p. 381.

30. Boyer, "Exotic Resonances," p. 307.

31. Michael Mandelbaum, "The Anti–Nuclear Weapons Movement," *PS* 17 (1984): 27, as cited in Boyer, "Exotic Resonances," p. 303.

32. McGeorge Bundy, *Danger and Survival: Choices About the Bomb in the First Fifty Years* (New York: Random House, 1988), pp. 58–79.

33. Barton J. Bernstein, "Eclipsed by Hiroshima and Nagasaki: Early Thinking About Tactical Nuclear Weapons," *International Security* 15 (1991): 164; quote from Truman diary, p. 159.

34. McGeorge Bundy suggests that this discrepancy was caused by the lack of "an air raid alert to send people to shelters." Bundy, *Danger and Survival,* p. 80. However, one wonders whether regular bomb shelters could have saved lives from the nuclear blast that flattened most of Hiroshima. Moreover, survivors would have been cooked alive in their shelters by the incredibly intense heat generated by the atomic explosion.

35. Michael S. Sherry, *Preparing for the Next War: American Plans for Postwar Defense, 1941–1945* (New Haven, CT: Yale University Press, 1977), p. 210.

36. Peter D. Feaver, *Guarding the Guardians: Civilian Control of Nuclear Weapons in the United States* (Ithaca, NY: Cornell University Press, 1992), p. 125.

37. Bundy, *Danger and Survival,* pp. 68–77; Bernstein, "Eclipsed," pp. 155–156.

38. Revisionist historians claim that the atomic bombing had more to do with the coming Cold War rather than the end of World War II. The argument goes that Japan was trying to surrender on terms that would protect the emperor (whose position was protected in the postwar Japanese constitution written by the US military), that US intelligence knew this, and that it used the bomb anyway to impress the Soviets. On this debate, see Rufus E. Miles Jr., "Hiroshima: The Strange Myth of Half a Million Lives Saved," *International Security* 10 (1985): 121–140; Robert Pape, "Why Japan Surrendered," *International Security* 18 (1993): 154–201; Alperovitz, *The Decision;* Gar Alperovitz, Robert L. Messer, and Barton J. Bernstein, "Correspondence: Marshall, Truman, and the Decision to Drop the Bomb," *International Security* 16, no. 3 (1991/1992): 204–221.

39. David S. Broscious, "Longing for International Control, Banking on Superiority," in John Lewis Gaddis et al. (eds.), *Cold War Statesmen Confront the Bomb* (Oxford: Oxford University Press, 1999), p. 32.

40. David Alan Rosenberg, "The Origins of Overkill: Nuclear Weapons and American Strategy, 1945–1960," *International Security* 7 (1983): 12–14, 26.

41. Broscious, "Longing for International Control," p. 27.

42. John Lewis Gaddis, *We Now Know: Rethinking Cold War History* (Oxford: Oxford University Press, 1997), p. 91.

43. Feaver, *Guarding the Guardians,* pp. 87–218; see also Peter J. Roman, "Ike's Hair-Trigger: US Nuclear Predelegation, 1953–1960," *Security Studies* 7 (1998): 121–164. The assertion of civilian control in the postwar United States may be seen in the context of the Republic's history, in which crisis-induced military growth has been typically followed by congressional-enforced military entrenchment. Aaron L. Friedberg, *In the Shadow of the Garrison State* (Princeton, NJ: Princeton University Press, 2000).

44. Marc Trachtenberg, *History and Strategy* (Princeton, NJ: Princeton University Press, 1991), pp. 103–107, 123–124.

45. William Burr and Jeffrey T. Richelson, "Whether to 'Strangle the Baby in the Cradle': The United States and the Chinese Nuclear Program, 1960–1964," *International Security* 25, no. 3 (Winter 2000–2001): 75.

46. US politicians and policymakers often had problems reading public views on national security matters. See Steven Kull and I. M. Destler, *Misreading the Public: The Myth of a New Isolationism* (Washington, DC: Brookings Institution, 1999).

47. Tannenwald, "Nuclear Taboo," pp. 442–462; Robert S. McNamara with Brian VanDeMark, *In Retrospect: The Tragedy and Lessons of Vietnam* (New York: Times Books, 1995), pp. 147, 160.

48. Eisenhower quotes taken from Gaddis, *We Now Know,* p. 108.

49. John Lewis Gaddis, *The Long Peace: Inquiries into the History of the Cold War* (Oxford: Oxford University Press, 1983), p. 141.

50. Tannenwald, "The Nuclear Taboo," p. 444.

51. Gaddis, *The Long Peace,* pp. 140–146.

52. On Eisenhower's and Dulles's beliefs about nuclear use, see chapters by Ned Rosendorf and Andrew Erdmann in John Lewis Gaddis et al. (eds.), *Cold War Statesmen Confront the Bomb* (Oxford: Oxford University Press, 1999).

53. Tannenwald, "The Nuclear Taboo," p. 460.

54. All quotes in this paragraph are taken from Scott D. Sagan, "The Commitment Trap: Why the United States Should Not Use Nuclear Threats to Deter Biological and Chemical Weapons Attacks," *International Security* 24, no. 4 (2000): 91–93.

55. Benjamin Friedman, "Mini-Nukes, Bunker-Busters, and Deterrence: Framing the Debate," 26 April 2002, http://www.cdi.org/.

56. William M. Arkin, "Secret Plan Outlines the Unthinkable," *Los Angeles Times,* 10 March 2002.

57. Nicholas Kralev, "US Drops Pledge on Nukes: Won't Rule Out Hitting Any States," *Washington Times,* 22 February 2002. In so doing, the United States was also breaking a similar pledge made by all five declared nuclear powers at the UN Security Council in 1995. See S/RES/984 (1995), http://www.un.org/documents/scres.htm.

58. Charles Kucia and Daryl Kimball, "New Nuclear Policies, New Weapons, New Dangers," Issue Brief, Arms Control Association, 28 April 2003, http://armscontrol.org/.

59. Excerpts from the Hearing of the Senate Armed Services Committee, 13 February 2003, http://www.fcnl.org.

60. Statement of the Honorable Douglas J. Feith, Undersecretary of Defense for Policy, Senate Armed Services Hearing on the Nuclear Posture Review, 14 February 2002, p. 5.

61. Statement of Admiral James O. Ellis, USN, CINC US Strategic Command Before the Senate Armed Services Committee on the Nuclear Posture Review, 14 February 2002, pp. 5–6.

62. Richard Sokolsky, "Demystifying the US Nuclear Posture Review," *Survival* 44, no. 3 (2002): 138.

63. This is the Spratt-Furse Amendment to the National Defense Authorization for Fiscal Year 1994 (PL 103-106), *Congressional Bills,* 103rd Congress (1993–1994).

64. *Report to the Congress on the Defeat of Hard and Deeply Buried Targets,* submitted by the Secretary of Defense in conjunction with the Secretary of Energy, July 2001, p. 18.

65. "Partial Victories on Nuclear Weapons in Congress," 14 November 2002, http://www.fcnl.org/.

66. David Appell, "Ground Below Zero," *Scientific American.Com,* 17 June 2002, http://www.sciam.com/; "20 Experts Urge Senate to Reject Nuclear Earth Penetrator Funds," Council for a Livable World, 20 June 2002, http://www.clw.org/; Mark Browley, David Grahame, and Christine Kucia, *Bunker Busters: Washington's Drive for New Nuclear Weapons,* BASIC Research Report (Washington, DC: British American Security Information Council, July 2002); Michael A. Levi, *Fire in the Hole: Nuclear and Non-nuclear Options for Counter-proliferation* (Washington, DC: Carneige Endowment for International Peace, November 2002), http://www.ceip.org/; "The Troubling Science of Bunker-Busting Nuclear Weapons," Union of Concerned Scientists, April 2003, http://ucsusa.org/; "Prominent Nuclear Weapons Scientists Urge Senate to Retain the 'Mini-Nuke' Ban," 19 May 2003, www.fcnl.org; Robert W. Nelson, "Low-Yield Earth-Penetrating Nuclear Weapons," *FAS Public Interest Report,* 2001, http://www.fas.org/.

67. 172 states have signed the 1996 CTBT (including the United States) and 115 states have ratified it. See http://www.ctbto.org/.

68. Vicki Allen, "Rumsfeld Pushes for New Nuclear Weapons Study," Reuters, 20 May 2003; Vicki Allen, "Senate Backs Bush on 'Mini-Nukes,'" Reuters, 21 May 2003, http://www.reuters.com/.

69. For a classic treatment on this, see Richard E. Neustadt, *Presidential Power: The Politics of Leadership from FDR to Carter* (New York: John Wiley and Sons, 1980).

70. Indeed, there was little scope for truth-seeking argument. As the next section discusses, the US military did not recognize the nuclear taboo. The US general in charge of executing the US nuclear war plan, General Curtis LeMay, thought the idea of non–first nuclear use was nonsense. Incredibly, he had arranged to circumvent pres-

idential and civilian control in 1950 by taking delivery of atomic weapons from military guards at AEC facilities. Rhodes, *Dark Sun,* p. 568.

71. Rosenberg, "Origins of Overkill," p. 11.

72. Steven T. Ross, *American War Plans, 1945–1950* (London: Frank Cass, 1996), p. 155; Bret J. Cillessen, "Embracing the Bomb: Ethics, Morality, and Nuclear Deterrence in the US Air Force, 1945–1955," *Journal of Strategic Studies* 21 (1998): 99–103.

73. Michael S. Sherry, *The Rise of American Air Power: The Creation of Armageddon* (New Haven, CT: Yale University Press, 1987), pp. 1–46.

74. Phillip S. Meilinger, "Trenchard, Slessor, and Royal Air Force Doctrine Before World War II," in Phillip S. Meilinger (ed.), *The Paths of Heaven: The Evolution of Airpower Theory* (Maxwell AFB, AL: Air University Press, 1997), pp. 41–78.

75. Jeffrey W. Legro, *Cooperation Under Fire: Anglo-German Restraint During World War II* (Ithaca, NY: Cornell University Press, 1995), pp. 129–135; Stephen Peter Rosen, *Winning the Next War: Innovation and the Modern Military* (Ithaca, NY: Cornell University Press, 1991), pp. 150–157; Williamson Murray, "Strategic Bombing: The British, American, and German Experiences," in Williamson Murray and Allan R. Millet (eds.), *Military Innovation in the Intrawar Period* (Cambridge: Cambridge University Press, 1996), pp. 116–127.

76. Ronald Schaffer, *Wings of Judgment: American Bombing in World War II* (Oxford: Oxford University Press, 1985); Sherry, *The Rise,* pp. 147–176; Tami Davis Biddle, "British and American Approaches to Strategic Bombing: Their Origins and Implementation in the World War II Combined Bomber Offensive," *Journal of Strategic Studies* 18, no. 1 (1995): 91–144; Hays W. Park, "'Precision' and 'Area' Bombing: Who Did Which and When?" *Journal of Strategic Studies* 18, no. 1 (1995): 145–174.

77. Rosenberg, "Origins of Overkill," p. 20. A similar argument about ideas traveling with veterans of World War II into SAC is developed in more detail in Eden, *Whole World on Fire,* pp. 93–121.

78. Sherry, *Preparing,* pp. 231–232.

79. Rosenberg, "Origins of Overkill," pp. 15, 21.

80. Bernstein, "Eclipsed," p. 170.

81. Cited in Rosenberg, "Origins of Overkill," p. 15; see also Ross, *American War Plans,* pp. 56–57.

82. Rhodes, *Dark Sun,* p. 347; David Alan Rosenberg, "American Atomic Strategy and the Hydrogen Bomb Decision," *Journal of American History* 66, no. 1 (1979): 71.

83. David Alan Rosenberg, "A Smoking Radiating Ruin at the End of Two Hours: Documents on American Plans for Nuclear War with the Soviet Union," *International Security* 6, no. 3 (1981/1982): 11.

84. Melvyn Leffler, *A Preponderance of Power: National Security, the Truman Administration, and the Cold War* (Stanford, CA: Stanford University Press, 1992), pp. 221–229.

85. Lynn Eden, "Capitalist Conflict and the State: The Making of United States Military Policy in 1948," in Charles Bright and Susan Harding (eds.), *Statemaking and Social Movements* (Ann Arbor: University of Michigan Press, 1984), pp. 233–261.

86. Frank Kofsky, *Harry S. Truman and the War Scare of 1948* (New York: St. Martin's, 1995).

87. David Goldfischer, *The Best Defense: Policy Alternatives for US Nuclear Security from the 1950s to the 1990s* (Ithaca, NY: Cornell University Press, 1993), pp. 79–146.

88. Samuel R. Williamson Jr. and Steven L. Reardon, *The Origins of US Nuclear Strategy, 1945–1953* (New York: St. Martin's, 1993); Matthew A. Evangelista, "Stalin's Postwar Army Reappraised," *International Security* 7 (1982/1983): 110–138.

89. Rosenberg, "American Atomic Strategy," pp. 72–73.

90. Ross, *American War Plans*, pp. 107–132.

91. Rosenberg, "American Atomic Strategy," p. 78.

92. Graham Spinardi, *From Polaris to Trident: The Development of US Fleet Ballistic Missile Technology* (Cambridge: Cambridge University Press, 1994), pp. 32–34.

93. McGeorge Bundy, "Early Thoughts on Controlling the Nuclear Arms Race: A Report to the Secretary of State, January 1953," *International Security* 7, no. 2 (1982): 14.

94. Brodie quoted in Rosenberg, "Origins of Overkill," p. 18.

95. Trachtenberg, *History and Strategy*, pp. 3–46.

96. Fred Kaplan, *The Wizards of Armageddon* (New York: Simon and Schuster, 1983), pp. 222–223.

97. Scott D. Sagan, *Moving Targets: Nuclear Strategy and National Security* (Princeton, NJ: Princeton University Press, 1989), chap. 1.

98. Saturation of the Soviet nuclear target base is discussed in Theo Farrell, *Weapons Without a Cause: The Politics of Weapons Acquisition in the United States* (New York: St. Martin's, 1997), pp. 48–49.

99. Kaplan, *The Wizards*, pp. 40–42, 104; Peter Pringle and William Arkin, *SIOP: Nuclear War from the Inside* (London: Sphere, 1983), pp. 24, 30.

100. Rosenberg, "Origins of Overkill," pp. 4–5, 36, 64–69.

101. Fred Charles Ikle, "Can Nuclear Deterrence Last Out the Century?" *Foreign Affairs* 51 (1973): 281.

102. Terry Terriff, *The Nixon Administration and the Making of US Nuclear Strategy* (Ithaca, NY: Cornell University Press, 1995), p. 178.

103. Cited in Desmond Ball, *Targeting for Strategic Deterrence* (London: International Institute for Strategic Studies, 1983, Alephi Paper 185), p. 33. This theme was reiterated in Brown's annual reports to Congress in 1979 and 1980.

104. Office of Technology Assessment, Congress of the United States, *The Effects of Nuclear War* (London: Croom Helm, 1980), p. 100.

105. Bruce G. Blair, *The Logic of Accidental Nuclear War* (Washington, DC: Brookings Institution, 1993), pp. 42–43.

106. Janne E. Nolan, *Guardians of the Arsenal: The Politics of Nuclear Strategy* (New York: Basic, 1989), pp. 251–255, 261.

107. US General Account Office, *Strategic Weapons: Nuclear Weapons Targeting Process*, GAO/NSIAD-91-319FS (Washington, DC: US GAO, September 1991), pp. 13, 16.

108. Ward Thomas, *The Ethics of Destruction: Norms and Force in International Relations* (Ithaca, NY: Cornell University Press, 2001), pp. 168–174; Benjamin S. Lambert, *The Transformation of American Air Power* (Ithaca, NY: Cornell University Press, 2000).

109. Bruce G. Blair, John E. Pike, and Stephen L. Schwartz, "Targeting and Controlling the Bomb," in Stephen L. Schwartz (ed.), *Atomic Audit* (Washington, DC: Brookings Institution, 1998), pp. 199, 203, 205.

110. The NRDC's nuclear war simulation may be downloaded from http://www.nrdc.org/nuclear/.

111. Jervis, *The Illogic*, pp. 48–49.

112. For a useful summary of the "easy school" and "difficult school" of nuclear deterrence, see Barry Buzan and Eric Herring, *The Arms Dynamic in World Politics* (Boulder, CO: Lynne Rienner, 1998), pp. 168–169. Detailed analysis of MAD versus nuclear warfighting is provided in Charles L. Glaser, *Analyzing Stratetgic Nuclear Policy* (Princeton, NJ: Princeton University Press, 1990).

113. Trachtenberg, *History and Strategy,* pp. 3–46.

114. Herman Kahn, *On Thermonuclear War* (Princeton, NJ: Princeton University Press, 1960), p. 21.

115. Bernard Brodie, *War and Politics* (London: Cassell, 1973), p. 421.

116. Hans Morgenthau similarly flirted with the idea of limited nuclear war in the 1950s before finally rejecting it in 1960. Nuclear war of any kind, he declared in 1961, was "an instrument of mass murder and suicide." Campbell Craig, *Glimmer of a New Leviathan: Total War in the Realism of Niebuhr, Morgenthau, and Waltz* (New York: Columbia University Press, 2003), p. 106.

117. Colin S. Gray, "Nuclear Strategy: The Case for a Theory of Victory," *International Security* 4, no. 1 (1979): 70.

118. Michael E. Howard, "On Fighting Nuclear War," *International Security* 5, no. 4 (1981): 3, 12.

119. David N. Schwartz, *NATO's Nuclear Dilemmas* (Washington, DC: Brookings Institution, 1983).

120. Jervis, *The Meaning of the Nuclear Revolution,* pp. 74–106.

121. Spurgeon M. Keeny Jr. and Wolfgang K. H. Panofsky, "MAD Versus NUTS," *Foreign Affairs* 60 (Winter 1981–1982): 287–304.

122. Howard, "On Fighting Nuclear War," p. 14.

123. This point is also developed in Sagan, *Moving Targets,* pp. 10–57.

124. Colin S. Gray, *The Second Nuclear Age* (Boulder, CO: Lynne Rienner, 1999), p. 108.

125. Schwartz, *NATO's Nuclear Dilemmas,* pp. 176–177. The dominant European preference was for rapid escalation to very small-scale tactical nuclear use, in order to demonstrate to the Soviets that NATO would risk nuclear war in defense of Europe. The logical extension of this was that NATO had to be prepared to make good on this promise. The United States favored avoiding early nuclear use, and instead wanted Europe to put more effort into building up their conventional forces. If nuclear use proved absolutely necessary, US policymakers wanted it to be confined to Europe but to still be large enough in scale to enable NATO to repulse a Soviet invasion. Terriff, *The Nixon Administration,* pp. 35–41.

126. McGeorge Bundy, George F. Kennan, Robert S. McNamara, and Gerard Smith, "Nuclear Weapons and the Atlantic Alliance," *Foreign Affairs* 60, no. 4 (1982): 757.

127. Karl Kaiser, Georg Leber, Alois Mertes, and Franz-Josef Schulze, "Nuclear Weapons and the Preservation of Peace: A Response to an American Proposal for Renouncing the First Use of Nuclear Weapons," *Foreign Affairs* 60, no. 5 (1982): 1159.

128. Malcolm N. Shaw, *International Law,* 5th ed. (Cambridge: Cambridge University Press, 2003), pp. 1063–1068.

129. Analysis on the ICJ opinion is provided in Theo Farrell and Hélène Lambert, "Courting Controversy: International Law, National Norms and American Nuclear Use," *Review of International Studies* 27, no. 3 (2001): 309–326.

130. General David C. Jones, Chairman, Joint Chiefs of Staff, speech to the American Newspaper Publishers Association on 28 April 1982, San Francisco. Reprinted in *Foreign Affairs* 60, no. 5 (Summer 1982): 1173.

131. Lawrence S. Wittner, *The Struggle Against the Bomb: 3 Volumes* (Stanford, CA: Stanford University Press, 1993, 1997, and 2003); Jeffrey W. Knopf, *Domestic Society and International Cooperation: The Impact of Protest on US Arms Control Policy* (Cambridge: Cambridge University Press, 1998).

132. Matthew A. Evangelista, *Unarmed Forces: The Transnational Movement to End the Cold War* (Ithaca, NY: Cornell University Press, 1999).

133. Wittner, *The Struggle Against the Bomb: Vol. 3,* p. 483.

5

Humanitarian War

The end of the twentieth century has seen greater humanitarianism both in the cause and conduct of Western war.[1] The rise of humanitarian intervention as a newly accepted practice reveals a new just cause for war.[2] At the same time, humanitarian law has gained greater force in law and state practice, with the creation of international criminal tribunals, and the clear recognition that humanitarian law is applicable to civil conflicts and also that individuals may be held liable for war crimes.[3]

Integral to this new humanitarianism in war is international law. In general, use of force is prohibited under Article 2(4) of the UN Charter—the keystone of modern international law. The two exceptions to this general prohibition are the use of force in self-defense and the use of force authorized by the UN Security Council (UNSC) for the purpose of protecting international peace and security. In addition, the conduct of war is regulated under humanitarian law, in order to protect civilians and prevent the unnecessary suffering of combatants. States have also agreed to outlaw some tools of war—such as use of chemical or biological weapons. But international law does more than regulate and (partially) restrain war, it also constitutes and enables war. By defining what is wrong in war, the law also seeks to define what is right. This is certainly true of humanitarian law, which provides rules for the moral conduct of warfare. In contrast, humanitarian intervention presents a challenge for international law. As we shall see, humanitarian necessity is not recognized in law as an exception to the nonuse of force norm. Yet, there are cases where the moral imperative for forcible intervention is all too evident. Humanitarian war—both in conduct and purpose—therefore, nicely captures the potential and limitations of the law in providing a normative order for war.

In this chapter, I consider legal norms to be beliefs about the legal capacities, rights, and duties of actors. Such norms determine who can and should do what in law. Not all norms in law are actually legally binding on states; those that are binding are called legal rules. When it comes to war, traditionally distinction is drawn between those rules that govern how force may be used (*jus in bello*) and those that govern when states may resort to force (*jus ad bellum*). *Jus in bello* rules are contained within modern humanitarian law. *Jus ad bellum* is covered by Charter rules on the use of force, as well as state custom on self-defense.

Legal norms are distinct from nonlegal norms by virtue of being institutionalized in either state custom or convention. Customary law comprises state practice and *opinio juris* (i.e., the belief that such practice embodies law). Generally speaking, there must be consistency and general conformity in state practice for it to form the basis of a rule in customary law. Note that conformity need not be absolute. What matters is that most states—especially, the most powerful states and those most closely concerned with the matter at hand—conform to the practice. States must also be engaging in such practice because they believe there to be a legal obligation to do so, as opposed to some other reason—courtesy, nicety, morality, or whatever. Often, *opinio juris* is found in state practice, or consensus in academic literature, or previous judgments of the International Court of Justice (ICJ) or some other international tribunal.[4] International conventions or treaties enable states to bind themselves legally to specific rules of conduct. There is a common a two-fold distinction between "law-making treaties" and "treaty-contracts." The former include "agreements whereby states elaborate their perception of international law."[5] Obviously, many states must be party to such law-making treaties for them to have any effect. While law-making treaties are, in principle, only binding on those states that sign up, they have the potential to produce customary law. Treaty contracts are limited in scope to specific issues and two or more parties, though they may constitute evidence of customary rules of international law.[6]

Legal norms may provide technical scripts for efficient action. For example, the body of soft law generated by the International Organization for Standardization is intended to smooth the flow of goods worldwide by producing common technical guidelines and standards for things like screw widths.[7] In the field of international security, legal norms are mostly principled beliefs about moral action in world politics. Indeed, targeting civilians is prohibited by law notwithstanding, as we saw in Chapter 4, a military belief in the efficiency of countercity bombing. Legal norms in international security are usually binding in law. In fact, the general prohibitions on the use of force and attacks on civilians are recognized to be peremptory norms of international law. Peremptory norms, also called *jus cogens,* embody fundamental values of the international community, the breach of which would be almost universally recognized as a crime; other examples include the prohibitions on genocide, slavery, and piracy. In other words, they are especially powerful legal rules that are binding on all states and from which no derogation is permitted.[8]

There is an obvious contradiction here. Legal norms, even when they are *jus cogens,* are regularly ignored in war. Thus even though the 1945 UN Charter codified a general prohibition on use of force, states have frequently resorted to force since then. Equally, states and insurgent groups have often breached norms of humanitarian law, in particular, by intentionally killing large numbers of civilians in war.[9] As Hersch Lauterpacht famously observed: "If international law is in some ways at the vanishing point of law, the law of war is, perhaps even more conspicuously, at the vanishing point of international law."[10] A key theme of this chapter then, is the tension between legal norms and actual military practice. This is explored in the context of legal norms that are designed to place humanitarian restrictions on the conduct of war, as well as breaches of international law that are humanitarian in purpose.

Chapter Outline

The first section of this chapter examines the relatively new state practice of humanitarian intervention. There is no provision for such practice in international law thus this section focuses on the role of norm violation as a mechanism for legal change. The section begins with an analysis of state practice, and then proceeds to a case study of NATO's intervention in Kosovo in 1999. This is commonly recognized as a crucial test case for the emergence of a new legal norm permitting humanitarian intervention. I discuss why norm violation has not resulted in legal change in this case. Using the model of cultural change outlined in Chapter 1, I argue that a *nonlegal* norm of humanitarian intervention has emerged nonetheless.

Humanitarian law is explored in the second section. Here, state compliance, particularly compliance by powerful states, is somewhat puzzling given that humanitarian law places considerable restrictions on the conduct of warfare. This section starts with an analysis of the development of humanitarian law, which provides considerable evidence of the extent to which it is embedded in the modern world system. I then return to the NATO Kosovo case to examine the application of humanitarian law. This case neatly presents the puzzle of restraint in war by the more powerful side: NATO pursued a very cautious bombing campaign against Yugoslavia, which it was slow to escalate even when there were compelling military reasons for doing so. I produce evidence to show that NATO restraint was down to humanitarian law nonetheless.

The two causal chains explored in the Kosovo case are shown in Table 5.1. For there to be a norm of humanitarian intervention in operation in this case, there must have been massive abuses of human rights by the Yugoslav authorities (which there clearly were) and evidence that NATO states felt some kind of moral obligation to intervene. I concentrate on one norm of humanitarian law in the Kosovo case: the prohibition against the targeting of civilians and civilian objects. If this norm were in operation we would expect to find some kind of legal checks built into NATO's target generation system and restrictive

Table 5.1   Causal Impacts of Humanitarian Norms

Independent Variables	Dependent Variables	Hypothesized Impact
Norm of humanitarian intervention	International response to humanitarian crisis	Prescribes forcible intervention to prevent massive human rights violations
Norms of humanitarian law	Target generation process and rules of engagement	Prohibits attacks on civilians and civilian objects

rules of engagement to ensure that pilots complied with humanitarian law. We might also expect to see such restraint even in the face of some cost to the progress of the military campaign.

Before proceeding to my examination of humanitarian intervention and humanitarian law, I briefly locate two major theoretical approaches to international law in relation to the constructivism in IR. I also consider two questions that are of central importance to our understanding of "the vanishing point of international law": Why do states comply with the law? and, What happens when they break international law?

International Law and Constructivism in IR

There are three major theoretical approaches to international law: Legal Positivism, Natural Law, and the New Haven School. Natural Law thinking, which focuses on the ethical roots and purpose of international law, does not concern us here.[11] But Legal Positivism and the New Haven School both deal with the ontology of international law and methodologies of legal scholarship, and, as such, are highly relevant to the constructivist approach to IR. Legal Positivism sees international law as a set of rules. By freely consenting to these rules, states have created the legal rights and responsibilities that structure international relations. This view highlights the concrete and fixed nature of international law—law is not passing fancy but rather involves real commitment on the part of states, and this gives it permanency, presence, and force.[12] The New Haven School takes an explicitly interdisciplinary approach in an effort to situate legal rules in their wider social context. Thus the New Haven School takes a broad perspective of the entire legal decisionmaking process, one that explores the interplay of values, interests, and rules. This perspective highlights the dynamic and changing character of international law, and the role of power and politics in shaping, maintaining, and changing the law.[13] For the New Haven School, the products of this process are not only binding rules but also nonbinding norms (often called "soft law").[14]

Both schools of thought are consistent with the constructivist approach to international relations. The New Haven School most obviously so, because of its concern with the process whereby law is constructed, and its acceptance of law as encompassing nonbinding norms. But equally, the Legal Positivism conception of legal rules is simply a more narrow focus on norms that are binding in law. Legal Positivism is also useful in terms of methodology. The New Haven School tends to attribute too much dynamism to law-making, leaving it open to the criticism that there is little left that is legal in their political process account of international law. In addition, as Anthony Clark Arend notes, "to make law equal to process ignores that, at a given point in time, certain concrete *rules* can be identified."[15] Arend's view typifies the Legal Positivist concern with empirically pinning down rules. This is also a concern for constructivists. Precisely because they are the meanings attached to social practices and artifacts, and not actual material things, norms must first be identified before we can uncover the processes whereby they were constructed and take causal effect.

The Logics of State Compliance

Why do states obey international law? Aside from matters of war, the record of state compliance with international law is a good one. Indeed, world politics is substantially law governed.[16] All three causal mechanisms identified in Chapter 1 operate to reinforce rule-following behavior. States (and organizations and individuals) obey international law for three reasons. First, because there is utility in doing so, consistent with the logic of consequences, states may see an immediate benefit for themselves in cooperating through legal regimes. Beyond immediate payoffs from specific legal agreements, states generally see a long-term benefit in rule-governed relations.[17] The role of structural inducements is most obvious in convention law. States conclude treaties on trade, arms control, environment, and so forth, because such treaties provide a legal structure for the achievement of mutually beneficial goals. Power plays a far lesser role. In theory, treaties express free consent to be bound to a legal regime. In the past, great powers could impose treaties on lesser states. But this is now explicitly prohibited under the 1969 Vienna Convention on the Law of Treaties (which entered into force in 1980); Article 52 provides that a "treaty shall be void if its conclusion has been procured by the threat or use of force" in violation of the UN Charter. However great powers do, on occasion, use more subtle forms of coercion to get lesser states to consent to treaties. The role of power hierarchy is more evident in customary law. As we saw, when it comes to making and breaking rules of customary international law, the words and deeds of the great powers matter most. Great powers also have a material advantage in the size of their diplomatic corps, and ability to track, and consent or object to developments worldwide that may have bearing on customary law.[18] Sanctions are also important in enforcing state responsibilities under convention and customary law. These may be broadly defined to include all lawful countermeasures, both diplomatic and economic.[19]

Second, following the logic of appropriateness, states comply with those international legal norms and rules that have been internalized in domestic discourse, and institutionalized in domestic laws, political structures, and social practices. We have already noted how states are literally constituted by legal norms of sovereignty.[20] Equally, they are constituted and reconstituted in numerous more specific ways by a dynamic transnational legal process that reaches across the international system and into the governance processes and structures of individual states.[21] Driving this is a process of social learning that occurs via transnational contacts between officials, policy experts, and lawyers.[22]

Third, states obey international law when they are persuaded that it is equitable and/or just to do so.[23] This sense of fair play is preserved by the role of the ICJ and other international tribunals in interpreting the content and application of legal norms and rules. When it comes to new norms, legalization involves moral pressure and persuasion, as advocates of a particular legal norm seek to rally support among states for legal change. Such norm entrepreneurs may be leading states, international governmental organizations (IGOs), and/or international nongovernmental organizations (INGOs). All played a part in mobilizing international support for the development of legal regimes prohibiting piracy, slavery, drug trafficking, and whaling.[24] Sometimes power and persuasion operate in tandem to produce the necessary support for a new legal norm—thus, the power of the Royal Navy was directed against the transatlantic slave trade in support of British efforts to outlaw slavery in the eighteenth and nineteenth centuries.[25] But equally, persuasion does not necessarily depend on power. Thus, notwithstanding firm opposition from the world hegemon, the United States, an international treaty banning antipersonnel landmines was signed by 122 states and came into force in 1997. This was thanks to the efforts of major states like Germany and Canada, and INGOs in the shape of the International Committee for the Red Cross (ICRC) and the International Campaign to Ban Landmines (ICBL). Supportive states gave legitimacy to the campaign, the ICRC hosted numerous conferences to persuade other states of the case for banning landmines, and the ICBL put pressure on resisting states by providing worldwide support and sponsorship to national campaigns.[26]

Norm Violation and Legal Change

Sometimes, however, states must break the law in order to make new law. Oscar Schachter notes that "at times, the line between violations and emerging law may be difficult to draw."[27] This is especially true of customary law.

Indeed, Michael Bothe argues that a "usual procedure to modify customary law is to break it and to accompany the breach by a new legal claim."[28] In contrast, norm violation is an awkward mechanism for changing convention law. In the normal run of things, treaties change by agreement. Violation by one or more parties would not necessarily result in termination or alteration of that treaty. Instead, the victims of the breach would be entitled to take a number of countermeasures, only one of which may be to seek to terminate the treaty.[29] Of course, violation of a convention norm may occur in the context of an attempt to establish a nascent customary norm.

Norm violation occurs when a state action manifestly breaches a norm of international law. Violation does not automatically invalidate a norm. As Yoram Dinstein points out, "the criminal codes of all states are constantly trampled underfoot by countless criminals, yet the unimpaired legal validity of these codes is universally conceded."[30] So when does norm violation contribute to legal change? Two factors determine whether such violation is norm-affirming or norm-undermining in character. First is the state's legal reasoning in carrying out the violating action. In noting the importance of such legal "articulation," the ICJ stated in the *Nicaragua* case that:

> If a State acts in a way prima facie incompatible with a recognized rule, but defends its conduct by appealing to exceptions or justifications contained within the rule itself, then whether or not the state's conduct is in fact justifiable on that basis, the significance of that attitude is to confirm rather than weaken the rule.[31]

Conversely, it may be reasoned that if a state justifies its action by rejecting the legal force or applicability of the norm concerned, then its violation may be norm-undermining.[32] The second factor is the response of the international community. Where a norm violation is met by condemnation by states, it will be norm-affirming in effect. State may make their views known in submissions before relevant international bodies (such as the UNSC and ICJ), in declarations in the UN General Assembly (UNGA), and in press announcements. There are degrees of condemnation here; condemnation gains increasing force when it is matched with increasingly forceful countermeasures and when these are authorized by the UNSC. Again, conversely, where the violation is accepted, it will be norm-undermining in effect.

As Table 5.2 charts, the legal justification for, and international response to, norm violation operate synergistically to determine whether the violation produces legal change. Norm violation is likely to undermine a norm when the violating state explicitly rejects the force and/or applicability of the norm, and when the act in question is accepted by the international community. Equally, legal change is unlikely when the violating state actually appeals to the norm itself, or to exceptions to it, and the action is condemned by the international

Table 5.2   Norm Violation and Legal Change

	Legal Justification for Violation	
International Response to Violation	Appeals to norm	Rejects norm
Condemnation	Norm-affirming	Indeterminate
Acquiescence	Indeterminate	Norm-undermining

community. In such cases, violation actually affirms the norm. It is harder to predict the effect of norm violation when these two conditions clash, that is to say, when the violating state accepts the norm but its violation is accepted, and vice versa.

The Norm of Humanitarian Intervention

Humanitarian intervention raises the question of the relationship between norm violation and possible legal change. Intervention is clearly forbidden in international law. By intervention, I mean forcible military intervention in humanitarian crises.[33] Each state's right to sovereignty, territorial integrity, and political independence is essentially guaranteed by a general prohibition on intervention in the affairs of any state. This norm is codified in Article 2(7) of the UN Charter, and it has been reiterated in numerous UNGA resolutions. Where intervention involves use of force, it is also prohibited by Article 2(4) of the UN Charter. So how can humanitarian intervention be reconciled with the nonintervention and nonuse of force norms? The UN Charter does aspire to promote fundamental human rights, but it does not contain any concrete enforcement provisions for this purpose. A right of humanitarian intervention was discussed but not adopted at the San Francisco conference on the draft UN Charter in 1945.[34] On the face of it then, there is no provision in convention law for humanitarian intervention. The legal basis for humanitarian intervention, if it exists at all, must be found in customary law.

The first half of this section examines the evidence for a customary norm of humanitarian intervention. Here I look at state practice, the justifications given for intervention, and the response of the international community. A basic distinction needs to be introduced here between unilateral and collective intervention. The former is military intervention by one or more states without the authorization of the UNSC, whereas the latter refers to intervention that has been authorized by the Security Council. I begin by examining these two forms of humanitarian intervention. I then go on to consider cases of quasi-collective intervention—where UN authorization was implied or retrospectively given. An initial conclusion as to the legality of humanitarian intervention is made based on this analysis of state practice and discourse. I turn to the Kosovo case study, as a critical test of a legal norm permitting humanitarian intervention, in the second half of this section. I conclude with an assessment of the implications of norm violation in this case, and of the current legal and normative status of humanitarian intervention.

The Practice of Humanitarian Intervention

States have used force on a number of occasions since 1945 to stop large-scale abuses of human rights. Included in this is the practice of armed intervention to protect nationals whose lives are in imminent danger. The notable thing is that in almost all cases, the states that engaged in this practice were Western powers and the interventions were carried out against non-Western states. Examples include armed intervention by Belgium in the Congo (1960 and 1964), Israel in Uganda (1976), France and Belgium in Zaire (1978), and by the United States in the Dominican Republic (1965), Iran (1980), Grenada (1983), and Panama (1989) (an exception is Turkish intervention in Cyprus [1964]). Some cases were manifestly more genuine than others. The Belgian, French, and Israeli interventions were clearly directed toward rescuing nationals who were being held hostage and whose lives were in peril. In contrast, there is little evidence that US lives were at risk in Grenada and Panama, and these interventions took the form of full-scale invasions designed to remove regimes that were hostile to the United States. The United States, Israel, and Belgium justified their armed interventions by appealing to Article 51 of the UN Charter, which provides for self-defense, and by appealing to pre-Charter customary law. While some states expressed sympathy for the plight of nationals at risk, and recognized the need for rescue in particular cases, there was and still is very little support for the legality of armed intervention in such cases.[35]

Unilateral intervention may also be directed toward stopping atrocities, that is, protecting the lives of nonnationals. This occurred four times during the Cold War: Indian intervention in East Pakistan (1971), Tanzanian intervention in Uganda (1978), Vietnamese intervention in Kampuchea (1978), and French intervention in the Central African Empire (1979). The first three of these armed interventions actually amounted to full-blown invasions resulting in regime change. But in each of these cases there was a compelling humanitarian necessity for the intervention; brutal government repression had killed a million people in East Pakistan and in Kampuchea, and 300,000 people in Uganda. In the Central African Empire, the French intervention was more discreet and supported a bloodless coup against a dictator who had killed hundreds of his own people. What is most striking is the reluctance of the intervening states to justify their use of force on humanitarian grounds. India did claim its intervention to be a humanitarian action, but equally said it was in self-defense even though East Pakistan had not actually attacked India. Tanzania and Vietnam both claimed to be acting in self-defense. Both had suffered some minor border incursions by Uganda and Kampuchea, respectively, but in neither case were these serious enough to justify an all-out war.[36] Peter Hilpold rightly observes: "The fact that both Vietnam and Tanzania have tried to justify their actions by allegations that do not withstand an even rudimentary scrutiny while the humanitarian argument would have been at hand speaks volumes for the legal quality both states have attributed to this concept."[37]

The reaction of the international community was mixed to these interventions. The interventions in Uganda and the Central African Empire both passed without discussion at the UNSC and UNGA. In these cases, the international community was glad to be rid of two mad and troublesome dictators. The UNSC and UNGA did not condemn or condone India's intervention but merely called for the cessation of hostilities and withdrawal of armed forces. In contrast, Vietnam's intervention was condemned by most developing countries and most Western states. In part, this was because of Cold War politics— Vietnam was an ally of the Soviet Union. Vietnam's humanitarian motives were also suspect because it stayed on for years in Kampuchea. But there was also a matter of legal principle, expressed thus by the French representative to the UNSC:

> The notion that because a regime is detestable foreign intervention is justified and forcible overthrow is legitimate is extremely dangerous. That could ultimately jeopardize the very maintenance of international law and order and make the continued existence of various regimes dependent on the judgment of their neighbours.[38]

This view captures the mood of the international community: unilateral intervention for humanitarian purposes may be excusable, but to make it legal would undermine Articles 2(4) and 2(7) of the UN Charter.

The 1990s saw a dramatic explosion in collective humanitarian interventions. The end of the Cold War broke the veto logjam in the UNSC. Conflicts around the world were no longer viewed as extensions of East-West rivalry, and this enabled the Security Council to authorize armed intervention in humanitarian crises. Nobody disputes the Security Council's right to do this. Under Chapter VII of the UN Charter, it is empowered to determine if a situation is a threat to international peace and security (Article 39) and where such a threat exists, to authorize an appropriate response, including use of force (Article 41). It is evident from the Dumbarton Oaks and San Francisco conferences on the draft UN Charter, that the Security Council was intended to have wide discretion in determining threats to peace and security.[39] And indeed, Christine Gray notes that "the Security Council has consistently taken a wide view of 'the threat to international peace and security' under Article 39."[40] Nonetheless, the elevation of humanitarian crises to Article 39 threats was new to the 1990s.

There is a problem insofar as the UNSC has tended not to provide reasoning to justify the characterization of a humanitarian crisis as a threat to international peace. This lack of justification was evident right from the first time that the UNSC invoked Chapter VII for a humanitarian operation. This was in December 1992 when it authorized intervention by a US-led force in the failed state of Somalia. The United Task Force (UNITAF) was mandated under UNSC resolution 794 to "use all necessary means to establish as soon as possible to create a secure environment for humanitarian relief operations in Somalia." Resolution 794 declared that the "magnitude of the human tragedy caused by the conflict in Somalia, further exacerbated by the obstacles being created by the distribution of humanitarian assistance, constitutes a threat to international peace and security."[41] To be sure, the situation in Somalia was appalling, but it was not a threat to international security as commonly understood, in that no neighboring states were threatened by it.

Antonio Cassese puts this slack reasoning by the Security Council down to expediency: "The SC is eager to retain discretionary power in this matter and tends to avoid explaining the nature of the link [between humanitarian crises and international peace] and the reasons for its action."[42] The Security Council has also sought to maximize its discretion in this matter by repeatedly declaring those humanitarian crises that it deems warrant action under Chapter VII to be unique in some way, thereby suggesting that these cases do not set precedent. Accordingly, Security Council resolutions recognized "the unique character of the situation in Somalia," as well as the "unique character" of the Haiti crisis, and again declared that the crisis in Rwanda was "a unique case which demands an urgent response by the international community."[43] This has implications regarding the possible emergence of a customary norm of humanitarian intervention, which I will discuss in the context of Kosovo. For the moment, it is sufficient to note that provided the UNSC invokes Article 39, then forcible military intervention may be legally authorized.

There have also been a number of cases of intervention by coalitions of states and regional organizations that proceeded without clear UNSC authorization. Indeed, the very first of the post–Cold War humanitarian interventions, Operation Provide Comfort, was not directly authorized by the UNSC. This intervention occurred in late April 1991 in the aftermath of the 1990–1991 war against Iraq. Brutal repression of Kurdish rebellion in early April by the Iraqi Army produced millions of displaced people practically overnight. In resolution 688, the Security Council condemned the Iraqi repression, declared the refugee flow to be a threat to international peace and security, and called for a humanitarian response. But the bottom line is that this resolution was not passed under Chapter VII and did not authorize the use of force. Nonetheless, the United States, Britain, and France intervened in force to create a "safe haven" for Kurds in northern Iraq. President George H. W. Bush pointed to the humanitarian necessity for action: "Some might argue that this is an intervention into the internal affairs of Iraq. But I think the humanitarian concern, the refugee concern, is so overwhelming that there will be a lot of understanding about this." However, this was not the legal justification advanced by the Coalition for Operation Provide Comfort. Instead, both Washington and London declared that the intervention was "consistent with" resolution 688.[44] The basis for reading consent for the intervention in resolution 688 comes from paragraph six which "appeals to all Member States and to all humanitarian organizations to contribute to these humanitarian relief efforts."[45] The Coalition had to make do with this because China threatened to veto any further UNSC resolution explicitly authorizing the intervention. Politically, the Coalition position was strong. Iraq was deeply unpopular in world opinion and had just lost a war to the United Nations. Legally, however, the Coalition position was weak. Thomas Franck notes that it "brought a quiet dissent from the UN Secretary-General and from his Legal Counsel, but no admonition either from the Security Council or the General Assembly."[46] The lack of condemnation was, in part, put down to political circumstances. But it was also attributed to the fact that, as Nicholas Wheeler notes, Operation Provide Comfort "was in conformity with the purposes laid down in Resolution 688."[47]

There have also been a number of collective interventions by regional organizations that went ahead without UNSC authorization. There is provision for action by regional organizations in the UN Charter. Article 52 gives regional organizations a role in dealing with international peace and security at a regional level. Article 53 also permits the Security Council to use regional organizations for enforcement action, but at the same time, it specifies that regional organizations may not engage in such action without UNSC authorization. As with the new interventionism in general, this mechanism was rarely invoked prior to 1989. But post-1991, there has been an explosion of activity by regional organizations in conflict prevention and resolution. Many such missions have proceeded with explicit UNSC authorization, but some have not. Military interventions by the Commonwealth of Independent States (CIS) in the internal conflicts in Tajikistan in 1993 and Georgia in 1992 were cautiously welcomed by the Security Council, but neither was actually authorized under Chapter VII. Equally, forcible interventions by the Economic Community of West African States (ECOWAS) in the civil wars in Liberia in 1990 and Sierra Leone in 1997 were both retrospectively authorized by the Security Council, even though neither was legal to begin with.[48]

Operation Provide Comfort was a harbinger of things to come—as we saw with the new interventionism of the 1990s. But it was not, in itself, norm-creating in character. Only Britain and France attempted to advance a legal justification for the intervention based on humanitarian need. And the main reason recognized by most members of the Security Council, and written into resolution 688, was the threat of refugee flows to regional security. Moreover, the intervention was tolerated but was not condoned by the international community. Indeed, the Security Council has acted to retard the development of a norm of humanitarian intervention. Through careful wording of resolutions authorizing use of force it has sought to avoid precedent. Equally, by retroactively authorizing interventions, it has neutralized the potential undermining effects of clear violations of the nonintervention and nonuse of force norms. However, in failing to openly condemn the notion that UNSC consent for use of force does not have to be explicit but may be implied, the Security Council was to open a Pandora's box—a precedent that was to haunt it in Kosovo.

NATO's Intervention in Kosovo

On 24 March 1999, NATO started bombing the Serbian-dominated Federal Republic of Yugoslavia (FRY). The aim was to stop violent Serb repression of ethnic Albanians in the Yugoslav province of Kosovo. This intervention by NATO was widely seen as responding to dire humanitarian need and hence legitimate. But serious doubts were expressed about its legality.

Trouble started in 1989 when Yugoslav president Slobodan Milosevic stripped Kosovo of its autonomy under the 1974 Constitution and placed it under direct rule from Belgrade. This was part of Milosevic's strategy to mobilize domestic support for his government by radicalizing Yugoslav politics, generating ethnic cleavages, and playing the Serb nationalist card. Albanians, who formed 90 percent of the population in Kosovo, also lost their rights and became second-class citizens. Kosovar Albanians responded in the early 1990s with a peaceful campaign of resistance, creating a parallel government, education, and healthcare system. However, they became disillusioned with peaceful means when settlement in Kosovo was not rolled into the Western-brokered 1995 Dayton Agreement ending the war between Serbs, Croats, and Bosnians. Thereafter, the Albanian populace increasingly supported the violent campaign for independence being pursued by the self-styled Kosovo Liberation Army (KLA). Between 1996 and 1998, the KLA stepped up its attacks on Serb security forces in Kosovo, who in turn retaliated with indiscriminate and disproportionate violence, mostly directed against the civilian populace. In March 1998 the UNSC passed resolution 1160, condemning Serb repression, calling for an end to violence on both sides, and declaring the situation to be a threat to international peace and security. Matters got far worse in the summer as the Serbs started to systematically drive hundreds of thousands of Albanians from their homes. In September, the Security Council reiterated its call under Chapter VII for a ceasefire in resolution 1199. This resolution also required Serb security forces to stop operations, and to permit the free movement of humanitarian aid and Albanians returning home. Resolution 1199 also stated that the Security Council would "consider further action" if these demands were not met. In negotiations in Rambouillet in February and Paris in March 1999, an agreement was reached on these points. But the FRY refused to sign it because the agreement also required free movement of NATO forces throughout the FRY as well as a referendum on Kosovo's independence in three years. In the face of Serb defiance and continued Serb atrocities in Kosovo, NATO decided to use force.[49]

What evidence is there of a norm of humanitarian intervention in NATO action? It is clear that there were massive violations of human rights in Kosovo prior to the NATO intervention. Arguably, not that many Kosovar civilians had been killed by Serb security forces: only around 500. But many, many more were being driven from their homes by a Serb terror campaign that included rape, torture, and looting. The UN High Commissioner for Refugees (UNHCR) estimated that by late March half a million ethnic Albanians had fled their towns and villages, and 90,000 of them had left Yugoslavia altogether.[50] It is also evident that NATO intervention was motivated out of a sense of moral obligation to do something about this humanitarian disaster on NATO's doorstep. The moral grounds for war were detailed in a British policy paper circulated to NATO capitals in October 1998, and included the scale and urgency of humanitarian distress, the lack of alternatives to forcible intervention, and that force used would be proportionate and limited.[51]

The importance of moral obligation, as a motive for NATO intervention, becomes evident when alternative explanations are considered. At best, neorealism provides a weak account for NATO action. NATO was not acting to balance power in Europe.[52] Yugoslavia was not a challenge to NATO power, either in itself or because it was about to join a Russian bandwagon against NATO.[53] Yugoslavia was *already* a long-standing ally of Russia. Moreover and nonetheless, Russia was cooperating with NATO's diplomatic efforts to resolve the Kosovo crisis. As for offensive realism: we often think of NATO as a "security-seeker," but could it have been acting as a "power-maximiser"?[54] Hardly. NATO was not out to conquer Yugoslavia, just to subdue it. Indeed, the alliance had nothing to gain by using force against Yugoslavia. The campaign promised to be (and was) very costly for NATO. For instance, the US Congress began to raise concerns about cost about 3 weeks into the military campaign. At this stage, the Congressional Budget Office estimated that the United States had spent $600 million, and was likely to spend over $1 billion per month of air operations.[55] Such costs were not going to be offset by conquest; NATO would not gain territory. One variant of neorealism—balance of threat theory—suggests that NATO might have acted to remove a threat to the alliance.[56] Indeed, there was a concern on the part of some in NATO that other countries, including Greece and Turkey, might be dragged into a wider Balkan conflict. But it is unlikely that this alone would have been enough to encourage NATO to undertake the great risks and costs of going to war with Yugoslavia.

Domestic politics does not fare any better as an explanation for NATO intervention. For domestic politics to be the driving force, the US and British executives (as the major proponents within NATO for military action) would have had to face strong pressure from domestic constituencies for military action in response to Serb atrocities.[57] Note moral imperatives are still present in such an account, as motivating domestic political agitation for use of force, but they are a second order explanation to domestic politics. But as it happens, neither President Bill Clinton nor Prime Minister Tony Blair was pushed to war by domestic constituencies. In fact, it was Blair and Foreign Secretary Robin Cook who raised media interest in the Kosovo crisis and mobilized support in the British polity for the possible military action by NATO.[58] Clinton actually faced significant domestic political opposition from Congress to NATO military action. Congress was already unhappy about the deployment of US peacekeepers in Bosnia, and deeply concerned about another open-ended US military commitment in the Balkans. Clinton was already skating on thin ice with Congress, as the Monica Lewinsky scandal was unfolding in mid-1998.[59] Significantly, the Lewinsky scandal had run its course shortly before NATO took military action (when Clinton was acquitted of impeachment by the Senate on 12 February 1999). All the same, Clinton was sufficiently nervous about the lack of congressional support for intervention in Kosovo to openly rule out the use of ground forces in order to placate Congress.[60]

Arguably the intervention was a crucial test for NATO credibility in the post–Cold War era. Indeed, the Alliance was in the process of redefining its role following the collapse of the Soviet threat. Some member states, especially the United States, were pushing for NATO to play a role in resolving "out-of-area" crises (i.e., conflicts not involving self-defense of NATO territory). The push for NATO to reinvent itself was played out at the height of the Kosovo intervention in the spring of 1999, as the Alliance celebrated its fiftieth anniversary and adopted the new Strategic Concept that incorporated "out-of-area" missions. As Michael MccGwire notes: "There was considerable pressure in official circles and the press to demonstrate that NATO at 50 still had a role to play."[61]

The concern with NATO credibility, along with the fear of the conflict widening to elsewhere in the Balkans, provided additional reasons for NATO to use force to stop Serb brutality in Kosovo. But it was primarily ideas—about what was right and required—not interests that drove the United States, Britain, and ultimately NATO to war over Kosovo. All the major powers agreed that international action was required to avoid a repetition of the massacres witnessed in Bosnia. Indeed, this point was hammered home on numerous occasions by the Clinton administration. As Secretary of State Madeleine Albright told her European counterparts in a meeting in London, in Lancaster House in March 1998: "In this very room our predecessors delayed as Bosnia burned, and history will not be kind to us if we do the same."[62] Furthermore, NATO was spurred further into action by each Serb atrocity. The gruesome massacre of 21 women, children, and elderly men in Gornji Obrinje in September 1998 prompted the Clinton administration to press NATO to issue an ultimatum to

Yugoslavia. The final straw came for the Clinton administration with the slaughter of 45 Kosovar civilians in Racak in January 1999. This galvanized them to push forward the Rambouillet process and, when this failed, to push within NATO for a coercive bombing strategy.[63]

In using force against Yugoslavia, NATO violated international law because such action was not authorized by the UNSC. In this case, however, the failure of NATO to articulate a legal justification for military action, combined with a mixed international response, prevented NATO's intervention in Kosovo from being law-changing in character.

Resolutions 1160 and 1199 provided the triggers for UN-authorized military action by identifying the situation in the province as a threat to international peace and security. But neither resolution actually authorized use of force, precisely because Russia and China would not agree to it. Given this, it was incumbent on NATO to lay out the legal case for war. This NATO did not do. In part this was because NATO governments were divided and uncertain as to what legal case to make. Drawing on precedent from the intervention in Iraq in 1991, the US and UK governments suggested that consent for use of force could be implied from resolutions 1160 and 1199. Arguably, this is what was meant by consideration of "further action." Such an argument had little credibility, however, as Russia and China both attached declaratory statements to their votes stating that these resolutions should not be interpreted as authorizing use of force. Unlike the US and UK governments, the Germans were more unsure of the legal basis for war. Germany changed government in the midst of the crisis and this added to the incoherence of its position. All the same, some German leaders were prepared to assert that NATO was acting within the "sense and logic" of UNSC resolutions. Likewise, in the debate that followed the bombing, the French, Canadians, and Dutch all adopted a similar line, namely that use of force was consistent with UNSC resolutions. The Italian government briefly alluded to collective self-defense on the part of NATO—a position without foundation since NATO had not been attacked by the FRY.[64]

The international community was equally divided in its response to NATO's humanitarian war. Two days after the bombing started, Russia, Belarus, and India tabled a draft resolution condemning NATO's action as a breach of Articles 2(4), 24, and 53 of the UN Charter.[65] Only Russia, China, and Namibia voted for this resolution; 12 states voted against it. Brazil, Costa Rica, and Mexico voiced misgivings about NATO action, but were not prepared to actually condemn it as illegal. Whereas the Bahrain, Malaysian, and Argentine governments all accepted the humanitarian necessity for NATO action.[66]

That NATO violated the nonuse of force norm is beyond doubt. Most lawyers put this down as a "technical violation." Not only were there compelling humanitarian grounds for military intervention, in the lead-up to the bombing the UN and NATO worked closely together in trying to resolve the Kosovo crisis. Even after NATO threatened to bomb the FRY in October 1998, the UNSC passed resolution 1203, which again did not authorize use of force, but did effectively support NATO's "gunboat diplomacy." Moreover, after the bombing stopped, the Security Council passed resolution 1244, which effectively endorsed the consequences of NATO action, namely an enforced peace in Kosovo.[67] This came close to the kind of retrospective authorization extended to the CIS interventions in Tajikistan and Georgia and ECOWAS interventions in Liberia and Sierra Leone.

NATO may be seen as only in "technical violation" in the sense that unilateral action was necessary because ultimately the UNSC was prevented from enforcing resolutions 1160 and 1199 by Russian and Chinese threats of veto. In other words, the international mechanism for maintaining peace and security failed and so NATO had to step in.[68] NATO did hint that it had to act because the UNSC was unable to do so.[69] But equally it could be argued that the international mechanism worked just fine. "In such cases, the [Security] Council is not in fact 'paralyzed' as it has been previously put, but is rather fulfilling its role as a discretionary, governing body of nations whose withholding of consent is indicative of their dissatisfaction with the proposed action."[70] Louis Henkin reckons that this is as it should be: "the law against unilateral intervention may reflect, above all, the moral-political conclusion that no individual state can be trusted with the authority to judge and determine wisely."[71]

Whatever the legitimacy of NATO's violation of international law, it was not norm-undermining in effect. It did not create a new exception to the nonuse of force norm. This is because NATO did not advance the case for a legal norm of humanitarian intervention. NATO could have possibly inferred an emerging state practice of humanitarian intervention, from the collective interventions of the 1990s and the unilateral interventions before then. It could also have pointed to the growing body of scholarly opinion supporting the emergence of a legal right to use force to prevent massive violations of human rights. As it happens, only Belgium claimed to be acting out of a sense of legal obligation to forcibly intervene in Kosovo on humanitarian grounds. As we saw, when it came to the legal basis for use of force, other NATO states came up with variants of the implied consent argument. In fact, once again, most states were concerned with preventing the emergence of a legal norm of humanitarian intervention. Accordingly, Kosovo was presented as an "exceptional case" by the US, British, French, and German governments.[72]

In any case, it is doubtful that a customary norm of humanitarian intervention would have emerged even if NATO had tried to advance one. As we noted earlier, there does not need to be absolute uniformity in state practice for it to sustain a new norm of customary international law. This is especially true of a norm of humanitarian intervention since it would be permissive rather than mandatory. However, the same cannot be said for *opinio juris*. Nonuse of force and nonintervention are peremptory norms and so exceptions to them must also be *jus cogens* in character. Given their fundamental character, such norms demand much higher levels of state support than is the case with ordinary norms of customary law. The Kosovo intervention clearly revealed that there was nothing like the required level of support in the international community for a norm of humanitarian intervention. Indeed following it, the G77 group of 133 nonindustrialized states issued a statement in April 2000 declaring: "We reject the so-called 'right' of humanitarian intervention, which has no legal basis in the United Nations Charter or in the general principles of international law."[73]

Humanitarian intervention has occurred with sufficient frequency in the post–Cold War period to suggest such practice as having some kind of normative force nonetheless. However, a legal right of humanitarian intervention has hardly ever been invoked either in unilateral or collective interventions. In fact, the UNSC has gone out of its way to avoid creating precedent on this. Moreover, there is not the level of support necessary in the international community to sustain a legal norm of humanitarian intervention. While there is no evidence that states have undertaken humanitarian intervention out of a sense of *legal* obligation (which is necessary for state practice to constitute customary law), there is evidence (as we saw in the Kosovo case) that humanitarian intervention has occurred out of a sense of *moral* obligation. In other words, that there is a moral code in operation. Furthermore, it appears that there is international acceptance of the need for humanitarian intervention on a case-by-case basis. The fact that this has happened repeatedly points to this as having normative weight in international society. Wheeler correctly notes that there is most support for this nonlegal norm among Western states. Given the history of Western imperialism, developing states are understandably nervous about legitimating an exception to the nonintervention norm.[74] However, developing states have played an active part in collective and quasi-collective interventions, and (as we noted) ECOWAS is strengthening its legal and military capacity to undertake regional humanitarian intervention. There is likely to be further pressure for the development of a norm of humanitarian intervention. This is evident from the final report of the High-Level Panel on Threats, Challenges and Change set up by the UN Secretary-General in November 2003 and including members from 16 countries. In its December 2004 report, the panel "endorse[d] the emerging norm that there is a collective international responsibility to protect, exercisable by the Security Council authorizing military intervention as a last resort, in the event of genocide and other large-scale killing, ethnic cleansing or serious violations of international humanitarian law."[75]

The enabling conditions of normative change identified in Chapter 1 have been present in this case. The genocide in Rwanda shocked the world into realizing the consequences of international inaction in the face of massive violations of human rights.[76] Between April and July 1994, the world stood by as Hutu extremists murdered up to 800,000 civilians and raped somewhere between 250,000 and 500,000 women (most of the victims were Tutsis, some were

Hutu moderates). The lesson the UN drew from this shocking experience was: never again.[77] Two leading norm entrepreneurs may also be identified: the UN Secretary-General, Kofi Annan, and the British government under Blair. Annan's ability to frame debate is derived from the legitimacy conferred by the office of Secretary-General. The fact that he was previously Assistant Secretary-General for Peacekeeping gives him added credibility in terms of his technical expertise on the subject of humanitarian intervention. Annan has been pushing forward a humanitarian intervention agenda within the UN. This has resulted in four major reports to the UNSC on "the protection of civilians in armed conflict." In his first such report, Annan explicitly referred to a "developing international norm" of humanitarian intervention.[78] Rwanda has been the major spur for Annan's campaign.[79] His fourth report begins by noting, as an "important milestone," the "10 years since the world's silent witnessing of genocide in Rwanda."[80]

In recent years, Britain has also played the leading part in developing a nonlegal norm of humanitarian intervention. The Blair government has the potential to be an effective norm entrepreneur given Britain's role as a "pivotal power" in the world system.[81] In a speech in Chicago in April 1999, Blair proclaimed humanitarian intervention to be part of a new "doctrine of international community," declaring that "we cannot turn our backs on conflicts and the violation of human rights within other countries."[82] That same year, Cook directed the Foreign Office to draw up general guidelines for humanitarian intervention that the UNSC could approve. Such guidelines were intended to lessen UNSC disagreements over future interventions and ensure that even where UNSC authorization was not forthcoming, that such interventions at least adhered to preagreed criteria. This innovation was rejected by the UNSC, but it does point to Britain's role as a norm entrepreneur.[83]

This effort may also be located in a broader ethical agenda in British foreign policy, unveiled by Cook (to much fanfare) in May 1997. In truth Britain has had a mixed ethical record in its foreign policy. In addition to promoting humanitarian intervention, it has also been the leading advocate in the West of debt relief for the poorest developing countries. But, against this, it has continued to sell arms to states that abuse human rights. Moreover, since 2000, the "ethical dimension" of foreign policy has been downplayed in public.[84] However, Britain continues to push humanitarian intervention (as well as debt relief) as a moral code on the world stage.[85] Thus, speaking at his Labour Party conference in 2001, Blair reiterated his belief that Britain had a "moral duty" to intervene in any country in order to prevent a repetition of Rwanda. In July 2004, the Blair government once again considered humanitarian intervention, this time in response to state-sponsored ethnic cleansing in Sudan. Blair's motive was to prevent another Rwanda. A source in the Foreign Office explained: "For [Foreign Secretary Jack] Straw and Blair, Rwanda was a marker for the world," adding, "A reprise of Rwanda chills everyone's blood."[86]

Norms of Humanitarian Law

Norms of humanitarian law are well established in international law. The principles underlying humanitarian law go back centuries in customary law, and the rules of modern humanitarian law are clearly codified in the Hague Conventions of 1899 and 1907, and the four Geneva Conventions of 1949 (and two Additional Protocols of 1977). In the first half of this section, I discuss the content, evolution, and institutionalization of humanitarian law. The reasons for compliance and noncompliance are also briefly considered. The second half of this section provides a detailed case study of compliance with humanitarian law, looking at NATO's military campaign against Yugoslavia in 1999. I examine how humanitarian law operated to restrain NATO's bombing campaign, even when there were compelling military reasons for escalation.

Content, Evolution, and Institutionalization

Humanitarian law provides moral codes for the conduct of armed conflict. It defines the subjects and objects of combat: who may lawfully fight and what are lawful targets (or more precisely, what must not be targeted). Humanitarian law also regulates the treatment of prisoners, wounded combatants, and civilians in conflict zones. It prohibits the causing of unnecessary suffering and the use of specific banned weapons in war. Three fundamental principles underpin humanitarian law: those of military necessity, proportionality, and discrimination. These principles establish that use of force must not be excessive to military requirements, must be proportional to anticipated military gains and proportional in response to enemy attack, and must discriminate between lawful and unlawful targets.[87]

Norms restricting warfare have a long history. As Christopher Greenwood notes: "laws on the conduct of hostilities have existed in most cultures for hundreds, if not thousands, of years."[88] Thus modern state custom (i.e., practice accepted by states as embodying law) on restrictions in war may be traced back through the Middle Ages to antiquity. From the late eighteenth century onward, states began to codify customary rules of humanitarian law through a series of treaties, the most important being the Hague and Geneva Conventions. The norms contained within these conventions are legally binding rules that all combatants must follow (the newer Additional Protocols are only binding on the signatories). Outright breaches of these rules constitute war crimes.[89]

The content and reach of modern humanitarian law has coevolved with international law as a professional field. Indeed, the development of the international law profession conforms nicely to new institutionalist theory (introduced in Chapter 2). Professional knowledge and standards were codified in convention law,[90] and propagated through international law associations, professional journals, and university law courses in Europe and North America from the mid-nineteenth century.[91] Statesmen and diplomats were also increasingly lawyers by training. In this way, Martha Finnemore notes how professional standards of international law came to inform state practice with the legalization of diplomacy in the twentieth century (especially with regard to the use of force).[92] Professional standards and knowledge of humanitarian law have also been developed through the work of nonstate legal actors (such as the International Committee for the Red Cross) and international war crimes tribunals (following World War II, and more recently wars in the former Yugoslavia and Rwanda).[93]

Early state adherence to humanitarian norms in the late nineteenth and early twentieth centuries followed the logic of consequences. Better treatment of battlefield wounded made military sense. Equally, better treatment of each other's prisoners has a powerful reciprocal logic.[94] Codification of these norms in the Geneva Conventions followed the logic of appropriateness: states agreed to be bound by these norms because by the mid-twentieth century, the alternatives—mistreating civilians, wounded, and prisoners—were no longer considered acceptable behavior by the international community.[95]

Norms of humanitarian law are now well embedded in the world system. All states (with the exception of Sudan)[96] have formally institutionalized humanitarian norms in their national legal system: in their constitution (e.g., Cambodia, Croatia, Guinea, Japan, Peru, Malaysia, the Philippines, and Samoa) or through constitutional amendment (e.g., Argentina, Burkina Faso, Ireland, and South Africa), legislative acts (e.g., Cook Islands, Hungary, India, Venezuela, Rwanda, Spain, Yemen, and Zimbabwe), and/or military penal codes (e.g., Côte d'Ivoire, Republic of Korea, Mali, Mexico, Norway, and Switzerland). Usually states have adopted some combination of these instruments—especially, states with well-developed legal systems (Australia, Britain, France, Germany, and the United States). Some states, especially former Soviet republics, have also established national committees to oversee implementation of humanitarian law (e.g., Azerbaijan, Belarus, Georgia, Kyrgyzstan, Moldova, Tajikistan, and Ukraine).[97] Norms of humanitarian law have been further institutionalized in the world system with the establishment of a permanent International Criminal Court (ICC). The ICC has jurisdiction over all breaches of humanitarian law and other war crimes committed on, by, or near the territory of any of the states that are party to the Rome Statute (the treaty creating the ICC). The ICC will try such cases where national courts prove unable or unwilling to do so. One hundred twenty states had signed the Rome Statute by 1998 and 94 states had ratified it (making them party to the treaty).[98]

Combatant compliance with humanitarian rules has not been consistent and universal, however. This is largely because compliance has depended on self-regulation—on states enforcing humanitarian rules through their national civilian and military legal systems. As noted earlier, practically all states in the world have created the instruments to do this. Moreover, many European states established military codes on the model of the Lieber Code in advance of the Hague Conventions.[99] In this sense, national military law and international humanitarian law are, to some extent, mutually constitutive. Nonetheless, breaches of these codes have often gone unpunished by national authorities. We must recognize the obvious tension here between the need to foster aggression in combat and the norm against unnecessary brutality. Given the difficulty of turning civilians into killers on the battlefield, far more emphasis is traditionally placed on the former than the latter in military training and discipline.[100] Moreover, sometimes states intentionally set out to commit war crimes in the process of waging genocidal wars.[101] In such cases, enforcement with humanitarian law requires international action through the setting up of tribunals to prosecute wrong-doers (a role that the ICC will take over). It may also require international armed intervention to halt war crimes in progress, as in the case of Kosovo.

NATO's Humane War

Right from the beginning, NATO conceived of its military intervention in Kosovo as a limited war—limited both in its political ends and military means. A land invasion of Yugoslavia was initially (and publicly) ruled out because of the risk of NATO casualties, and instead NATO relied on air power alone. Moreover, NATO planes flew above 15,000 feet in order to lessen the threat from the formidable Yugoslav air defense system. Political considerations led the alliance to pursue a graduated bombing campaign designed to coerce Yugoslav leadership, especially President Slobodan Milosevic, to back down at minimum cost to the Serb people. Targets and weapons were also carefully vetted to minimize the risk of civilian deaths and collateral damage. NATO's cautious bombing campaign helped maintain alliance cohesion for an illegal humanitarian war but, at the same time, it limited NATO's ability to force the Serbs to back down.[102]

In Operation Allied Force, NATO began with air strikes against the Yugoslav air defense system and against Serb field forces in southern Yugoslavia (including Kosovo). As the campaign wore on, NATO gradually began to extend the bombing to "strategic targets" in Belgrade and elsewhere in northern Yugoslavia. NATO officials have subsequently claimed that it "had been hoped, but never assumed" that the Serbs would quickly capitulate.[103] In fact, the evidence suggests that, at the time, NATO *expected* a quick and easy victory. As Ivo Daalder and Michael O'Hanlon wrote in 2000: "Many alliance leaders deny that assertion to this day, but the evidence is overwhelming."[104] Indeed, NATO political leaders initially authorized only 71 targets, all of which had been destroyed 3 days into the bombing campaign.[105] In the end, Operation Allied Force lasted 78 days.

NATO was slow to escalate the bombing in response to Serb intransigence. NATO restraint was reflected both in the tempo of operations and in the choice of targets. During the first month, NATO was averaging only 92 sorties a day. By way of contrast, 1,300 sorties were flown per day in the 1991 war against Iraq. As one critic of NATO's Kosovo campaign observes: "In terms of level of effort, it took NATO 30 days to do what General Norman Schwarzkopf and the Coalition did in about three days of the (1991) Gulf War."[106] Senior US Air Force officers were similarly disenchanted with Operation Allied Force. One US Air Force general called it a "disgrace" and noted that "senior officers think that the tempo is so disgustingly slow it makes us look inept."[107]

NATO was also reluctant to move on from purely military targets to political ones. The declared objective of the bombing campaign was to stop Serb atrocities in Kosovo, principally by targeting Serb security forces on the ground. The day bombing began, NATO's Supreme Allied Commander in Europe (SACEUR), General Wesley Clark, announced: "The military mission is to attack Yugoslav military and security forces and associated facilities with sufficient effect to degrade its capacity to continue repression of the civilian population." Even military barracks were excluded initially in a campaign that was designed to discriminate between the ethnic cleansers and innocent Serbs.[108] However, the problems of targeting small mobile units in wooded and mountainous terrain from 15,000 feet, combined with poor weather and effective deception by Serb ground forces, meant that NATO was not able to significantly disrupt Serb operations in Kosovo. Indeed, the ethnic cleansing accelerated following the onset of NATO bombing.[109]

NATO responded to the accelerated ethnic cleansing by intensifying its sorties against Serb field forces. At the same time, General Clark began lobbying Washington and the other NATO capitals in late March for authorization to go after "strategic targets." Clark met resistance from all NATO governments. But as the war dragged on into April (raising the possibility that a ground intervention by NATO might be required) Washington and London began to push for escalation in the bombing. Officially the air campaign had three phases. Three days into the campaign, Clark was authorized to move on from phase 1 (attacking the Yugoslav air defense system) to phase 2 (strikes against Serb military forces and military infrastructure in southern Yugoslavia). He was never given authority to proceed to phase 3, namely strikes against "strategic targets" north of the 44th parallel including Belgrade. Indeed, Clark never sought authorization because he knew that it would be opposed by Germany because of its antimilitaristic foreign policy, by France on logistical grounds, by Greece because of its pro-Serb sympathies, and by Italy, which was concerned about the impact on Balkan stability. Instead, these strategic targets—which included bridges, railway yards, television and radio stations, power stations, the electricity grid, and government offices—were incrementally authorized (in what became known as "phase 2-plus") throughout April and May. This involved a laborious process of persuading doubting allies of the merits of each target.[110]

In addition to gradually expanding the target list, NATO also picked up the tempo of operations. Ever more assets were committed to the war: NATO commanders kicked off the campaign with 121 strike aircraft but by June they had over 350.[111] The steady increase in the daily sortie rate is a particularly good indicator of escalation in NATO's air campaign. As Table 5.3 shows, the sortie rate steadily grew through April and May. The culminative rise was dramatic: NATO was flying 10 times as many daily strike sorties by the end of the campaign as at the beginning. By the end of May, NATO bombing got even bolder. The bombing of downtown Belgrade became more intensive, the power and telephone grids were destroyed, and government buildings and the homes of Serb leaders were also hit.[112] This escalation in the bombing finally undercut domestic support for Milosevic, and persuaded the Serb leader that he had to back down. Serb public defiance at NATO bombing in March had given way to Serb public desperation in May and June for the bombing to stop.[113]

The US Air Force general in charge of executing Operation Allied Force would have fought the war very differently. In a subsequent interview, General Mike Short said that he would have gone "downtown from the first night" and caused "significant destruction" in order to shock the Serb people and political leaders into realizing just how powerful and determined NATO was. Indeed, in a meeting with Milosevic in October 1998, Short warned the Serb leader of a quick and devastating air campaign by NATO. This was reflected in the war plan Short submitted to Clark, which was for NATO to take out the Serb transportation, communication, and energy grids. In effect, to shut down Serbia overnight.[114]

So why did NATO not adopt Short's plan to blitz Belgrade on day 1? More generally, how can we explain NATO reluctance to escalate the bombing? Neorealist balance of power theory does not help much. NATO restraint was not the product of fear, either of a Yugoslav response (Yugoslavia was, after all, completely outgunned by NATO), or of counterbalancing action by Russia. Russia was outraged at NATO bombing. As we noted earlier, it con-

Table 5.3 Daily Sortie Rate in NATO's Kosovo Campaign

Date	All Sorties	Strike Sorties
March 24–31	Data unavailable	30–50
April	300	100
Most of May	500	150
End of May–June 10	600–700	Up to 300

Source: Data from Daalder and O'Hanlon, *Winning Ugly,* pp. 143–144.

demned NATO action as illegal. In late March, it also sent a flotilla of warships into the Mediterranean, close to the NATO naval force off Yugoslav waters in the Adriatic. But nobody expected Russian military action against NATO. The concern with the Russian flotilla was not that it might attack NATO ships, but that it could gather and pass on information about NATO flight operations to Serb forces. Moreover, at the same time as condemning NATO military action, Russia was collaborating with NATO's diplomatic efforts to persuade Milosevic to surrender.[115]

An alternative approach might be to explain NATO military operations in terms of intra-alliance politics. In a consensual alliance, such as NATO, variation in the strategic preferences of member states can profoundly impact on alliance policy. Such preferences are presumed to flow from the distribution of costs for proposed actions. Where significant variation in preferences exists, policy choices result from an intra-alliance bargaining process.[116] The biggest states (i.e., the United States) cannot simply push the smaller European members around, as this is prevented by norms of consultation that are deeply embedded in the alliance.[117] In this case, it would seem that intra-alliance politics was important in shaping NATO strategy. All states wanted a limited air campaign. But as the war dragged on into April, the United States and Britain joined Clark in advocating escalation in the bombing. As discussed above, the other European allies resisted escalation. The product of this intra-alliance politics was NATO restraint. But, significantly, this was not a bargaining process whereby alliance members were seeking to advance national interests and offset national costs. The United States was a leading advocate of escalation, even though it was going to bear the lion's share of the cost for this since it provided the bulk of air forces for the campaign.[118] In contrast, restraint in the bombing threatened to greatly increase costs for all alliance members because if the bombing failed, then this would have increased the pressure for massive land invasion by NATO (which would have involved sizable contributions from the European allies).[119] In short, NATO member states did have different strategic preferences as regards escalating the bombing, but this preference variation was not the product of a clash of interests but rather a clash of ideas.

All in the alliance agreed on the basics of humanitarian law. Targeting of civilians was prohibited, and collateral damage (i.e., the unintended causing of civilian deaths and damage to civilian structures) was to be kept to a minimum. This made it very difficult to hit strategic targets in and around heavily populated major urban centers (such as Belgrade). Checks for compliance with humanitarian law were built into the process of generating targets and assigning munitions. Legal checks were conducted by targeting teams at the NATO Combined Air Operations Center (which planned, directed, and executed the air campaign), as well as by military lawyers from the US Judge Advocate General's Office based in Germany (and likewise, by military lawyers from other NATO countries for operations involving their warplanes). Legal constraints were also built into strict rules of engagement for NATO pilots: including pilots having to observe the assigned targets and radio for final authorization before releasing their munitions.[120] Clark notes in his memoirs that originally NATO political leaders were to sign off on categories of targets, which he could then authorize for attack on his discretion. But, NATO capitals ended up imposing "a target-by-target approval requirement" on SACEUR.[121] Some targets ended up being vetted by up to nine people. Sensitive targets, especially those in Belgrade, "were reviewed by officials in each of the nineteen NATO capitals,"[122] and often also by the US president when there was any risk of civilian casualties.[123] According to a report by the US Center for Naval Analysis, 64 percent of the fixed targets in the air campaign required approval by higher authorities above Clark.[124]

Mistakes were made, and NATO bombs did kill innocent civilians. Clark claims that "everything possible was being undertaken to ensure that [NATO] strikes met strict legal standards and minimized risks of harm to innocent civilians."[125] After the war, the US secretary of defense and the chairman of the Joint Chiefs of Staff told the Senate Armed Services Committee that Operation Allied Force was "the most precise and lowest–collateral damage air campaign in history."[126] Was it? The NATO campaign was found compliant with humanitarian law by the prosecutor for the International Criminal Tribunal for the former Yugoslavia.[127] Amnesty International was likewise satisfied.[128] The Independent International Commission on Kosovo reported that "NATO's overall record was unprecedented to the extent that it avoided civilian damage through the accuracy of its targeting."[129]

Such close compliance with humanitarian law came at a military price, however. It hindered NATO's ability to coerce the Serbs. When Clark wanted to escalate in late March to strategic targets around Belgrade he was blocked by NATO capitals (including Washington) nervous about collateral damage. The strict rules of engagement requiring pilots to physically observe targets made operations very difficult as most sorties were flown at high altitudes and often in poor weather.[130] Given the problems NATO was having in destroying Serb field forces, and from this coercing Milosevic to surrender, the alliance should have responded by rapidly escalating to strikes against Belgrade. Instead, it took the alliance some 9 weeks to escalate to really punishing air strikes (punishing both in the range of targets and tempo of sorties). Problems continued even as NATO began to finally escalate. A report by the US General Accounting Office found that: "The high level concern about collateral damage also led to some approved targets being canceled, which caused some missions to be canceled at the last minute." The report further notes that: "At the end of the operation, over 150 targets were still waiting approval."[131] Even when targets were finally approved the delays alone caused problems for military planners. According to the GAO report:

> Officials at the [NATO] air operations center stated that the high level approval process also led to approved targets being provided on a sporadic basis, which limited the military's ability to achieve planned effects and mass and parallel operations as recommended in doctrine.[132]

This was a problem both in respect of disabling particular facilities (e.g., approval being denied for all the targets necessary to take out an oil refinery) and in terms of destroying a sufficient volume of targets in a sufficiently compressed time period to achieve synergistic strategic effects. These military problems were caused by NATO compliance with norms of humanitarian law.

At the same time, norms of humanitarian law ensured that the air campaign was integrated with the political goals of the alliance. The main goal was to achieve a humanitarian end (stop Serb oppression in Kosovo) by humane means (precision bombing). Throughout the bombing campaign, the Serbs were trying to portray themselves as the victims of NATO aggression, especially by publicizing civilian deaths from NATO bombing.[133] Minimizing collateral damage was crucial to NATO's public relations effort to undercut Serb propaganda and shore-up domestic support in NATO countries for the war. NATO restraint was also crucial in keeping the alliance together. Clark and other NATO military chiefs believed that blitzing Belgrade on day 1 would have broken alliance cohesion on the war.[134] It is clear that some NATO countries—France, Germany, Italy, and Greece especially—were particularly reluctant for NATO to bomb targets around Belgrade. For instance, the Italian chief of defense called Clark in late March to warn "that if we tried to move ahead too quickly on targeting, then Italy might face another governmental crisis." When Washington began to push aggressively for a widening of the target set, Clark warned his superiors that to unilaterally do so could well shatter the alliance.[135] By imposing restraint on NATO operations then, norms of humanitarian law served to provide a common moral vision for the conduct of the war that NATO capitals and publics could agree on.

As the war dragged on alliance unity began to fry. A clash of ideas developed between Clark's command, Washington, and London on one hand, and the other European capitals on the other, over the legality of hitting civilian infrastructure targets. Humanitarian law expressly forbids the targeting of civilian populations and "civilian objects." This injunction is pretty straightforward when it comes to people: only combatants and, in some circumstances, noncombatant military personnel may be targeted. With objects it becomes more complex given that many—such as roads and railway yards—have both civilian and military uses. Additional Protocol I tackles this problem by defining military objects as those "which by their nature, location, purpose or use make an effective contribution to military action."[136] Not all NATO members are party to Additional Protocol I (the United States, France, and Turkey are not signatories) but most of its content (including its definition of military objects)

is considered to have become customary international law and therefore binding on all states (including nonsignatories).[137] Nonetheless, this still leaves
plenty of room for disagreement. A strict reading of Additional Protocol I
would suggest that dual-use facilities may only be targeted where the object
concerned is making a direct contribution to enemy action (e.g., a bridge may
not be targeted unless it is on a route used for the movement of enemy
forces).[138] However, US air war planners (like General Short) believed that
civilian infrastructure invariably contributed to the enemy war effort and so was
fair game. They also believed that undermining enemy morale through such
targeting was legitimate.[139]

The bombing campaign culminated in NATO taking out the Serbian electricity grid. This was especially controversial because up to 100,000 civilians
had died through indirect effects when the US-led coalition had destroyed the
Iraqi electricity grid in the 1991 Gulf War. Following this, even US Air Force
officers debated in their professional journal whether such attacks could be carried out in the future. In early May, NATO disabled the electricity grid using
graphite bombs (which short-circuited the electricity transformers). But the
Serbs had the power on 8–24 hours later, and repeatedly knocking out the electricity grid in this way exposed NATO aircraft to Serb air defenses. Eventually,
NATO destroyed the electricity grid using conventional munitions. NATO's
military lawyers were uncertain about the legality of this action. French military chiefs were also doubtful, but were persuaded when their US counterparts
were able to demonstrate that Serb hospitals (and other vital civilian facilities)
had back-up generators. NATO claimed that these strikes would cripple the
Serb air defense system and military command and control networks.[140] But
there are reasons to doubt this. Otherwise, why was the Serb civilian power
supply not targeted early on in the campaign? And if hospitals had back-up
generators, then would not Serb military systems? NATO also later claimed
that "strikes against strategic targets, such as government ministries and re-
fineries, had *a longer-term and broader impact* on the Serb military machine."[141] Here NATO was being "a strategic user of culture" (as discussed in
Chapter 1) by stretching the definition of military objects in Additional Protocol I (a poorly established norm) to include less immediate contributions to
military action. In sum, NATO was on uncertain legal ground and this explains
its reluctance to destroy Serbian civilian infrastructure. Only when all else
failed, did it selectively do so. In the context of a long and careful air campaign, such isolated desperate measures were excusable and excused. The Independent International Commission on Kosovo concluded: "NATO succeeded better than any air war in history in selective targeting that adhered to
principles of discrimination, proportionality, and necessity, with only relatively
minor breaches that were themselves reasonable interpretations of 'military necessity' in the context."[142]

Conclusion

International law provides states with the rules of the game—telling them who can and should do what in world politics. When it comes to war, the law provides moral codes that must be obeyed. We noted how norms have evolved over time in state custom and have increasingly been codified in convention law. This is clearly evident in humanitarian law. Of course, it is possible for legal norms to clash with nonlegal norms that also provide moral imperatives for state action. This would appear to be the case with humanitarian intervention. This raises the question of what happens when a legal norm is violated in practice.

Most of the time states obey international law, and they do so for any one of a number of reasons: because they think it is advantageous, appropriate, and/or fair to do so. Crucially, in terms of showing the autonomous casual effect of legal norms, states will obey international law even when it goes against their self-interests. This was illustrated in NATO's military campaign in Kosovo: humanitarian law led NATO to exercise restraint in its bombing campaign even though military logic favored rapid escalation. Arguably inducement may still have played a role, in terms of the causal mechanism for NATO compliance with humanitarian law. We noted that restraint was crucial to NATO's public relations campaign to maintain domestic support in NATO states for the war. One may infer inducement of political elites for norm compliance, with feared sanctions taking the form of a decline in public support for the government. One could also read this in terms of maintaining public support for the campaign (rather than for the government in question). The prospect of a possible ground invasion would have produced powerful countervailing inducements to escalate the bombing campaign. Given this, I conclude that the main causal mechanism operating in this case was social learning—primarily social learning of norms of humanitarian law by NATO militaries as encoded in (and evidenced by) military doctrine and targeting procedures. One may also infer secondary social learning by Western publics of the moral and legal prohibitions against unrestrained bombing.

The Kosovo case also usefully highlights what happens when states violate international law. Violation may undermine or may affirm the legal norm in question—depending on the justification given by the violating state, and the response of the international community. We explored this dynamic in the evolution of humanitarian intervention. The failure of intervening states and the UNSC to provide a legal justification for humanitarian intervention, combined with general hostility from the international community, has prevented the emergence of a legal norm supporting this new state practice. The Kosovo case illustrated that states do still feel some kind of moral obligation all the same to on occasion intervene to stop massive human rights abuses. There is also evidence for two enabling conditions supporting cultural change: a shocking event in the form of the Rwandan genocide, and the UN Secretary-General and Britain as norm entrepreneurs. This suggests that while there is little prospect for the evolution of a legal norm of humanitarian intervention, a *non-legal* norm supporting such practice may be emerging.

Notes

1. This is noted and explored in Christopher Coker, *Humane Warfare* (London: Routledge, 2001).

2. Ian Holliday, "When Is a Cause Just?" *Review of International Studies* 28, no. 3 (2002): 557–576.

3. Kriangsak Kittichaisaree, *International Criminal Law* (Oxford: Oxford University Press, 2001).

4. Obviously, it is tautological to see in state practice evidence of the legal obligation that is supposed to generate such practice in the first place. Nonetheless, this is often how the ICJ (which makes authoritative findings regarding the existence of customary law) sees it. Only occasionally has the ICJ required actual proof of *opinio juris*—some measure of state recognition of legal obligation underpinning the practice in question. Michael Byers, *Custom, Power and the Power of Rules* (Cambridge: Cambridge University Press, 1999), pp. 133–141; Ian Brownlie, *Principles of Public International Law,* 5th ed. (Oxford: Oxford University Press, 1998), p. 7.

5. Malcolm Shaw, *International Law,* 5th ed. (Cambridge: Cambridge University Press, 2003), p. 90.

6. Lawmaking treaties can create customary rules in one of three ways: they may *codify* existing rules, *crystallize* emerging rules, or *contribute momentum* toward new rules of customary law. Sir Robert Jennings and Sir Arthur Watts (eds.), *Oppenheim's International Law: Vol. 1, Peace: Introduction and Part 1,* 9th ed. (London: Longman, 1996), pp. 33–35.

7. Naomi Roht-Arriaza, "'Soft Law' in a 'Hybrid Organization': The International Organization for Standardization," in Dinah Shelton (ed.), *Commitment and Compliance: The Role of Non-Binding Norms in the International Legal System* (Oxford: Oxford University Press, 2000), pp. 263–281.

8. Antonio Cassese, *International Law,* 2nd ed. (Oxford: Oxford University Press, 2005), pp. 202–203. See also Convention on the Law of Treaties, 1969, Article 53, in Malcolm D. Evans (ed.), *Blackstone's International Law Documents,* 6th ed. (Oxford: Oxford University Press, 2003), p. 133.

9. Martin Shaw, *War and Genocide* (Cambridge: Polity, 2003).

10. Hersch Lauterpacht, "The Problem of Revision of the Law of War," *British Yearbook of International Law* 29 (1952), p. 382.

11. International law owes its origins to Natural Law thinking, but Legal Positivism has dominated the discipline since the nineteenth century. Stephen C. Heff, "A Short History of International Law," in Malcolm D. Evans (ed.), *International Law* (Oxford: Oxford University Press, 2003), pp. 31–58.

12. The classic statement on this approach is H. L. A. Hart, *The Concept of Law* (Oxford: Oxford University Press, 1961). For a recent development of this approach, see Anthony Clark Arend, *Legal Rules and International Society* (Oxford: Oxford University Press, 1999).

13. For a classic statement of this school, see Myres S. McDougal and Harold D. Lasswell, "The Identification and Appraisal of Diverse Systems of Public Order," *American Journal of International Law* 53 (1959): 1–29. For a review, see Gidon Gottlieb, "The Conceptual World of the Yale School of International Law," *World Politics* 21 (1968): 120–129. For a recent application, see Rosalyn Higgins, *Problems and Process: International Law and How We Use It* (Oxford: Oxford University Press, 1994).

14. Dinah Shelton (ed.), *Commitment and Compliance: The Role of Non-Binding Norms in the International Legal System* (Oxford: Oxford University Press, 2000); Kenneth Abbott and Duncan Snidal, "Hard and Soft Law in International Governance," *International Organization* 54 (2000): 421–456.

15. Arend, *Legal Rules*, p. 26, emphasis in original.

16. Judith L. Goldstein, Robert O. Keohane, and Anne-Marie Slaughter (eds.), *Legalization and World Politics* (Cambridge, MA: MIT Press, 2001).

17. Abram Chayes and Antonia Handler Chayes, *The New Sovereignty: Compliance with International Regulatory Agreements* (Cambridge, MA: Harvard University Press, 1995).

18. Byers, *Custom*, pp. 35–50.

19. N. D. White and A. Abass, "Countermeasures and Sanctions," in Malcolm Evans (ed.), *International Law* (Oxford: Oxford University Press, 2003), pp. 502–528.

20. J. Samuel Barkin and Bruce Cronin, "The State and the Nation: Changing Norms and the Rules of Sovereignty in International Relations," *International Organization* 48, no. 1 (1994): 107–130.

21. Harold Hongju Koh, "Why Do Nations Obey International Law," *The Yale Law Journal* 106 (1997): 2645–2658.

22. This is explored in Anne-Marie Slaughter, *A New World Order* (Princeton, NJ: Princeton University Press, 2004); see also Shelton, *Commitment and Compliance* (especially chapters by Reinickle and Witte, Rothwell, de Chazournes, and Cassel).

23. Thomas M. Franck, *Fairness in International Law and Institutions* (Oxford: Clarendon, 1995).

24. Ethan A. Nadelman, "Global Prohibition Regimes: The Evolution of Norms in International Society," *International Organization* 44, no. 4 (1990): 479–526.

25. Alfred Rubin, *Ethics and Authority in International Law* (Cambridge: Cambridge University Press, 1997), pp. 97–130. As noted in Chapter 1, in theory, persuasion stands apart from power under the logic of argumentation. The point being made here is that, in the real world, the two can often operate in tandem.

26. Richard M. Price, "Reversing the Gun Sights: Transnational Civil Society Targets Land Mines," *International Organization* 52, no. 3 (1998): 613–644.

27. Oscar Schachter, "Self-Defense and the Rule of Law," *American Journal of International Law* 83, no. 2 (1989): 267.

28. Michael Bothe, "Terrorism and the Legality of Pre-emptive Force," *European Journal of International Law* 14, no. 2 (2003): 116.

29. Shaw, *International Law,* pp. 694–752; Cassese, *International Law,* pp. 180–182, 258–262.

30. Yoram Dinstein, *War, Aggression and Self-Defence,* 2nd ed. (Cambridge: Cambridge University Press, 1994), p. 95.

31. Military and Paramilitary Activities in and Against Nicaragua, *(Nicaragua v. United States of America),* Merits Judgment, ICJ Reports, 1986, http://www.icj-cij.org/icjwww/idecisions.htm.

32. This is argued in Allen Buchanan, "Reforming the International Law of Humanitarian Intervention," in J. L. Holzgrefe and Robert O. Keohane (eds.), *Humani-*

tarian Intervention: Ethical, Legal, and Political Dilemmas (Cambridge: Cambridge University Press, 2003); Michael Byers, "Preemptive Self-Defense: Hegemony, Equality and Strategies of Legal Change," draft paper, 2003, p. 16.

33. This is the standard definition of humanitarian intervention. On this, see Adam Roberts, "The Price of Protection," *Survival* 44, no. 4 (2002–2003): 158.

34. Thomas M. Franck, *Recourse to Force: State Action Against Threats and Armed Attacks* (Cambridge: Cambridge University Press, 2002), p. 136; Thomas M. Franck, "Interpretation and Change in the Law of Humanitarian Intervention," in J. L. Holzgrefe and Robert O. Keohane (eds.), *Humanitarian Intervention: Ethical, Legal, and Political Dilemmas* (Cambridge: Cambridge University Press, 2003), p. 207.

35. Franck, *Recourse,* pp. 76–94; Christine Gray, *International Law and the Use of Force* (Oxford: Oxford University Press, 2001), pp. 63–65, 108–111; *The Responsibility to Protect: Research, Bibliography, Background,* Supplementary Volume to the Report of the International Commission on Intervention and State Sovereignty (Ottawa, ON: International Research Development Centre, 2001), pp. 43–67.

36. For analysis of these case studies, see *The Responsibility to Protect,* pp. 49–67; Nicholas J. Wheeler, *Saving Strangers: Humanitarian Intervention in International Society* (Oxford: Oxford University Press, 2000), pp. 55–138; Frederik Harhoff, "Unauthorised Humanitarian Interventions: Armed Violence in the Name of Humanity?" *Nordic Journal of International Law* 70 (2001): 85–88.

37. Peter Hilpold, "Humanitarian Intervention: Is There a Need for a Legal Reappraisal?" *European Journal of International Law* 12, no. 3 (2001): 443.

38. Franck, *Recourse,* p. 148.

39. J. L. Holzgrefe, "The Humanitarian Intervention Debate," in J. L. Holzgrefe and Robert O. Keohane (eds.), *Humanitarian Intervention: Ethical, Legal, and Political Dilemmas* (Cambridge: Cambridge University Press, 2003), p. 41.

40. Gray, *International,* p. 146.

41. S/RES/794 (1992), 3 December 1992, p. 1, http://www.un.org/Docs/sc/unsc_resolutions.htm.

42. Cassese, *International Law,* p. 347.

43. Hilpold, "Humanitarian," pp. 445–447.

44. *The Responsibility to Protect,* pp. 87–88.

45. Wheeler, *Saving,* p. 153.

46. Franck, *Recourse,* p. 153.

47. Wheeler, *Saving,* p. 167.

48. Gray, *International,* pp. 200, 212–214, 224–227.

49. For detail on this case, see Independent International Commission on Kosovo, *The Kosovo Report: Conflict, International Response, Lessons Learned* (Oxford: Oxford University Press, 2000); Lord Robertson, Secretary of State for Defence, *Kosovo: An Account of the Crisis* (London: Ministry of Defence, 1999).

50. *The Responsibility to Protect,* p. 113.

51. Adam Roberts, "NATO's 'Humanitarian War' over Kosovo," *Survival* 41, no. 3 (1999): 106.

52. The classic work on this is Kenneth N. Waltz, *Theory of International Politics* (Reading, MA: Addison-Wesley, 1979).

53. For Waltz, Russia is way down on the list of potential counterbalancers to US power. Instead, he sees Japan, China, and the European Union as much more likely candidates. Kenneth N. Waltz, "Structural Realism After the Cold War," *International Security* 25, no. 1 (2000): 30–39.

54. The major work on offensive realism is John. J. Mearsheimer, *The Tragedy of Great Power Politics* (New York: W. W. Norton, 2001).

55. "Capitol Hill Pushes for Cost of Kosovo," CNN web report, 15 April 1999, http://www.cnn.com/ALLPOLITICS/stories/1999/04/15/kosovo.costs/.

56. On balance of threat theory, see Stephen M. Walt, *The Origins of Alliances* (Ithaca, NY: Cornell University Press, 1987).

57. This model of domestic pressure prompting states to undertake humanitarian intervention is advanced in Karin Von Hippel, *Democracy by Force: US Military Intervention in the Post–Cold War World* (Cambridge: Cambridge University Press, 2000), pp. 161–171.

58. Wheeler, *Saving*, p. 259.

59. This scandal involved President Clinton having sex with Monica Lewinsky, a White House intern, and then lying about it under oath.

60. David Halberstam, *War in a Time of Peace: Bush, Clinton and the Generals* (London: Bloomsbury, 2001), pp. 387, 423–424.

61. Michael MccGwire, "Why Did We Bomb Belgrade?" *International Affairs* 76, no. 1 (2000): 17; see also pp. 8–9. For contemporaneous analysis of the challenges then facing the alliance, see David S. Yost, "The New NATO and Collective Security," *Survival* 40, no. 2 (1998): 135–160.

62. Cited in Ivo H. Daalder and Michael E. O'Hanlon, *Winning Ugly: NATO's War to Save Kosovo* (Washington, DC: Brookings Institution, 2000), p. 24.

63. Ibid., pp. 43–44, 62–69.

64. Catherine Guicherd, "International Law and the War in Kosovo," *Survival* 41, no. 2 (1999): 25–29; Wheeler, *Saving*, pp. 275–277.

65. Article 24 gives the UNSC primary responsibility for the maintenance of international peace and security.

66. Wheeler, *Saving*, pp. 278–280.

67. Bruno Simma, "NATO, the UN and Use of Force: Legal Aspects," *European Journal of International Law* 10 (1999): 6–14; Thomas M. Franck, "Lessons of Kosovo," *American Journal of International Law* 93, no. 4 (1999): 859; Alain Pellet, "Brief Remarks on the Unilateral Use of Force," *European Journal of International Law* 11, no. 2 (2000): 389.

68. W. Michael Reisman, "Unilateral Action and the Transformations of the World Constitutive Process: The Special Problem of Humanitarian Intervention," *European Journal of International Law* 11, no. 1 (2000): 3–18; W. Michael Reisman, "Kosovo's Antinomies," *American Journal of International Law* 93, no. 4 (1999): 860–862.

69. Guicherd, "International Law," p. 27.

70. Daniel H. Joyner, "The Kosovo Intervention: Legal Analysis and a More Persuasive Paradigm," *European Journal of International Law* 13, no. 3 (2002): 608.

71. Louis Henkin, "Kosovo and the Law of 'Humanitarian Intervention,'" *American Journal of International Law* 93, no. 4 (1999): 825.

72. See Joyner, "The Kosovo Intervention," pp. 603, 609; Jonathan I. Charney, "Anticipatory Humanitarian Intervention in Kosovo," *American Journal of International Law* 93, no. 4 (1999): 836–837; Michael Byers and Simon Chesterman, "Changing the Rules About the Rules? Unilateral Humanitarian Intervention and the Future of International Law," in J. L. Holzgrefe and Robert O. Keohane (eds.), *Humanitarian Intervention: Ethical, Legal, and Political Dilemmas* (Cambridge: Cambridge University Press, 2003), p. 199; Buchanan, "Reforming," pp. 168–170; Simma, "NATO," p. 13; Roberts, "NATO's," p. 107; Franck, *Recourse*, p. 167.

73. Antonio Cassese, "A Follow-Up: Forcible Humanitarian Countermeasures and *Opinio Nessitatis*," *European Journal of International Law* 10, no. 4 (1999): 791–799; Vera Gowlland-Debbas, "The Limits of Unilateral Enforcement of Commu-

nity Objectives in the Framework of UN Peace Maintenance," *European Journal of International Law* 11, no. 2 (2000): 377; J. L. Holzgrefe, "The Humanitarian Intervention Debate," p. 47; Charney, "Anticipatory," p. 837; Joyner, "The Kosovo Intervention," pp. 603–604; Hilpold, "Humanitarian," pp. 460–461; Declaration of the Group of 77 South Summit, Havana, Cuba, 10–14 April 2000, http://www.g77.org/Declaration_G77Summit.htm.

74. Nicholas J. Wheeler, "The Humanitarian Responsibilities of Sovereignty: Explaining the Development of a New Norm of Military Intervention for Humanitarian Purposes in International Society," in Jennifer M. Welsh (ed.), *Humanitarian Intervention and International Relations* (Oxford: Oxford University Press, 2004), p. 48. This view is echoed in Adam Roberts, "The United Nations and Humanitarian Intervention," in Jennifer M. Welsh (ed.), *Humanitarian Intervention and International Relations* (Oxford: Oxford University Press, 2004), p. 88.

75. Report of the Secretary-General's High-Level Panel on Threats, Challenges and Change, *A More Secure World: Our Shared Responsibility* (New York: United Nations, 2004), paragraph 203, p. 66.

76. Independent International Commission on Kosovo, *The Kosovo Report,* p. 170.

77. See *Report of the Independent Inquiry into the Actions of the United Nations During the 1994 Genocide in Rwanda* (New York: United Nations, 1999), http://www.un.org/Depts/dpko/lessons/.

78. Cited in Wheeler, "The Humanitarian Responsibilities," p. 29.

79. Roberts, "The United Nations and Humanitarian Intervention," p. 87.

80. Report of the Secretary-General to the Security Council on the Protection of Civilians in Armed Conflict, 28 May 2004, S/2004/431, paragraph 2.

81. This potential is explored in Tim Dunne, "'When the Shooting Starts': Atlanticism in British Security Strategy," *International Affairs* 80, no. 5 (2004): 811–833.

82. Tony Blair, "Doctrine of the International Community," Economic Club of Chicago, Chicago, 22 April 1999. This particular new "doctrine" was the product of Blair's own conviction rather than policy work from within the British government. John Kampfner, *Blair's Wars* (London: Free Press, 2003), pp. 51–53.

83. Wheeler, "The Humanitarian Responsibilities," pp. 46–47.

84. For critical appraisal, see Paul Williams, "The Rise and Fall of the 'Ethical Dimension': Presentation and Practice in New Labour's Foreign Policy," *Cambridge Review of International Affairs* 15, no. 1 (2002): 53–63.

85. Nicholas J. Wheeler and Tim Dunne, *Moral Britannia? Evaluating the Ethical Dimension in Labour's Foreign Policy* (London: The Foreign Policy Centre, 2004).

86. Ewen MacAskill, "Blair Draws Up Plans to Send Troops to Sudan," *The Guardian,* 22 July 2004, p. 1.

87. Adam Roberts and Richard Guelff, "Editors' Introduction," in Adam Roberts and Richard Guelff (eds.), *Documents on the Laws of War,* 3rd ed. (Oxford: Oxford University Press, 1999), pp. 9–10.

88. Christopher Greenwood, "The Law of War (International Humanitarian Law)," in Malcolm Evans (ed.), *International Law* (Oxford: Oxford University Press, 2003), p. 790.

89. Antonio Cassese, *International Criminal Law* (Oxford: Oxford University Press, 2003).

90. Codification was precisely about creating a knowledge base of agreed and precise legal rules. Jennings and Watts, *Oppenheim's,* pp. 97–115.

91. Frederic L. Kirgis, "The Formative Years of the American Society of International Law," *American Journal of International Law* 90, no. 4 (1996): 559–589; John

M. Raymond and Barbara J. Frischholz, "Lawyers Who Established International Law in the United States, 1776–1914," *American Journal of International Law* 76, no. 4 (1982): 802–829; Martti Koskenniemi, *The Gentle Civilizer of Nations: The Rise and Fall of International Law 1870–1960* (Cambridge: Cambridge University Press, 2001).

92. Martha Finnemore, *The Purpose of Intervention: Changing Beliefs About the Use of Force* (Ithaca, NY: Cornell University Press, 2003), chapter 2.

93. Christopher Rudolph, "Constructing an Atrocities Regime: The Politics of War Crimes Tribunals," *International Organization* 55, no. 3 (2001): 655–691.

94. James D. Morrow, "The Institutional Features of the Prisoners of War Treaties," *International Organization* 55, no. 4 (2001): 971–991.

95. Martha Finnemore, *National Interests in International Society* (Ithaca, NY: Cornell University Press, 1996), pp. 69–88.

96. Sudan has only established, by presidential decree, a national commission on implementing humanitarian law.

97. Data from the ICRC database on national implementation of humanitarian law, http://www.icrc.org/ihl-nat.

98. Data from the official ICC website, http://www.icc-cpi.int/home.html&l=en. For analysis on this development in international criminal law, see Rolf Einar Fife, "The International Criminal Court: Whence It Came, Where It Goes," *Nordic Journal of International Law* 69 (2000): 63–85.

99. Roberts and Guelff, "Editors' Introduction," pp. 12–13.

100. For testimony on this, see Joanna Burke, *An Intimate History of Killing* (London: Granta, 1999).

101. This is explored in Martin Shaw, *War and Genocide* (Cambridge: Polity, 2003); Omer Bartov, *Germany's War and the Holocaust* (Ithaca, NY: Cornell University Press, 2003).

102. This tension is also recognized in Ward Thomas, *The Ethics of Destruction: Norms and Force in International Relations* (Ithaca, NY: Cornell University Press, 2001), p. 164.

103. NATO brief, "The Conduct of the Air Campaign," 30 October 2000, http://www.nato.int/kosovo/repo2000/conduct.htm.

104. Daalder and O'Hanlon, *Winning Ugly,* p. 103.

105. Interview with General Mike Short, NATO Air Commander, in *War in Europe: 2 Vanishing Targets,* Channel 4 documentary, 2000.

106. Stephen P. Aubin, "Operation Allied Force: War or 'Coercive Diplomacy'?" *Strategic Review* (Summer 1999): 6.

107. Cited in Benjamin S. Lambeth, *The Transformation of American Air Power* (Ithaca, NY: Cornell University Press, 2000), pp. 217–218.

108. Aubin, "Operation Allied Force," pp. 5–6.

109. Lambeth, *The Transformation,* pp. 196–197.

110. General Wesley K. Clark, *Waging Modern War: Bosnia, Kosovo, and the Future of Conflict* (New York: Public Affairs, 2001), pp. 220–242; Daalder and O'Hanlon, *Winning Ugly,* pp. 118–119.

111. House of Commons, Defence Select Committee, Fourteenth Report, 23 October 2000, paragraph 86.

112. Barry Posen, "The War for Kosovo: Serbia's Political-Military Strategy," *International Security* 24, no. 4 (2000): 72.

113. Stephen T. Hosmer, *Why Milosevic Decided to Settle When He Did* (Santa Monica, CA: RAND, 2001), pp. 49–52. Daalder and O'Hanlon conclude that the growing threat of land invasion by NATO was as crucial as the escalating air campaign

in persuading Milosevic to surrender; Daalder and O'Hanlon, *Winning Ugly,* pp. 198–206. For more recent analysis that comprehensively critiques this argument (principally on the grounds that the NATO threat was not clearly and convincingly communicated to Milosevic), see Andrew L. Stigler, "A Clear Victory of Air Power: NATO's Empty Threat to Invade Kosovo," *International Security* 27, no. 3 (2002–2003): 124–157.

114. Halberstam, *War,* pp. 440, 445. For a defense of this approach to strategic bombing by the intellectual father of "system shut-down" air strategy, see John A. Warden III, "Success in Modern War: A Response to Robert Pape's *Bombing to Win,*" *Security Studies* 7, no. 2 (1997–1998): 172–190.

115. Daalder and O'Hanlon, *Winning Ugly,* pp. 127–128.

116. John S. Duffield, *Power Rules: The Evolution of NATO's Conventional Force Structure* (Stanford, CA: Stanford University Press, 1995), pp. 18–21. This tension between the costs and benefits of alliance membership is also explored in Glenn Synder, *Alliance Politics* (Ithaca, NY: Cornell University Press, 1997).

117. Thomas Risse-Kappen, *Cooperation Among Democracies: The European Influence on US Foreign Policy* (Princeton, NJ: Princeton University Press, 1995).

118. In total, US aircraft flew 60 percent of all sorties, and 53 percent of all strike sorties in Operation Allied Force. Daalder and O'Hanlon, *Winning Ugly,* p. 149.

119. Pressure began to build within the NATO military hierarchy in late May and early June for the alliance to prepare for ground invasion. Clark told NATO leaders that he would need 175,000 troops, of which 75,000 were expected to come from the European allies. Daadler and O'Hanlon, *Winning Ugly,* pp. 156–160.

120. Michael Ignatief, *Virtual War: Kosovo and Beyond* (London: Chatto and Windus, 2000), pp. 100–101. Weapon payloads were also adjusted to comply with humanitarian law. See Lambeth, *The Transformation,* p. 204.

121. Clark, *Waging Modern War,* p. 224.

122. Thomas, *The Ethics of Destruction,* pp. 162–163.

123. Clark, *Waging Modern War,* p. 201.

124. Cited in US General Accounting Office, *Kosovo Air Operations: Need to Maintain Alliance Cohesion Resulted in Doctrinal Departures,* GAO-01-784 (Washington, DC: GAO, July 2001), p. 8.

125. Clark, *Waging Modern War,* p. 225.

126. Nicholas J. Wheeler, "The Kosovo Bombing Campaign," in Christian Reus-Smit (ed.), *The Politics of International Law* (Cambridge: Cambridge University Press, 2004), p. 197.

127. Paolo Benvenuti, "The ICTY Prosecutor and the Review of the NATO Bombing Campaign Against the Federal Republic of Yugoslavia," *European Journal of International Law* 12, no. 3 (2001): 503–529.

128. Amnesty International, *NATO/Federal Republic of Yugoslavia: "Collateral Damage" or Unlawful Killings?* June 2000 (AL Index: EUR 70/18/00). For a more critical report, see Human Rights Watch, *Civilian Deaths in the NATO Air Campaign,* 2000, http://www.hrw.org/reports/2000/nato/Natbm200.htm.

129. Independent International Commission on Kosovo, *The Kosovo Report,* p. 181.

130. Clark, *Waging Modern War,* p. 304.

131. US General Accounting Office, *Kosovo Air Operations,* p. 8.

132. Ibid., p. 9.

133. Daniel L. Byman and Matthew C. Waxman, "Kosovo and the Great Air Power Debate," *International Security* 24, no. 4 (2000): 33–34; Lawrence Freedman, "Victims and Victors: Reflections on the Kosovo War," *Review of International Studies* 26, no. 3 (2000): 356–358.

134. Interview with SACEUR in *War in Europe,* House of Commons, Defence Select Committee, paragraph 94.

135. Clark, *Waging Modern War,* pp. 213, 240. Undoubtedly, compounding the unease of some NATO members about the use of force in this case was the fact that it was not actually authorized by the UN Security Council.

136. Greenwood, "The Law of War," pp. 797–798.

137. Independent International Commission on Kosovo, *The Kosovo Report,* p. 177.

138. A. P. V. Rogers, *Law on the Battlefield* (Manchester: Manchester University Press, 1996), pp. 33–41.

139. This orthodoxy can be traced back to pre–World War II US air power doctrine. For discussion, see Tami Davis Biddle, *Rhetoric and Reality in Air Warfare: The Evolution of British and American Ideas About Strategic Bombing, 1914–1945* (Princeton, NJ: Princeton University Press, 2002).

140. Ignatief, *Virtual War,* pp. 107–108; Thomas, *The Ethics of Destruction,* pp. 165–166; Wheeler, "The Kosovo Bombing Campaign," pp. 204–206.

141. NATO brief, "The Conduct of the Air Campaign," emphasis added. Similarly, the North Atlantic Council refers to "Alliance air operations against the Yugoslav war machine" in its "Statement on Kosovo" from the Washington, DC, summit, 23 April 1999, http://www.nato.int/docu/pr/1999/p99-062e.htm.

142. Independent International Commission on Kosovo, *The Kosovo Report,* p. 184.

6

The Changing Culture of War

Culture makes war possible. It does this by providing the moral codes and technical scripts for war, telling communities why and how they should fight. Even at the most basic technical level of organizing for war, culture has a determining impact. As Chapter 2 showed, military professionals the world over share core beliefs about how they should organize themselves, and this translates into worldwide homogeneity in military organization. As we saw in the peculiar case of the Irish Army, even when strategic imperatives strongly suggest otherwise, norms of conventional warfare drive small states to build regular armies. Chapter 2 also examined another transnational norm of military professionalism that is profoundly important to democratic government, that is, a moral code that prescribes civilian supremacy in civil-military relations. Again, the Irish case illustrates the power of this norm of civilian supremacy.

The role of culture in motivating war was explored in Chapter 3, in the context of the mass industrialized wars of the twentieth century. Mass participation in World War II is somewhat puzzling given the horrors of World War I. In the case of Germany, it may be understood in terms of the way national memory of the first Great War was framed, as well as how popular imagination was captured for a project of state expansion. Chapter 3 also looked at how imagination shaped technical scripts for machine warfare. It discussed how imagemaking enabled the United Sates to harness technology to pursue a fierce air and land war in the Pacific during World War II.

Cultural beliefs have been particularly important to nuclear strategy because, in the absence of any experience of nuclear combat, ideas are all policymakers and nuclear planners have had to go on. Taking the case of the world's foremost nuclear power, the United States, Chapter 4 examined how military practice was shaped by a moral code prohibiting first nuclear use, and a technical script prescribing the nuclear targeting of cities. Even thinking about nuclear war is crazy; culture makes sense of this madness.

173

Some norms of war have force in law. Chapter 5 considered the power and limitations of international law in the context of humanitarian war. States have increasingly codified norms on the conduct of war in humanitarian law. These legal rules produce restraint in military operations even, as in the case of NATO's war over Kosovo, when such restraint contradicts self-interest. Chapter 5 also explored the evolving practice of humanitarian intervention. This is a moral code for the purpose of war, which in practice violates international law. Kosovo provides a crucial test case for the norm-changing character of such violation—a test case in which humanitarian intervention fails to gain sufficient justification or support to become a lawful reason for use of force.

Chapter 1 identified three causal mechanisms for norms in military action (see Table 6.1). The first, coercion and inducement, was least in evidence in the cases discussed here. In only one case was this mechanism present, in that the origins of the nuclear taboo do owe something to the coercive power of President Harry Truman. In general terms, various inducements also support norms of conventional warfare and norms of humanitarian law. In the case studies examined, however, inducement did not play a part. Indeed, the Irish Army had strong inducements not to follow norms of conventional warfare, just as NATO had inducements to breach strictures of humanitarian law in its Kosovo campaign. Far more in evidence was the second mechanism, moral pressure and persuasion. In Chapter 1, I argued that this mechanism actually comes in two forms—rhetorical action and truth-seeking argument. Chapter 2 showed how rhetorical action partly explains the encoding of norms of conventional warfare and the norm of civilian supremacy in the Irish Army culture. Chapter 4 noted how Truman also engaged in rhetorical action to supplement his coercive efforts to promote the nuclear taboo. Chapter 5 revealed states engaging in truth-seeking argument over legality of humanitarian intervention: this is a norm to which many (especially Western) states are open to persuasion. The final

Table 6.1   Causal Mechanisms for Normative Action

Case	Norm	Causal Mechanism
Irish Army	Conventional warfare	Rhetorical action followed by social learning
	Civilian supremacy	Rhetorical action followed by social learning
United States	Nuclear taboo	Coercion combined with rhetorical action followed by social learning
	Countercity targeting	Social learning
NATO	Humanitarian intervention	Truth-seeking argument
	Humanitarian law	Social learning

mechanism, social learning, was also in evidence in Chapters 2, 4, and 5. Norms of conventional warfare were further entrenched in Irish Army culture through reinforcing social learning of these norms, especially by and through officers returning from foreign training. Social learning ensured adherence to the nuclear taboo by post-Truman administrations; while norms of countercity targeting were grafted from conventional bombing into nuclear war planning through a process of social learning. Finally (and in contrast to US nuclear war planning), military doctrine and targeting practice reveal that NATO militaries have been socialized into complying with norms of humanitarian law.

In this book, I have taken a broad view of my subject—ranging historically from the late nineteenth to the early twenty-first century and thematically from the large canvas of state-society relations to the arcane detail of nuclear strategy. In this chapter, I explore some conclusions regarding how we theorize normative change and how Western norms of war have changed in substance. A final section reflects on the book's findings for the 2003 Iraq War.

How Norms Evolve

The first set of conclusions concerns developing constructivist theory. Two areas previously understudied by constructivists are the origins of norms and the processes of normative change.

I approach the origins of norms from two angles, that of agency and that of structure. Constructivists have tended to take a narrow view of agency in their accounts of culture and war, concentrating on the role of military and political elites. As Chapter 3 argued, however, a whole range of agents in civil society are motivated for aesthetic, emotional, and/or financial reasons to shape images of wars present and future, and collective memories of wars past. These are the building blocks of norms of war. Thus, shared beliefs about what a tank could do in World War I and how a bomber should be used in World War II owe their origins to images of armored and air warfare, respectively, images generated as much by the media and industry as by military and political elites. Equally, in addition to the government, all manner of agents—from performance artists, to the press, to opposition politicians—were involved in shaping collective memories of Germany's wars in 1870–1871 and 1914–1918. Nurtured by the Nazis, these memories fed into a popular will for war, once again.

Of course, not all norms are homegrown. In terms of social structure, I have argued that norms exist at multiple levels: organizational, national, international, and transnational (some of which are worldwide). Norms interact and travel across these levels, thus worldwide norms may be transplanted on local cultural systems and, equally, local culture may end up being institutionalized in, and transmitted through, transnational networks. As Chapter 2 showed, the military culture of the twentieth-century Irish Army embraced worldwide norms of conventional warfare that, in turn, originated in the strategic culture of the sixteenth-century Dutch Republic. Given that militaries are eyeing-up and emulating each other all the time, we may expect that much of what a military believes and does has been learned elsewhere.[1] Therefore, this process of norm transplantation accounts for the origins of some of the content of national military cultures.

Constructivist work has been criticized for failing to account for the process of normative change.[2] Certainly, constructivists face a challenge here. By definition, norms are taken to be rigid in some sense. Indeed, this is central to the methodology of those constructivists who seek to trace the causal impact of norms on world politics; norms must first be "fixed" before their causal effect can be demonstrated. Rigidity may be expected especially of norms that have been institutionalized in law, doctrine, or policy. Such norms will enjoy the backing of these institutions, as well as the support of those that practice them. Once institutionalized, norms are usually internalized by actors and come to be taken for granted. Changing them then becomes almost unthinkable. Yet, cultures do change.

That said, constructivists *do* have ideas about how culture changes. Chapter 1 drew on these ideas, and on the military innovation literature, to identify three enabling conditions of cultural change: effective norm entrepreneurs, external shock to the cultural system, and personnel change (either of key or large numbers of people) in the community undertaking change. I discussed the evidence for these enabling conditions in Chapters 2, 4, and 5. The results are illustrated in Table 6.2—each "X" indicates the presence of an enabling condition.

These enabling conditions are relevant both to norm transplantation and to domestic cultural change. Chapter 2 revealed norm transplantation occurring in the new Irish Army when military leaders were able to mobilize support in their own organization for foreign norms of conventional warfare and civilian supremacy. In addition to effective norm entrepreneurs, external shock (in the

Table 6.2   Enabling Conditions of Cultural Change

Case Study	Norm	Norm Entrepreneur	Shock	Personnel Change
Irish Army	Conventional warfare	X	X	X
	Civilian supremacy	X	X	X
United States	Nuclear taboo	X	X	
	Countercity targeting			X
NATO	Humanitarian intervention	X	X	
	Humanitarian law	n/a	n/a	n/a

Note: The enabling conditions are not applicable in the NATO case for humanitarian law because it does not concern legal change.

form of civil war) and personnel turnover (with seasoned rebels being replaced by raw recruits) were both important enablers of normative change in the Irish case. As Chapter 4 showed, these three causal mechanisms also apply to home-grown cultural change. The devastation caused by the atomic bombing of Japan jolted President Truman, as the lead norm entrepreneur, into mobilizing support in the US polity for the nuclear taboo. At the same time, a norm of countercity targeting developed when ideas traveled with US Air Force officers with wartime experience of bombing cities into the new command responsible for nuclear war planning.

As Chapter 5 noted, change in international law is particularly difficult. So much so, in fact, that normative violation is an important mechanism for legal change. Breaching a norm does not automatically undermine the norm in question. However, when those breaching the norm declare that they do so because they no longer recognize it, and the breach is accepted by the rest of the international community, then the norm loses its authority and a new one takes its place. Chapter 5 examined this process in the context of the growing state practice of humanitarian intervention. It found insufficient justification or support to sustain legal change in this case. It did find evidence of shock (the Rwandan genocide) and norm entrepreneurs (the UN Secretary-General and Britain under Blair), which, combined with persistent state practice in recent decades, does suggest the emergence of a nonlegal norm of humanitarian intervention.

Further research on cases across space and time is required to establish the relative importance of these enabling conditions and to identify if any are sufficient conditions for radical cultural change. The crucial question is, must voluntary radical change be preceded by an external shock to the cultural system? The countercity targeting norm does not present an example of this. While there was only one enabling condition present in this case (personnel change), this was not a case of radical cultural change—it did not challenge the existing norm hierarchy in the US Air Force, and accordingly was freely adopted by the organization. Further research might also home in on and test the relative importance of the attributes of norm entrepreneurs (policymaking proximity versus persuasiveness) and the character of personnel change (leadership versus mass turnover).

The New Norms of War

The second set of conclusions concerns the normative place of force in the twenty-first century. Substantively speaking, how have the norms of war changed?

For Martha Finnemore and John Mueller the main trend is, in Finnemore's words, "the steady erosion of force's normative value in international politics." Finnemore notes that, whereas "war was glorious and honourable" in the seventeenth century, now "force is viewed as legitimate only as a last resort, and only for defensive or humanitarian purposes."[3] Mueller likewise finds that, whereas war has "for almost all of history been accepted as a natural, inevitable, and, often, desirable element in human affairs," it has become for many developed states "subrationally unthinkable," even "absurd."[4] There is further evidence of the declining value of war in the West.[5] Chapter 3 discussed a growing appreciation among Western publics of the moral and mortal hazards of war in the mass industrial age. As noted in Chapter 5, following World War II states only recognize the use of force to be lawful when it is in self-defense or is authorized by the United Nations for the purpose of maintaining international peace and security.

This normative shift away from war has not lessened the occurrence of war. As Finnemore notes: "The twentieth century was certainly one of the bloodiest on record despite eighty years of international discourse about the evils of war and attempts to curb or even outlaw war in various ways."[6] Indeed, for Martin Shaw, war increasingly "degenerated" as the twentieth century wore on, with the deliberate destruction of homelands and civilian populations. The "ethnic wars" of the late twentieth century—in Central Europe, Africa, and Asia—continued this pattern with attacks on civilians becoming the main mode of warfare (as opposed to a supplementary tactic or by-product).[7] These "new wars" have a normative dynamic of their own, combining ethnic symbolism, popular beliefs, and elite myth-making to generate lethal cocktails of fear and murderous hostility.[8] However, when it comes to the West and war (the focus of this book), the normative devaluation of war is both evident in political discourse and military practice. A new Western way of warfare has evolved in line with public expectations, legal prohibitions, and professional prescriptions of the late twentieth and early twenty-first centuries.

Not only did Western publics go off mass industrialized war following the two world wars, as the twentieth century progressed the wars that the West fought were increasingly by choice rather than necessity. This created clear political imperatives to contain the cost of such wars to the states that waged them. Where the costs could not be contained, as in the US war in Vietnam, the political fallout was considerable.[9] This growing public intolerance of war is reflected in a new style of Western warfare, what Shaw calls "risk-transfer war." Western states now seek to limit the political risks of war through use of airpower and to redirect the costs through use of locally provided proxy ground forces.[10] This was demonstrated in Kosovo when NATO sought to bomb Serbia into submission, and instead of deploying NATO ground forces relied on the Kosovo Liberation Front to generate what limited land power it could.[11] In Afghanistan, the United States also sought to limit the size of the US "combat footprint" through reliance on airpower and local proxy ground forces.[12] Where the costs cannot be contained, we may expect wars of choice to be dressed up as wars of necessity in order to achieve popular mobilization for war.

Moreover, the new Western way of war is shaped by international law. The UN Charter now provides the main legitimating framework for Western use of force. As noted in Chapter 5, Western states usually seek to situate justifications for use of force, even when force serves humanitarian ends, in the context of UN Security Council authorization. Self-defense is less often invoked by Western states because these days they rarely suffer direct attack. The new Western way of war also enacts the prescriptions contained in humanitarian law and Western military doctrine. Chief among these is the norm prohibiting the targeting of civilians. This norm was codified in the Fourth Geneva Convention of 1949, further clarified in Additional Protocol I in 1977, and is now considered a peremptory norm of customary international law.[13]

Rules of humanitarian law are also institutionalized in Western military codes, doctrine, training, and rules of engagement.[14] Chapter 2 discussed the importance of military doctrine and education in producing and diffusing technical scripts for war. As Chapter 5 showed, Western militaries now go into battle with legal advisers to ensure that they do not break international law. Indeed, the US military has embedded military lawyers in all levels of command since 1989.[15] For the most part, Western militaries do go to considerable lengths to avoid causing collateral damage even though the inadvertent killing of civilians is permitted under international law. In part, this is a happy marriage of hardware and software; that is to say, Western technological prowess and Western-derived norms of international law.[16] Western militaries can limit civilian deaths during combat because they have unprecedented capability to create discriminate destruction.[17] This greater appreciation of humanitarian law by Western military professionals also owes something to broader political and legal change. Western military chiefs and political leaders fear that their publics will not stomach operations that cause many foreign civilian deaths.[18] Chapter 5 also noted that, with the creation of the International Criminal Court, Western militaries now have instrumental reasons (i.e., fear of prosecution) for observing norms of humanitarian law.

Reflections on the Iraq War

The 2003 war with Iraq is a dramatic reminder of the fact that Western war is hardly a thing of the past. It revealed the power of norms of conventional warfare and the importance of civil society in mobilizing support for wars of choice. However, it also showed that the new norms of war do operate to delimit Western use of force.

Norms of conventional warfare were evident in the behavior of the Iraqi Army. The Iraqi military mounted a mostly conventional defense of their country, despite taking a real beating from a US-led coalition in the 1990–1991 Gulf War. They were in even worse shape in 2003 following 12 years of crippling sanctions. Predictably, Iraqi Army units were decimated in conventional engagements with US and British forces. Following the war, former members of the Iraqi regime and various Islamic militant groups have mounted a robust guerrilla insurgency against coalition forces.[19] There is some evidence to suggest that the Iraqi regime may have taken some measures to prepare for such an insurgency should their conventional defense fail.[20] However, insufficient effort was put into preparing a guerrilla-style defense of the country. Only in the run-up to the war did the Iraqi regime pull together a force of irregular troops, comprised of loyal civilians and foreign fanatics, called the fedayeen. The fedayeen were not trained or prepared for guerrilla warfare: for the most part they acted as untrained light infantry, and were slaughtered when they launched direct assaults against heavily armed US units.[21] As a poor country facing off against a military giant, the Iraqis should have fashioned a guerrilla-style defense. Indeed, the effectiveness of a more concerted effort in this regard is suggested by the continuing problems faced by the US forces in suppressing insurgency in postwar Iraq in 2005.

The 2003 Iraq war also demonstrated the importance of secondary agents in mobilizing society for war. This "war of choice" was framed as a "war of necessity" by political leaders in the United States seeking to raise support at home and abroad for the war.[22] Political and military elites also tried to generate support for the war by framing public imagination as to how it would be conducted. It was promised to be swift and precisely targeted on the regime (and not ordinary Iraqis).[23] Civil society produced both supportive impulses and sites of resistance to official efforts to frame the 2003 war. Antiwar movements around the world provided foci for widespread popular opposition to the war.[24] More influential on the American public, however, was the uncritical press coverage that served to communicate the official case for war.[25] As in World War II, war imagery was also used by various groups in civil society in order to increase the popular appeal of their rhetoric, products, and services. Thus, the war was used by corporate groups in the United States to attack environmentalists ("eco-Al-Qaida") and teachers unions ("terrorism in the classroom"), as well as to market products such as large sports utility vehicles. Such commercial activity domesticated the war for Americans and furthered the government's efforts to generate public support.[26]

The new norms of war were also in evidence in the conduct of the coalition military campaign. While fast and furious, it was restrained all the same by humanitarian law. The US military made great claims in this respect: the coalition air component commander told reporters that an operational priority in the 2003 war against Iraq was to "absolutely totally minimize the collateral damage and absolutely totally minimize the effect on the civilian population."[27] As it happens, US Central Command was subject to considerable external scrutiny when it was generating the target lists for the air campaign. A number of agencies— from the National Security Council staff to the US Agency for International Development—specified thousands of "no-strike targets," and the evolving target lists were reviewed by the secretary of defense and the president.[28] Moreover, during the campaign itself, the targeting of structures by ground forces required approval by the Coalition Land Force Component Command, Central Command, and the secretary of defense.[29]

To be sure, there has been criticism of the claimed precision of US bombing.[30] Moreover, as US ground forces pushed into Iraq they encountered circumstances—such as Iraqi irregulars and operations in urban environments—that severely tested their ability to distinguish between civilians and combatants.[31] Even more challenging have been continued military operations in postwar Iraq. The US military has left a wake of destruction in its efforts to combat the insurgency. Most notable, in this regard, is the city of Falluja. It was emptied of its 500,000 occupants and practically flattened in order to root out some 1,300 insurgents (many of whom probably escaped the city).[32] There has also been some abuse of detained Iraqis—both prisoners of war (POWs) and civilian looters—by US and UK military personnel. It is not clear whether such abuse was knowingly tolerated or even sanctioned by senior military officers; though it does seem to be the case that senior officers lacked full knowledge of the rules of the Geneva Conventions with regard to the protection of civilians and humane treatment of POWs. However, the fact that these cases of prisoner abuse have triggered international outrage and have been condemned by political leaders in the United States and Britain is indicative of the normative force of humanitarian law. In this case, norm violation has clearly resulted in norm affirmation.[33]

Ultimately, the crucial test of the impact of humanitarian law on US military operations is to look at how many civilians were killed, and compare this with previous US military campaigns. There is one alarming study in the medical journal *The Lancet* that estimates that between March 2003 (when the coalition invaded Iraq) and May 2004 there were upward of 100,000 excess deaths (mostly of women and children) as a consequence of coalition military operations.[34] However, this finding contradicts the widely cited Iraq Body Count project (IBC), which by January 2005 recorded a civilian death toll of 15,000 to 17,000.[35] In response, IBC has raised two concerns about the *Lancet* study: first that it is a "projection" of the total Iraqi death toll based on a relatively small sample survey; and second that it fails (indeed is not equipped) to distinguish between combatant and noncombatant casualties. Accordingly, IBC stands by its lower figure, which records only civilian deaths as confirmed from impartial sources (e.g., media, NGOs, hospitals, and morgues).[36] Certainly the *Lancet* figure, if accurate, would suggest that nothing has changed: US forces are still paying scant regard to international humanitarian law. But the IBC figure would appear to be more reliable. While many thousands of civilian dead is horrendous, it is a vast improvement on the campaigns waged by US forces during World War II and the Vietnam War, when many hundreds of thousands of civilians were killed. The bottom line is that Human Rights

Watch was probably right when they concluded in their overall report on the conduct of the war that "US-led coalition forces took precautions to spare civilians and, for the most part, made efforts to uphold their legal obligations."[37]

The United States is trying to expand the normative range of legitimate military action. As described in Chapter 4, the current US administration is undertaking a number of measures, including the targeting of nonnuclear states and the development of very low-yield nuclear weapons, the effect of which will be to water down the nuclear taboo. The 2003 war in Iraq is also illustrative of US efforts to widen the self-defense norm to permit use of force to prevent a threat from emerging. The United States (and Britain) went to war to disarm Iraq without explicit authorization by the UN Security Council for the use of force (they claimed an authorization from a prior resolution that was 12 years old).[38] The United States declared in its 2002 *National Security Strategy* that it had the right to use force to prevent a threat from emerging, and that this constituted lawful self-defense.[39] Preemptive self-defense (i.e., use of force against an imminent threat) is arguably legal under customary law. Preventive use of force against some future anticipated threat is clearly unlawful, however, and very few states are prepared to support any change in the law on this.[40] This message was reiterated by the UN Secretary-General, Kofi Annan, in an address to the General Assembly in September 2003. In a thinly veiled critique of the US-led war against Iraq, Annan noted that "some states" argue that they "are not obliged to wait until there is agreement in the Security Council" on emerging international threats, "instead they reserve the right to act unilaterally, or in ad hoc coalitions." Annan warned that "this logic represents a fundamental challenge to the principles on which, however imperfectly, world peace and stability have rested for fifty years."[41] The Secretary-General's High-Level Panel on Threats, Challenges and Change has similarly found that "the risk to the global order and the norm of nonintervention on which it continues to be based is simply too great for the legality of unilateral preventive action, as distinct from collectively endorsed action, to be accepted."[42]

The political fallout from Iraq, and international rejection of the legality of preventive use of force, demonstrate the limit of US hegemony. To secure itself, the United States needs allies, and accordingly needs to work within accepted norms of international society.[43] In short, might does not make right in world politics; norms have a power of their own.

Conclusion

Any treatment of norms and war invites grand observations. To be sure, recent history shows progress in the decline of Western warfare. There is a substantial literature suggesting that much of this has to do with the growth of stable liberal democracy in the West.[44] Liberal norms and democratic institutions provide a potent mix for peace.[45] While liberal democracies are still capable of acts of great violence, they show less warlike tendencies (especially toward each other) and more civility than do autocratic regimes.[46] Further progress is possible, however.[47] This is certainly true in terms of how the West uses force. For example, the extraordinary care taken to avoid civilian deaths in NATO's Kosovo campaign was less evident in the subsequent US campaign in Afghanistan, where less than half as many air missions produced over twice as many civilian dead. The total number of civilians killed by the US military in Afghanistan—approximately 1,000 to 1,300—was still remarkably low for a major war. The point is, however, the Kosovo campaign showed that the US military could probably have done better.[48] Progress may also be hampered by the US ambivalence toward international law. Sometimes the United States is a vital defender of the rule of law in world politics. On other occasions its actions threatened to undermine particular legal rules.[49] The current US effort to create a norm permitting it to engage in preventive use of force is one such worrying example. Perhaps it is understandable that the United States should want to adapt the postwar legal order—one designed to accommodate a number of great powers—to better suit the unipolar world. Ultimately, however, as Lawrence Freedman notes, the United States cannot have its cake and eat it too: "If [the United States] wants to encourage a restrictive framework when it comes to the use of force then it cannot claim a permissive one for itself."[50]

The main point of this book is not to make sweeping generalizations, however.[51] Rather it is to make the case for an interdisciplinary approach to uncovering the role of norms in modern warfare. Norms directly impact how states organize for war, mobilize for war, and conduct war. Sometimes norms are supported by interests and incentives, and sometimes they defy material power. Sometimes norms produce military efficiency, and sometimes they result in suboptimal and even suicidal military activity. In short, no scholar or student of war can afford to ignore the causal force of norms.

This book has pointed to vibrant literatures in political science, sociology, history, and law on norms and war. These various literatures demonstrate norms operating at multiple levels above and within states to shape military activity. They show a variety of agents involved in creating and enacting norms of war. They reveal norms interacting with the material things (military technology) and clashing with each other. The normative fabric of war is thick and remarkably complex. This book has suggested some rules of the road for scholars wishing to navigate this potentially bewildering social world. Recognize that norms may act both as moral codes and technical scripts for war. Be attentive to the causal mechanisms that make norms work, and look out for enabling conditions for normative change. Finally, home in on particular norms and track their causal effect through case studies. My hope is that through such careful interdisciplinary scholarship we can build a better foundation from which to generalize about norms and war, not just in the West, but also across the world.

Notes

1. Kimberly Zisk argues that competitor states may even engage in "doctrinal races" as each reacts to military developments in the other. Kimberly Martin Zisk, *Engaging the Enemy: Organization Theory and Soviet Military Development, 1955–1991* (Princeton, NJ: Princeton University Press, 1993).

2. Paul Kowert and Jeffrey Legro, "Norms, Identity and Their Limits: A Theoretical Reprise," in Peter J. Katzenstein (ed.), *The Culture of National Security: Norms and Identity in World Politics* (New York: Columbia University Press, 1996), pp. 488–490.

3. Martha Finnemore, *The Purpose of Intervention: Changing Beliefs About the Use of Force* (Ithaca, NY: Cornell University Press, 2003), p. 19. A good illustration of this trend is European use of force to recover debt from non-European states, a common practice before the twentieth century. Finnemore shows how this was outlawed in 1907 and steadily fell into disuse thereafter.

4. John Mueller, *The Remnants of War* (Ithaca, NY: Cornell University Press, 2004), p. 161.

5. Finnemore's book also echoes *The Norms of War* in its discussion of the mechanisms of normative change as encompassing coercion and inducement, persuasion and social learning, and the agents of change as including states, transnational professional networks (of lawyers), and social movements (human rights and antiwar advocacy groups). See Finnemore, *The Purpose,* pp. 141–162.

6. Ibid., p. 19.

7. Martin Shaw, *War and Genocide* (Cambridge: Polity, 2003).

8. Mary Kaldor, *New and Old Wars: Organized Violence in a Global Era* (Cambridge: Polity, 1999); Stuart J. Kaufman, *Modern Hatreds: The Symbolic Politics of Ethnic War* (Ithaca, NY: Cornell University Press, 2001). These "new wars" are also sustained by a political economy that combines cheap military labor, natural resource exploitation, and the free transborder flow of illegal goods, which lowers the cost of war and raises the price of peace. See Herfried Munkler, *The New Wars* (Cambridge: Polity, 2005).

9. Robert D. Schulzinger, *A Time for War: The United States and Vietnam, 1941–1975* (Oxford: Oxford University Press, 1997).

10. Shaw, *War,* pp. 238–240. See also Elliot A. Cohen, "The Mystique of US Air Power," *Foreign Affairs* 73, no. 1 (1994): 109–124.

11. Daniel A. Byman and Matthew C. Waxman, "Kosovo and the Great Air Power Debate," *International Security* 24, no. 4 (2000): 5–38.

12. Colin McInnes, "A Different Kind of War? September 11 and the United States' Afghan War," *Review of International Studies* 29, no. 2 (2003): 165–184.

13. Malcolm N. Shaw, *International Law,* 5th ed. (Cambridge: Cambridge University Press, 2003), pp. 1061–1064.

14. See, for example, The International and Operational Law Department, Judge Advocate General's School, US Army, *Operational Law Handbook* (2002); US Army, AR 3504-41, *Training in Units* (19 March 1993), chapter 14; Chairman, US Joint Chiefs of Staff, Instruction 3121.01A, *Standing Rules of Engagement for US Forces*

(15 January 2000); North Atlantic Military Committee, MC 362 encl. 1, *NATO Rules of Engagement* (9 November 1999).

15. Charles J. Dunlap Jr., "Law and Military Interventions: Preserving Humanitarian Values in Twenty-first Century Conflicts," working paper, Project on the Means of Intervention, Carr Center for Human Rights Policy, Harvard University, http://www.ksg.harvard.edu/cchrp/UseofForcePapers.shtml, 16–17. The impact of embedding Judge Advocate General's Corps officers on US military operations is well explored in Michael W. Lewis, "The Law of Aerial Bombardment in the 1991 Gulf War," *American Journal of International Law* 97, no. 3 (2003): 481–509.

16. Thomas W. Smith, "The New Law of War: Legitimating Hi-Tech and Infrastructural Violence," *International Studies Quarterly* 46, no. 3 (2002): 355–374.

17. This is especially true of the United States. See Benjamin S. Lambert, *The Transformation of American Air Power* (Ithaca, NY: Cornell University Press, 2000).

18. In fact, US policy and military elites are more sensitive to this issue than US public opinion, which is quite tolerant of foreign civilian casualties. See Alan Vick et al., *Aerospace Operations in Urban Environments: Exploring New Concepts*, RAND report MR-1187-AF (2000), pp. 52–69, http://www.rand.org/publications/MR/MR1187/.

19. "US Faces Complex Insurgency in Iraq," 5 October 2004, http://www.military.com/.

20. Bryan Bender, "Study Ties Hussein, Guerrilla Strategy," *Boston Globe,* 11 October 2004, http://www.boston.com/.

21. Williamson Murray and Robert H. Scales Jr., *The Iraq War: A Military History* (Cambridge, MA: Belknap Press of Harvard University Press, 2003), p. 84. On feyadeen tactics, see pp. 213–216, 1001–1002; see also David Zucchino, *Thunder Run: Three Days in the Battle for Baghdad* (London: Atlantic, 2005).

22. David Usborne, "WMD Just a Convenient Excuse for War, Admits Wolfowitz," *The Independent,* 30 May 2003, p. 5. A special agency called the Office of Special Plans was set up by US defense secretary Donald Rumsfeld for the express purpose of selecting intelligence that could be used to make the case for war against Iraq. See Julian Borger, "The Spies Who Pushed for War," *The Guardian,* 17 July 2003, pp. 1–2. The official case for war with Iraq is carefully and comprehensively critiqued in Anup Shah, "Media, Propaganda and Iraq," 30 March 2003, http://www.globalissues.org/HumanRights/Media/Propaganda.

23. Kathleen T. Rhem, "US Military Works to Avoid Civilian Deaths, Collateral Damage," American Armed Forces Information Service, 5 March 2003; "DOD News: Background Briefing on Targeting," 5 March 2003, both at http://www.defenselink.mil/news/Mar2003/.

24. For a guide to the antiwar movements, see http://www.guardian.co.uk/antiwar/. For some specific antiwar movement websites, see http://www.stopwar.org.uk/; http://www.votenowar.org/; http://www.peacepledge.org/. On the increasingly transnational nature of popular opposition movements, see Roland Bleiker, *Popular Dissent, Human Agency and Global Politics* (Cambridge: Cambridge University Press, 2000).

25. *Correspondent: War Spin,* BBC2 documentary, broadcast 16 May 2003; see also Kate Holton, "Embedding Hampered Iraq Media Independence," *Reuters,* 30 January 2004, http://www.reuters.com/.

26. Sheldon Rampton and John Stauber, *Weapons of Mass Distraction: The Uses of Propaganda in Bush's War on Iraq* (London: Robinson, 2003), pp. 131–160.

27. News Transcript, US Department of Defense, News Briefing, Lieutenant-General Michael Moseley, CFACC, 5 April 2003 (Pentagon–Saudi Arabia Two-Way Briefing), http://www.usinfo.state.gov/topical/pol/terror/texts/03040502.htm.

28. Bob Woodward, *Plan of Attack* (New York: Simon and Schuster, 2004), pp. 277–278, 331–332.

29. Third Infantry Division (Mechanized), *After Action Report: Operation Iraqi Freedom* (July 2003), p. 287, http://www.globalsecurity.org/military/ops/oif-lessons-learned.htm.

30. See, for example, Peter Spang Goodrich, "The Surgical Precision Myth: After the Bomb Explodes," 11 June 2003, http://www.providence.edu/mba/goodrich/war/surgical/.

31. Anthony Dworkin, "Guerrilla War, 'Deadly Deception,' and Urban Combat," Crimes of War Project, 26 March 2003, http://www.crimesofwar.org/print/onnews/iraq-guerrilla-print.html. See also Evan Wright, *Generation Kill: Living Dangerous on the Road to Baghdad with the Ultraviolent Marines of Bravo Company* (Bantam Press, 2004).

32. Ali Fadhil, "City of Ghosts," *The Guardian,* 11 January 2005, G2 supplement, pp. 1–5.

33. Vicki Allen, "Senators Grill Military on Prison Abuses," *Reuters,* 11 May 2004, http://www.reuters.com/; Audrey Gillan, "Shocking Images Revealed at Britain's 'Abu Ghraib Trial,'" *The Guardian,* 19 January 2005, p. 1.

34. Lee Roberts, Riyadh Lafta, Richard Garfield, Jamal Khudhairi, and Gilbert Burnham, "Mortality Before and After the 2003 Invasion of Iraq: Cluster Sample Survey," *The Lancet* (published online 29 October 2004), pp. 1–8, http://image.thelancet.com/extras/04art10342web.pdf.

35. Civilian body count as of 4 January 2005, http://www.iraqbodycount.net/.

36. IBC Press Release, "IBC Response to the Lancet Study Estimating '100,000' Iraqi Deaths," PR10, 7 November 2004, http://www.iraqbodycount.net/press.

37. Human Rights Watch, *Off Target: The Conduct of the War and Civilian Casualties in Iraq* (New York, December 2003), p. 5, http://www.hrw.org/reports/2003/usa1203/. The report does criticize the coalition, however, for using millions of submunitions that do not explode on impact, for launching counterleadership air strikes in populated areas, and for targeting dual-use facilities such as power stations.

38. Adam Roberts, "Law and the Use of Force After Iraq," *Survival* 45, no. 2 (2003): 39–45.

39. *The National Security Strategy of the United States of America* (Washington, DC: 2002), p. 15, http://www.whitehouse.gov/nsc/nss.html.

40. Only Russia, Israel, and Australia have supported this new formulation of the right of preemptive self-defense. Michael Byers, "Preemptive Self-Defense: Hegemony, Equality and Strategies of Legal Change," draft paper, 2003, p. 12. See also Roberts, "Law and the Use of Force After Iraq," pp. 45–48. On the blurring of the distinction between preemptive and preventive use of force, see Jeffrey Record, "The Bush Doctrine and War with Iraq," *Parameters* (Spring 2003): 3–4, http://carlislewww.army.mil/usawc/Parameters/03spring/record.htm.

41. "The Secretary-General Address to the General Assembly," New York, 23 September 2003, p. 2, http://www.un.org/webcast/ga/58/statements/sgeng030923.htm.

42. Report of the Secretary-General's High-Level Panel on Threats, Challenges, and Change, *A More Secure World: Our Shared Responsibility* (New York: United Nations, 2004), paragraph 191, p. 63.

43. This is argued in Antony J. Blinken, "From Preemption to Engagement," *Survival* 45, no. 4 (2003–2004): 33–60; see also Christian Reus-Smit, *American Power and World Order* (Cambridge: Polity, 2004). The benefits of institutional restraint for hegemonic powers is explored historically in G. John Ikenberry, *After Victory: Institu-*

tions, Strategic Restraint, and the Rebuilding of Order After Major Wars (Princeton, NJ: Princeton University Press, 2001).

44. Key works in this literature include Michael Doyle, "Liberalism and World Politics," *American Political Science Review* 80, no. 4 (1986): 1152–1169; Zeev Maoz and Bruce Russett, "Normative and Structural Causes of Democratic Peace," *American Political Science Review* 87, no. 3 (1993): 624–638; Bruce Russett, *Grasping the Democratic Peace* (Princeton, NJ: Princeton University Press, 1993).

45. The importance of this mix is emphasized in John M. Owen, "How Liberalism Produces Democratic Peace," *International Security* 19, no. 2 (1994): 87–125.

46. The "civility" of democracies is explored in John Keane, *Violence and Democracy* (Cambridge: Cambridge University Press, 2004).

47. In an ironic twist, Christopher Coker suggests that too much progress in this regard might be counterproductive. He argues that as Western states take measures to reduce the human costs of war (to home societies and target states) they are likely to become "re-enchanted" with war. See Coker's provocative *The Future of War: The Re-Enchantment of War in the Twenty-First Century* (Oxford: Blackwell, 2004).

48. Anthony Burke, "Just War or Ethical Peace? Moral Discourses of Strategic Violence After 9/11," *International Affairs* 80, no. 2 (2004): 342–343. See also Carl Conetta, *Strange Victory: A Critical Appraisal of Operation Enduring Freedom and the Afghanistan War* (Cambridge, MA: Commonwealth Institute Project on Defense Alternatives, 2002), http://www.comw.org/pda/0201strangevic.pdf.

49. This overall conclusion is offered in John F. Murphy, *The United States and the Rule of Law in International Affairs* (Cambridge: Cambridge University Press, 2004); Shirley V. Scott, "Is There Room for International Law in *Realpolitik*? Accounting for the US 'Attitude' Towards International Law," *Review of International Studies* 30, no. 1 (2004): 71–88.

50. Lawrence Freedman, *Deterrence* (Cambridge: Polity, 2004), p. 108.

51. The classic study on the dangers of stereotyping military cultures is Ken Booth, *Strategy and Ethnocentrism* (London: Croom Helm, 1979).

Bibliography

Abbott, Kenneth, and Duncan Snidal. "Hard and Soft Law in International Governance," *International Organization* 54, no. 3 (2000): 421–456.

Acharya, Amitav. "How Ideas Spread: Whose Norms Matter? Norm Localization and Institutional Change in Asian Regionalism," *International Organization* 58, no. 2 (2004): 239–275.

Addison, P., and A. Calder (eds.). *Time to Kill: The Soldier's Experience of War in the West, 1939–1945*. London: Pimlico, 1997.

Allen, Vicki. "Rumsfeld Pushes for New Nuclear Weapons Study," *Reuters,* 20 May 2003. Available at http://www.reuters.com/.

Allison, Graham T. *The Essence of Decision*. Boston: Little, Brown, 1973.

Almond, Gabriel A., and Sidney Verba. *The Civic Culture: Political Attitudes and Democracy in Five Nations*. Princeton, NJ: Princeton University Press, 1963.

Alperovitz, Gar. *The Decision to Use the Atomic Bomb*. London: Fontana, 1996.

Alperovitz, Gar, Robert L. Messer, and Barton J. Bernstein. "Correspondence: Marshall, Truman, and the Decision to Drop the Bomb," *International Security* 16, no. 3 (1991–1992): 204–221.

Amnesty International. *NATO/Federal Republic of Yugoslavia: "Collateral Damage" or Unlawful Killings?* June, AL Index: EUR 70/18/00, 2000.

Appell, David. "Ground Below Zero," *Scientific American.Com*, 17 June 2002. Available at http://www.sciam.com/.

Archer, Christon I., et al. *World History of Warfare*. Lincoln: University of Nebraska Press, 2002.

Arend, Anthony Clark. *Legal Rules and International Society*. Oxford: Oxford University Press, 1999.

Arkin, William M. "Secret Plan Outlines the Unthinkable," *Los Angeles Times,* 10 March 2002.

Armstrong, David, Theo Farrell, and Bice Maiguashca (eds.). *Governance and Resistance in World Politics*. Cambridge: Cambridge University Press, 2003.

Arreguín-Toft, Ivan. "How the Weak Win Wars: A Theory of Asymmetric Conflict," *International Security* 26, no. 1 (2001): 93–128.

Ashplant, T. G., Graham Dawson, and Michael Roper (eds.). *The Politics of War Memory and Commemoration*. London: Routledge, 2000.

Aubin, Stephen P. "Operation Allied Force: War or 'Coercive Diplomacy'?" *Strategic Review* 6 (Summer 1999): 4–12.

Augusteijn, Joost. *From Public Defiance to Guerrilla Warfare*. Dublin: Irish Academic Press, 1996.

Avant, Deborah D. *Political Institutions and Military Change*. Ithaca, NY: Cornell University Press, 1994.

———. "From Mercenaries to Citizen Armies: Explaining Change in the Practice of War," *International Organization* 54, no. 1 (2000): 41–72.

Axelrod, Robert. "An Evolutionary Approach to Norms," *American Political Science Review* 80, no. 4 (1986): 1095–1111.

Badie, Bertrand. *The Imported State: The Westernization of the Political Order*. Stanford, CA: Stanford University Press, 2000.

Baer, George W. *One Hundred Years of Sea Power: The US Navy, 1890–1990*. Stanford, CA: Stanford University Press, 1994.

Ball, Desmond. *Targeting for Strategic Deterrence*, Alephi Paper 185. London: International Institute for Strategic Studies, 1983.

Barkawi, Tarak. "Peoples, Homelands, and Wars? Ethnicity, the Military, and Battle Among British Imperial Forces in the War Against Japan," *Comparative Studies in Society and History* 46, no. 1 (2004): 132–163.

Barkin, J. Samuel, and Bruce Cronin. "The State and the Nation: Changing Norms and the Rules of Sovereignty in International Relations," *International Organization* 48, no. 1 (1994): 107–130.

Bartov, Omer. *Germany's War and the Holocaust*. Ithaca, NY: Cornell University Press, 2003.

———. *Hitler's Army: Soldiers, Nazis, and War in the Third Reich*. Oxford: Oxford University Press, 1992.

———. "Trauma and Absence: France and Germany, 1914–1945," in P. Addison and A. Calder, eds., *Time to Kill: The Soldier's Experience of War in the West, 1939–1945*. London: Pimlico, 1997.

Bender, Bryan. "Study Ties Hussein, Guerrilla Strategy," *Boston Globe*, 11 October 2004. Available at http://www.boston.com/.

Benvenuti, Paolo. "The ICTY Prosecutor and the Review of the NATO Bombing Campaign Against the Federal Republic of Yugoslavia," *European Journal of International Law* 12, no. 3 (2001): 503–529.

Berger, Thomas U. *Cultures of Antimilitarism: National Security in Germany and Japan*. Baltimore: Johns Hopkins University Press, 1998.

———. "Norms, Identity, and National Security in Germany and Japan" in Peter J. Katzenstein, ed., *The Culture of National Security*. New York: Columbia University Press, 1996.

———. "The Power of Memory and Memories of Power: The Cultural Parameters of German Foreign Policy-Making Since 1945," in Jan-Werner Muller, ed., *Memory and Power in Post-War Europe*. Cambridge: Cambridge University Press, 2002.

Bernstein, Barton J. "Eclipsed by Hiroshima and Nagasaki: Early Thinking About Tactical Nuclear Weapons," *International Security* 15, no. 4 (1991): 149–173.

———. "Seizing the Contested Terrain of Early Nuclear History: Stimson, Conant, and Their Allies Explain the Decision to Use the Atomic Bomb," *Diplomatic History* 17 (1993): 35–72.

Best, Geoffrey. *Humanity in Warfare*. London: Weidenfeld and Nicolson, 1980.

Biddle, Tami Davis. "British and American Approaches to Strategic Bombing: Their Origins and Implementation in the World War II Combined Bomber Offensive," *Journal of Strategic Studies* 18, no. 1 (1995): 91–144.

———. *Rhetoric and Reality in Air Warfare: The Evolution of British and American*

Ideas About Strategic Bombing, 1914–1945. Princeton, NJ: Princeton University Press, 2002.

Bijker, Wiebe E., Thomas P. Hughes, and Trevor J. Pinch (eds.). *The Social Construction of Technological Systems: New Directions in the Sociology and History of Technology*. Cambridge, MA: MIT, 1987.

Bird, Chris. "KLA to Give Birth to Kosovo's New Army," *The Guardian,* 3 September 1999.

Blair, Bruce G. *The Logic of Accidental Nuclear War.* Washington, DC: Brookings Institution, 1993.

Blair, Bruce G., John E. Pike, and Stephen L. Schwartz. "Targeting and Controlling the Bomb," in Stephen I. Schwartz, ed., *Atomic Audit*. Washington, DC: Brookings Institution, 1998.

Bleiker, Roland. *Popular Dissent, Human Agency and Global Politics*. Cambridge: Cambridge University Press, 2000.

Blinken, Antony J. "From Preemption to Engagement," *Survival* 45, no. 4 (2003–2004): 33–60.

Boemeke, Manfred F., Roger Chickering, and Stig Forster (eds.). *Anticipating Total War: The German and American Experiences, 1871–1914*. Cambridge: Cambridge University Press, 1999.

Boli, John, and George M. Thomas (eds.). *Constructing World Culture*. Stanford, CA: Stanford University Press, 1999.

Booth, Ken. *Strategy and Ethnocentrism*. London: Croom Helm, 1979.

Booth, Ken, and Russell Trood (eds.). *Strategic Cultures in the Asia-Pacific Region*. New York: St. Martin's, 1999.

Borger, Julian. "The Spies Who Pushed for War," *The Guardian,* 17 July 2003.

Bothe, Michael. "Terrorism and the Legality of Pre-emptive Force," *European Journal of International Law* 14, no. 2 (2003): 227–240.

Bowden, Tom. "The Irish Underground and the War of Independence, 1919–1921," *Journal of Contemporary History* 8 (1973): 3–23.

Boyer, Paul. *By the Bomb's Early Light: American Thought and Culture at the Dawn of the Atomic Age,* 2nd ed. Chapel Hill: University of North Carolina Press, 1994.

———. "Exotic Resonances: Hiroshima in American Memory," *Diplomatic History* 19, no. 2 (1995): 297–318.

Bright, Charles, and Susan Harding (eds.). *Statemaking and Social Movements*. Ann Arbor: University of Michigan Press, 1984.

Brodie, Bernard. *War and Politics*. London: Cassell, 1973.

Brodie, Bernard (ed.). *The Absolute Weapon: Atomic Power and World Order.* New York: Harcourt, Brace, 1946.

Brooks, Risa. "Institutions at the Domestic/International Nexus: The Political-Military Origins of Strategic Integration, Military Effectiveness and War." Ph.D. dissertation, University of California, San Diego, 2000.

Broscious, S. David. "Longing for International Control, Banking on Superiority: Harry S. Truman's Approach to Nuclear Weapons," in John Lewis Gaddis et al., eds., *Cold War Statesmen Confront the Bomb: Nuclear Diplomacy Since 1945*. Oxford: Oxford University Press, 1999.

Browley, Mark, David Grahame, and Christine Kucia. *Bunker Busters: Washington's Drive for New Nuclear Weapons*. BASIC Research Report, Washington, DC: British American Security Information Council, July 2002.

Brown, M. Kathryn, and Travis W. Stanton (eds.). *Ancient Mesoamerican Warfare*. Lanham, MD: Altamira, 2003.

Brownlie, Ian (1998). *Principles of Public International Law,* 5th ed. Oxford: Oxford University Press, 1998.

Buchanan, Allen. "Reforming the International Law of Humanitarian Intervention," in J. L. Holzgrefe and Robert O. Keohane, eds., *Humanitarian Intervention: Ethical, Legal, and Political Dilemmas.* Cambridge: Cambridge University Press, 2003.

Bucholz, Arden (ed.). *Moltke, Schlieffen, and Prussian War Planning.* New York: Berg, 1990.

Buhl, Lance C. "Maintaining an American Navy, 1865–1873," in Kenneth J. Hagan, ed., *In Peace and War: Interpretations of American Naval History, 1775–1984,* 2nd ed. Westport, CT: Greenwood, 1984.

Bundy, McGeorge. *Danger and Survival: Choices About the Bomb in the First Fifty Years.* New York: Random House, 1988.

———. "Early Thoughts on Controlling the Nuclear Arms Race: A Report to the Secretary of State, January 1953," *International Security* 7, no. 2 (1982): 3–27.

Bundy, McGeorge, George F. Kennan, Robert S. McNamara, and Gerard Smith. "Nuclear Weapons and the Atlantic Alliance," *Foreign Affairs* 60, no. 4 (1982): 753–768.

Burk, James. "Public Support for Peacekeeping in Lebanon and Somalia: Assessing the Casualties Hypothesis," *Political Science Quarterly* 114 (1999): 53–78.

Burke, Anthony. "Just War or Ethical Peace: Moral Discourses of Strategic Violence After 9/11," *International Affairs* 80, no. 2 (2004): 329–353.

Burke, Joanna. *An Intimate History of Killing.* London: Granta, 1999.

Burr, William, and Jeffrey T. Richelson. "Whether to 'Strangle the Baby in the Cradle': The United States and the Chinese Nuclear Program, 1960–1964," *International Security* 25, no. 3 (Winter 2000–2001): 54–99.

Buzan, Barry, and Eric Herring. *The Arms Dynamic in World Politics.* Boulder, CO: Lynne Rienner, 1998.

Buzan, Barry, and Ole Waever. *Regions and Powers: The Structure of International Security.* Cambridge: Cambridge University Press, 2003.

Byers, Michael. *Custom, Power and the Power of Rules.* Cambridge: Cambridge University Press, 1999.

———. "Preemptive Self-Defense: Hegemony, Equality and Strategies of Legal Change." Draft paper, 2003.

Byers, Michael (ed.). *The Role of Law in International Relations: Essays in International Relations and International Law.* Oxford: Oxford University Press, 2000.

Byers, Michael, and Simon Chesterman. "Changing the Rules About the Rules? Unilateral Humanitarian Intervention and the Future of International Law," in J. L. Holzgrefe and Robert O. Keohane, eds., *Humanitarian Intervention: Ethical, Legal, and Political Dilemmas.* Cambridge: Cambridge University Press, 2003.

Byman, Daniel A., and Matthew C. Waxman. "Kosovo and the Great Air Power Debate," *International Security* 24, no. 4 (2000): 5–38.

Cameron, Craig M. *American Samurai: Myth, Imagination and the Conduct of Battle in the First Marine Division, 1941–1951.* Cambridge: Cambridge University Press, 1994.

Campbell, David. "Cultural Governance and Pictorial Resistance," in David Armstrong, Theo Farrell, and Bice Maiguashca, eds., *Governance and Resistance in World Politics.* Cambridge: Cambridge University Press, 2003.

Cassese, Antonio. "A Follow-Up: Forcible Humanitarian Countermeasures and *Opinio Nessitatis,*" *European Journal of International Law* 10, no. 4 (1999): 791–799.

———. *International Criminal Law.* Oxford: Oxford University Press, 2003.

————. *International Law,* 2nd ed. Oxford: Oxford University Press, 2005.
Chairman, US Joint Chiefs of Staff. Instruction 3121.01A, *Standing Rules of Engagement for US Forces.* 15 January 2000.
Chambers II, John Whiteclay. "American Debate over Modern War, 1871–1914," in Manfred F. Boemeke, Roger Chickering, and Stig Forster, eds., *Anticipating Total War: The German and American Experiences, 1871–1914.* Cambridge: Cambridge University Press, 1999.
Charney, Jonathan I. "Anticipatory Humanitarian Intervention in Kosovo," *American Journal of International Law* 93, no. 4 (1999): 834–841.
Chayes, Abram, and Antonia Handler Chayes. *The New Sovereignty: Compliance with International Regulatory Agreements.* Cambridge, MA: Harvard University Press, 1995.
Checkel, Jeffrey T. "The Constructivist Turn in International Relations Theory," *World Politics* 50, no. 2 (1998): 324–348.
————. "International Norms and Domestic Politics: Bridging the Rationalist-Constructivist Divide," *European Journal of International Relations* 3, no. 4 (1997): 473–495.
————. "Norms, Institutions and National Identity in Contemporary Europe," *International Studies Quarterly* 43, no. 1 (1999): 83–114.
————. "Social Constructivisms in Global and European Politics," *Review of International Studies* 30, no. 2 (2002): 229–245.
Chickering, Roger. "Total War: The Use and Abuse of a Concept," in Manfred F. Boemeke, Roger Chickering, and Stig Forster, eds., *Anticipating Total War: The German and American Experiences, 1871–1914.* Cambridge: Cambridge University Press, 1999.
Chickering, Roger, and Stig Forster (eds.). *Great War, Total War: Combat and Mobilization on the Western Front, 1914–1918.* Cambridge: Cambridge University Press, 2000.
Christensen, Thomas J. *Useful Adversaries.* Princeton, NJ: Princeton University Press, 1996.
Cillessen, Bret J. "Embracing the Bomb: Ethics, Morality, and Nuclear Deterrence in the US Air Force, 1945–1955," *Journal of Strategic Studies* 21 (1998): 99–103.
Clark, Ann Marie. *Diplomacy of Conscience: Amnesty International and Changing Human Rights Norms.* Ithaca, NY: Cornell University Press, 2001.
Clark, Anthony Arend. *Legal Rules and International Society.* Oxford: Oxford University Press, 1999.
Clark, Wesley K. *Waging Modern War: Bosnia, Kosovo, and the Future of Conflict.* New York: Public Affairs, 2001.
Clarke, I. F. "Future-War Fiction: The First Main Phase, 1871–1900," *Science Fiction Studies* 24, no. 3 (1997). Available from http://www.depauw.edu/sfs/clarkeess.htm.
————. *Voices Prophesying War: Future Wars, 1763–3749,* 2nd ed., Oxford: Oxford University Press, 1992.
Clodfelter, Mark. *The Limits of Air Power: The American Bombing of North Vietnam.* New York: Free Press, 1989.
CNN Web Report. "Capitol Hill Pushes for Cost of Kosovo," 15 April 1999. Available at http://www.cnn.com/ALLPOLITICS/stories/1999/04/15/kosovo.costs/.
Cohen, Elliot A. "The Mystique of US Air Power," *Foreign Affairs* 73, no. 1 (1994): 109–124.
Cohen, Stephen P. *The Indian Army: Its Contribution to the Development of a Nation.* Oxford: Oxford University Press, 1990.

Coker, Christopher. *The Future of War: The Re-Enchantment of War in the Twenty-First Century.* Oxford: Blackwell, 2004.
──────. *Humane Warfare.* London: Routledge, 2001.
Conetta, Carl. *Strange Victory: A Critical Appraisal of Operation Enduring Freedom and the Afghanistan War.* Cambridge, MA: Commonwealth Institute Project on Defense Alternatives, 2002. Available at http://www.comw.org/pda/0201strangevic.pdf.
Cope, John A. *International Military Education and Training: An Assessment,* McNair Paper no. 44. Washington, DC: National Defense University, Institute for National Strategic Studies, 1995.
Correspondent: War Spin. BBC2 documentary broadcast, 16 May 2003.
Cortell, Andrew P., and James W. Davis Jr. "How Do International Institutions Matter? The Domestic Impact of International Rules and Norms," *International Studies Quarterly* 40 (1996): 451–478.
──────. "Understanding the Domestic Impact of International Norms: A Research Agenda," *International Studies Review* 2, no. 1 (2000): 65–90.
Council for a Liveable World. "20 Experts Urge Senate to Reject Nuclear Earth Penetrator Funds," 20 June 2002. Available at http://www.clw.org/.
Craig, Campbell. *Glimmer of a New Leviathan: Total War in the Realism of Niebuhr, Morgenthau, and Waltz.* New York: Columbia University Press, 2003.
Crawford, Neta C. *Argument and Change in World Politics: Ethics, Decolonization and Humanitarian Intervention.* Cambridge: Cambridge University Press, 2002.
Curtin, Philip D. *The World and the West: The European Challenge and the Overseas Response in the Age of Empire.* Cambridge: Cambridge University Press, 2002.
Daalder, Ivo H., and Michael E. O'Hanlon. *Winning Ugly: NATO's War to Save Kosovo.* Washington, DC: Brookings Institution, 2000.
Danopoulos, Constantine P. (ed.). *From Military to Civilian Rule.* London: Routledge, 1992.
Dean Jr., Eric. *Shook over Hell: Post-Traumatic Stress, Vietnam and the Civil War.* Cambridge, MA: Harvard University Press, 1997.
Declaration of the Group of 77 South Summit. Havana, Cuba, 10–14 April 2000. Available at http://www.g77.org/Declaration_G77Summit.htm.
Deist, Wilhelm. "Strategy and Unlimited Warfare in Germany: Moltke, Falkenhayn, and Ludendorff," in Roger Chickering and Stig Forster, eds., *Great War, Total War: Combat and Mobilization on the Western Front, 1914–1918.* Cambridge: Cambridge University Press, 2000.
Demchak, Chris. "Complexity and Theory of Networked Militaries," in Theo Farrell and Terry Terriff, eds., *The Sources of Military Change: Culture, Politics, Technology.* Boulder, CO: Lynne Rienner, 2002.
──────. "Creating the Enemy: Structuration, Adaptation and Autopoesis in the International Military Community." Unpublished manuscript, n.d.
──────. *Military Organizations, Complex Machines: Modernization and the US Armed Services.* Ithaca, NY: Cornell University Press, 1991.
Dening, B. C. "Problems of Guerrilla Warfare," *An t-Óglách* (October 1927): 45–50.
Diamond, Larry, and Mark F. Plattner (eds.). *Civil-Military Relations and Democracy.* Baltimore: Johns Hopkins University Press, 1996.
DiMaggio, Paul J., and Walter W. Powell. "Introduction," in Walter W. Powell and Paul J. DiMaggio, eds., *The New Institutionalism in Organizational Analysis.* Chicago: University of Chicago Press, 1991.
──────. "The Iron Cage Revisited: Institutional Isomorphism and Collective Rationality in Organizational Fields," in Walter W. Powell and Paul J. DiMaggio, eds.,

The New Institutionalism in Organizational Analysis. Chicago: University of Chicago Press, 1991.

Dinstein, Yoram. *War, Aggression and Self-Defence*, 2nd ed. Cambridge: Cambridge University Press, 1994.

Dittmer, Lowell. "Political Culture and Political Symbolism: Toward a Theoretical Synthesis," *World Politics* 29, no. 4 (1977): 552–583.

Doorn, Jacques van. *The Soldier and Social Change: Comparative Studies in the History and Sociology of the Military*. Beverly Hills, CA: Sage, 1975.

Doubler, Michael D. *Closing with the Enemy: How GIs Fought the War in Europe, 1944–1945*. Lawrence: University Press of Kansas, 1994.

Dower, John W. "The Bombed: Hiroshima and Nagasaki in Japanese Memory," *Diplomatic History* 19 (1995): 275–296.

———. *War Without Mercy: Race and Power in the Pacific War*. New York: Pantheon, 1986.

Doyle, Michael. "Liberalism and World Politics," *American Political Science Review* 80, no. 4 (1986): 1152–1169.

Duffield, John S. *Power Rules: The Evolution of NATO's Conventional Force Structure*. Stanford, CA: Stanford University Press, 1995.

———. *World Power Forsaken: Political Culture, International Institutions, and German Security Policy After Unification*. Stanford, CA: Stanford University Press, 1998.

Duggan, John P. *A History of the Irish Army* Dublin: Gill and Macmillan, 1991.

Dunlap Jr., Charles J. "Law and Military Interventions: Preserving Humanitarian Values in Twenty-first Century Conflicts." Working paper, Project on the Means of Intervention, Carr Center for Human Rights Policy, Harvard University, 2002. Available at http://www.ksg.harvard.edu/cchrp/UseofForcePapers.shtml.

Dunne, Tim. "'When the Shooting Starts': Atlanticism in British Security Strategy," *International Affairs* 80, no. 5 (2004): 811–833.

Eden, Lynn. "Capitalist Conflict and the State: The Making of United States Military Policy in 1948," in Charles Bright and Susan Harding, eds., *Statemaking and Social Movements*. Ann Arbor: University of Michigan Press, 1984.

———. *Whole World on Fire: Organizations, Knowledge and Nuclear Weapons Devastation*. Ithaca, NY: Cornell University Press, 2004.

Edkins, Jenny. *Trauma and the Memory of Politics*. Cambridge: Cambridge University Press, 2003.

Elman, Colin, and Miriam Fendius Elman (eds.). *Bridges and Boundaries: Historians, Political Scientists and the Study of International Relations*. Cambridge, MA: MIT Press, 2001.

Erickson, John. *The Road to Berlin: Stalin's War with Germany, Vol. 2*. London: Grafton, 1983.

———. *The Road to Stalingrad, Vol. 1*. London: Panther, 1975.

Evangelista, Matthew A. "Stalin's Postwar Army Reappraised," *International Security* 7 (1982–1983): 110–138.

———. *Unarmed Forces: The Transnational Movement to End the Cold War*. Ithaca, NY: Cornell University Press, 1999.

Evans, Malcolm D. (ed.). *Blackstone's International Law Documents*, 6th ed. Oxford: Oxford University Press, 2003.

———. *International Law*. Oxford: Oxford University Press, 2003.

Evans, Martin, and Ken Lunn (eds.). *War and Memory in the Twentieth Century*. Oxford: Berg, 1997.

Eyre, Dana P. "The Very Model of the Major Modern Military: World System Influences on the Proliferation of Military Weapons, 1960–1990." Ph.D. dissertation, Stanford University, 1997.

Eyre, Dana P., and Mark C. Suchman. "Status, Norms, and the Proliferation of Conventional Weapons," in Peter J. Katzenstein, ed., *The Culture of National Security.* New York: Columbia University Press, 1996.

Farish, Matthew. "Modern Witnesses: Foreign Correspondents, Geopolitical Vision, and the First World War," *Transactions of the Institute of British Geographers* 26, no. 3 (2001): 273–287.

Farrell, Brian. *The Foundation of Dáil Éireann.* Dublin: Gill and Macmillan, 1971.

Farrell, Brian (ed.). *The Creation of the Dáil.* Dublin: Gill and Macmillan, 1994.

Farrell, Theo. "Constructivist Security Studies: Portrait of a Research Program," *International Studies Review* 4, no. 1 (2002): 50–72.

———. "Culture and Military Power," *Review of International Studies* 24, no. 3 (1998): 407–416.

———. "Figuring Out Fighting Organisations: The New Organisational Analysis in Strategic Studies," *Journal of Strategic Studies* 19, no. 1 (1996): 122–135.

———. "Memory, Imagination and War," *History* 87, no. 285 (2002): 61–73.

———. "The Model Army: Military Imitation and the Enfeeblement of the Army in Post-Revolutionary Ireland, 1922–1942," *Irish Studies in International Affairs* 8 (1997): 111–127.

———. "Professionalization and Suicidal Defence Planning by the Irish Army, 1921–1941," *Journal of Strategic Studies* 21, no. 3 (1998): 67–85.

———. *Weapons Without a Cause: The Politics of Weapons Acquisition in the United States.* New York: St. Martin's, 1997.

Farrell, Theo, and Hélène Lambert. "Courting Controversy: International Law, National Norms and American Nuclear Use," *Review of International Studies* 27, no. 3 (2001): 309–326.

Farrell, Theo, and Terry Terriff (eds.). *The Sources of Military Change: Culture, Politics, Technology.* Boulder, CO: Lynne Rienner, 2002.

Feaver, Peter D. *Armed Servants: Agency, Oversight, and Civil-Military Relations.* Cambridge, MA: Harvard University Press, 2003.

———. *Guarding the Guardians: Civilian Control of Nuclear Weapons in the United States.* Ithaca, NY: Cornell University Press, 1992.

Feld, M. D. "Middle-Class Society and the Rise of Military Professionalism," *Armed Forces and Society* 1 (1975): 419–442.

———. "Military Professionalism and the Mass Army," *Armed Forces and Society* 1 (1975).

Fields, Frank E., and Jack J. Jensen. "Military Professionalism in Post-Communist Hungary and Poland," *European Security* 7, no. 1 (1998): 117–156.

Fife, Rolf Einar. "The International Criminal Court: Whence It Came, Where It Goes," *Nordic Journal of International Law* 69 (2000): 63–85.

Finer, S. E. *Man on Horseback.* London: Pall Mall, 1962.

Finnemore, Martha. *National Interests in International Society.* Ithaca, NY: Cornell University Press, 1996.

———. "Norms, Culture, and World Politics: Insights from Sociology's Institutionalism," *International Organization* 50 (1996): 325–348.

———. *The Purpose of Intervention: Changing Beliefs About the Use of Force.* Ithaca, NY: Cornell University Press, 2003.

Finnemore, Martha, and Kathryn Sikkink. "International Norm Dynamics and Political Change," *International Organization* 52, no. 4 (1998): 887–917.

Fisk, Robert. *In Time of War.* Dublin: Gill and Macmillan, 1983.

Fitch, Samuel J. *The Armed Forces and Democracy in Latin America.* Baltimore: Johns Hopkins University Press, 2000.

Fitzpatrick, David. "The Geography of Irish Nationalism, 1910–1921," *Past and Present* 78 (1978): 113–144.

Forster, Stig. "Dreams and Nightmares: German Military Leadership and the Images of Future Warfare, 1871–1914," in Manfred F. Boemeke, Roger Chickering, and Stig Forster, eds., *Anticipating Total War: The German and American Experiences, 1871–1914.* Cambridge: Cambridge University Press, 1999.

———. "Introduction," in Roger Chickering and Stig Forster, eds., *Great War, Total War: Combat and Mobilization on the Western Front, 1914–1918.* Cambridge: Cambridge University Press, 2000.

Forster, Stig, and Jorg Nagler (eds.). *On the Road to Total War: The American Civil War and the German Wars of Unification, 1861–1871.* Cambridge: Cambridge University Press, 1997.

Foster, Kevin. *Fighting Fictions: War, Narrative and National Identity.* London: Pluto, 1999.

Franck, Thomas M. *Fairness in International Law and Institutions.* Oxford: Clarendon, 1995.

———. "Interpretation and Change in the Law of Humanitarian Intervention," in J. L. Holzgrefe and Robert O. Keohane, eds., *Humanitarian Intervention: Ethical, Legal, and Political Dilemmas.* Cambridge: Cambridge University Press, 2003.

———. "Lessons of Kosovo," *American Journal of International Law* 93, no. 4 (1999): 857–860.

———. *Recourse to Force: State Action Against Threats and Armed Attacks.* Cambridge: Cambridge University Press, 2002.

Freedman, Lawrence. *Deterrence.* Cambridge: Polity, 2004.

———. *The Evolution of Nuclear Strategy.* Basingstoke: Macmillan, 1981.

———. *The Revolution in Strategic Affairs.* Oxford: Oxford University Press for the International Institute for Strategic Studies, 1998.

———. "Victims and Victors: Reflections on the Kosovo War," *Review of International Studies* 26, no. 3 (2000): 335–358.

Friedberg, Aaron L. *In the Shadow of the Garrison State.* Princeton, NJ: Princeton University Press, 2000.

Friedman, Benjamin. "Mini-Nukes, Bunker-Busters, and Deterrence: Framing the Debate," April 26, 2002. Available at http://www.cdi.org/.

Fussell, Paul. *The Great War and Modern Memory.* Oxford: Oxford University Press, 1975.

Gaddis, John Lewis. *The Long Peace: Inquiries into the History of the Cold War.* Oxford: Oxford University Press, 1983.

———. *We Now Know: Rethinking Cold War History.* Oxford: Oxford University Press, 1997.

Gaddis, John Lewis, et al. *Cold War Statesmen Confront the Bomb: Nuclear Diplomacy Since 1945.* Oxford: Oxford University Press, 1999.

Garvin, Tom. *1922: The Birth of Irish Democracy.* Dublin: Gill and Macmillan, 1996.

Gat, Azar. *Fascist and Liberal Visions of War: Fuller, Liddell Hart, Douhet and Other Modernists.* Oxford: Oxford University Press, 1998.

Geintz, Christian. "The First Air War Against Noncombatants: Strategic Bombing of German Cities in World War I," in Roger Chickering and Stig Forster, eds., *Great War, Total War: Combat and Mobilization on the Western Front, 1914–1918.* Cambridge: Cambridge University Press, 2000.

Glaser, Charles L. *Analyzing Strategic Nuclear Policy.* Princeton, NJ: Princeton University Press, 1990.

Glover, Jonathan. *Humanity: A Moral History of the Twentieth Century.* London: Pimlico, 2001.

Goldfischer, David. *The Best Defense: Policy Alternatives for US Nuclear Security from the 1950s to the 1990s.* Ithaca, NY: Cornell University Press, 1993.

Goldman, Emily O. "The Spread of Western Military Models to Ottoman Turkey and Meiji Japan," in Theo Farrell and Terry Terriff, eds., *The Sources of Military Change: Culture, Politics, Technology.* Boulder, CO: Lynne Rienner, 2002.

Goldman, Emily O., and Leslie C. Eliason (eds.). *The Diffusion of Military Technology and Ideas.* Stanford, CA: Stanford University Press, 2003.

Goldstein, Joshua. *War and Gender.* Cambridge: Cambridge University Press, 2001.

Goldstein, Judith, and Robert O. Keohane (eds.). *Ideas and Foreign Policy: Beliefs, Institutions, and Political Change.* Ithaca, NY: Cornell University Press, 1993.

Goldstein, Judith L., Robert O. Keohane, and Anne-Marie Slaughter (eds.). *Legalization and World Politics.* Cambridge, MA: MIT Press, 2001.

Golinski, Jan. *Making Natural Knowledge: Constructivism and the History of Science.* Cambridge: Cambridge University Press, 1998.

Goodrich, Peter Spang. "The Surgical Precision Myth: After the Bomb Explodes," 11 June 2003. Available at http://www.providence.edu/mba/goodrich/war/surgical/.

Gottlieb, Gidon. "The Conceptual World of the Yale School of International Law," *World Politics* 21 (1968): 120–129.

Goulding Jr., Vincent J. "Back to the Future with Asymmetric Warfare," *Parameters* (Winter 2000–2001): 21–30.

Gowlland-Debbas, Vera. "The Limits of Unilateral Enforcement of Community Objectives in the Framework of UN Peace Maintenance," *European Journal of International Law* 11, no. 2 (2000): 361–383.

Gray, Christine. *International Law and the Use of Force.* Oxford: Oxford University Press, 2001.

Gray, Colin S. *Modern Strategy.* Oxford: Oxford University Press, 1999.

———. *Nuclear Strategy and National Style.* Lanham, MD: Hamilton, 1986.

———. "Nuclear Strategy: The Case for a Theory of Victory," *International Security* 4, no. 1 (1979): 54–87.

———. *The Second Nuclear Age.* Boulder CO: Lynne Rienner, 1999.

———. "Strategic Culture as Context: The First Generation of Theory Strikes Back," *Review of International Studies* 25, no. 1 (1999): 49–70.

———. *Weapons Don't Make War.* Lawrence: University of Kansas Press, 1993.

Greenwood, Christopher. "The Law of War (International Humanitarian Law)," in Malcolm Evans, ed., *International Law.* Oxford: Oxford University Press, 2003.

Greenwood, Royston, and C. R. Hinings. "Understanding Strategic Change: The Contribution of Archetypes," *Academy of Management Journal* 36, no. 5 (1993): 1052–1081.

Griffith, Paddy. *Battle Tactics of the Western Front: The British Army's Art of Attack, 1916–1918.* New Haven, CT: Yale University Press, 1994.

Guicherd, Catherine. "International Law and the War in Kosovo," *Survival* 41, no. 2 (1999): 19–34.

Haas, Peter M. "Epistemic Communities and International Policy Coordination," *International Organization* 46 (1992): 1–35.

Hacker, Barton C. "Engineering a New Order: Military Institutions, Technical Education, and the Rise of the Industrial State," *Technology and Culture* 34 (1993): 1–27.

Hagan, Kenneth J. (ed.). *In Peace and War: Interpretations of American Naval History, 1775–1984*, 2nd ed. Westport, CT: Greenwood, 1984.

Hagerman, Edward. *The American Civil War and the Origins of Modern Warfare*. Bloomington: Indiana University Press, 1988.

Halberstam, David. *War in a Time of Peace: Bush, Clinton and the Generals*. London: Bloomsbury, 2001.

Hall, Peter A., and Rosemary C. R. Taylor. "Political Science and the Three New Institutionalisms," *Political Studies* 44, no. 5 (1996): 936–957.

Hall, Rodney Bruce. "Moral Authority as a Power Resource," *International Organization* 51, no. 4 (1997): 591–622.

Halperin, Morton H. *Bureaucratic Politics and Foreign Policy*. Washington, DC: Brookings Institution, 1974.

Hansenclever, Andreas, Peter Mayer, and Volker Rittberger. *Theories of International Regimes*. Cambridge: Cambridge University Press, 1997.

Hanson, Victor Davis. *The Western Way of War: Infantry Battle in Classical Greece*, 2nd ed. Los Angeles: University of California Press, 2000.

Harhoff, Frederik. "Unauthorised Humanitarian Interventions: Armed Violence in the Name of Humanity?" *Nordic Journal of International Law* 70 (2001): 65–119.

Harper, Sue. "Popular Film, Popular Memory: The Case of the Second World War," in Martin Evans and Ken Lunn, eds., *War and Memory in the Twentieth Century*. Oxford: Berg, 1997.

Harris, J. P. *Men, Ideas and Tanks: British Military Thought and Armoured Forces, 1903–1939*. Manchester: Manchester University Press, 1995.

Hart, H. L. A. *The Concept of Law*. Oxford: Oxford University Press, 1961.

Hart, Peter. *The IRA and Its Enemies*. Oxford: Oxford University Press, 1998.

———. "The Social Structure of the Irish Republican Army, 1916–1923," *The Historical Journal* 42 (1999): 207–231.

Hartigan, Richard S. *Lieber's Code and the Law of War*. Chicago: Precedent, 1983.

Heff, Stephen C. "A Short History of International Law," in Malcolm D. Evans, ed., *International Law*. Oxford: Oxford University Press, 2003.

Henkin, Louis. "Kosovo and the Law of 'Humanitarian Intervention,'" *American Journal of International Law* 93, no. 4 (1999): 824–828.

Herring, Eric. "Nuclear Totem and Taboo." Paper presented at the British International Studies Association Annual Conference, Leeds, December 1997.

———. "The Power of the Nuclear Taboo." Paper presented at the British International Studies Association Annual Conference, Swansea, December 1992.

Higgins, Rosalyn. *Problems and Process: International Law and How We Use It*. Oxford: Oxford University Press, 1994.

Hilpold, Peter. "Humanitarian Intervention: Is There a Need for a Legal Reappraisal?" *European Journal of International Law* 12, no. 3 (2001): 437–467.

Hippel, Karin Von. *Democracy by Force: US Military Intervention in the Post–Cold War World*. Cambridge: Cambridge University Press, 2000.

Hironaka, Ann. "Boundaries of War: Historical Change in Patterns of War-making, 1815–1980." Ph.D. dissertation, Stanford University, 1998.

———. "From Conflict to Consensus: The Decline of Wars of Colonial Independence, 1770–1985." Unpublished manuscript, 2000.

Holden, Wendy. *Shell Shock*. London: Channel Four Books, 1998.

Holliday, Ian. "When Is a Cause Just?" *Review of International Studies* 28, no. 3 (2002): 557–576.

Holton, Kate. "Embedding Hampered Iraq Media Independence," *Reuters,* 30 January 2004. Available at http://www.reuters.com/.

Holzgrefe, J. L. "The Humanitarian Intervention Debate," in J. L. Holzgrefe and Robert O. Keohane, eds., *Humanitarian Intervention: Ethical, Legal, and Political Dilemmas.* Cambridge: Cambridge University Press, 2003.

Holzgrefe, J. L., and Robert O. Keohane (eds.). *Humanitarian Intervention: Ethical, Legal, and Political Dilemmas.* Cambridge: Cambridge University Press, 2003.

Hopf, Ted. "The Promise of Constructivism in International Relations Theory," *International Security* 23, no. 1 (1998): 171–200.

———. *Social Construction of International Politics: Identities and Foreign Policies, Moscow, 1955 and 1999.* Ithaca, NY: Cornell University Press, 2002.

Hosmer, Stephen T. *Why Milosevic Decided to Settle When He Did.* Santa Monica, CA: RAND, 2001.

House of Commons, Defence Select Committee, Fourteenth Report, 23 October 2000.

Howard, Michael E. "On Fighting Nuclear War," *International Security* 5, no. 4 (1981): 3–17.

———. *War in European History.* Oxford: Oxford University Press, 1976.

Human Rights Watch. *Civilian Deaths in the NATO Air Campaign.* 2000. Available at http://www.hrw.org/reports/2000/nato/Natbm200.htm.

———. *Off Target: The Conduct of the War and Civilian Casualties in Iraq.* New York, December 2003. Available at http://www.hrw.org/reports/2003/usa1203/.

Humphreys, Leonard A. *The Way of the Heavenly Sword: The Japanese Army in the 1920s.* Stanford, CA: Stanford University Press, 1995.

Hunt, Terence. "Iraq Inquiry Could Be Risky for Bush," *Long Beach Press Telegram,* 13 February 2004. Available at http://www.presstelegram.com/.

Hunter, Wendy. *State and Soldier in Latin America.* Washington, DC: US Institute for Peace, 1996.

Huntington, Samuel P. *Political Order in Changing Societies.* New Haven, CT: Yale University Press, 1968.

———. "Reforming Civil-Military Relations," in Larry Diamond and Mark F. Plattner, eds., *Civil-Military Relations and Democracy.* Baltimore: Johns Hopkins University Press, 1996.

———. *The Soldier and the State: The Theory and Politics of Civil-Military Relations* (Cambridge: Harvard University Press, 1957).

Hurd, Ian. "Legitimacy and Authority in International Politics," *International Organization* 53, no. 2 (1999): 379–408.

IBC Press Release. "IBC Response to the Lancet Study Estimating 100,000 Iraqi Deaths," PR10, 7 November 2004. Available at http://www.iraqbodycount.net/press.

Ignatief, Michael. *Virtual War: Kosovo and Beyond.* London: Chatto and Windus, 2000.

Ikenberry, G. John. *After Victory: Institutions, Strategic Restraint, and the Rebuilding of Order After Major Wars.* Princeton, NJ: Princeton University Press, 2001.

Ikenberry, G. John, and Charles A. Kupchan. "Socialization and Hegemonic Power," *International Organization* 44, no. 3 (1990): 283–315.

Ikle, Fred Charles. "Can Nuclear Deterrence Last Out the Century?" *Foreign Affairs* 51 (1973): 267–285.

Independent International Commission on Kosovo. *The Kosovo Report: Conflict, International Response, Lessons Learned.* Oxford: Oxford University Press, 2000.

Inglehart, Ronald. *Culture Shift in Advanced Industrial Societies.* Princeton, NJ: Princeton University Press, 1990.

————. *The Silent Revolution: Changing Values and Political Styles Among Western Publics*. Princeton, NJ: Princeton University Press, 1977.

International and Operational Law Department, Judge Advocate General's School, US Army, *Operational Law Handbook*. 2002.

International Institute for Strategic Studies (IISS). *The Military Balance, 2003–2004*. Oxford: Oxford University Press for the IISS, 2003.

Interview with General Mike Short, NATO Air Commander. In *War in Europe: 2 Vanishing Targets,* Channel 4 documentary, 2000.

Irish Free State, Department of Defence. *Defence Force Regulations: Annual Training*. Dublin: Stationery Office, 1926.

Jeffrey, Simon. "Rumsfeld Apologises for Iraq Jail Abuse," *The Guardian,* 7 May 2004. Available at http://www.guardian.co.uk/.

Jenkins, Dominick. *The Final Frontier: America, Science and Terror.* London: Verso, 2003.

Jennings, Sir Robert, and Sir Arthur Watts (eds.). *Oppenheim's International Law: Vol. 1, Peace: Introduction and Part 1,* 9th ed. London: Longman, 1996.

Jervis, Robert. *The Illogic of American Nuclear Strategy*. Ithaca, NY: Cornell University Press, 1984.

————. *The Meaning of the Nuclear Revolution: Statecraft and the Prospects for Armageddon*. Ithaca, NY: Cornell University Press, 1989.

Johnston, Alastair Iain. *Cultural Realism: Strategic Culture and Grand Strategy in Chinese History*. Princeton, NJ: Princeton University Press, 1995.

————. "Thinking About Strategic Culture," *International Security* 19, no. 4 (1995): 32–65.

Johnston, Mark. *Fighting the Enemy: Australian Soldiers and Their Adversaries in World War II*. Cambridge: Cambridge University Press, 2000.

Jones, General David C. (Chairman, Joint Chiefs of Staff). Speech to the American Newspaper Publishers Association, San Francisco, 28 April 1982. Reprinted in *Foreign Affairs* 60, no. 5 (1982): 1172–1174.

Joyner, Daniel H. "The Kosovo Intervention: Legal Analysis and a More Persuasive Paradigm," *European Journal of International Law* 13, no. 3 (2000): 597–619.

Kahn, Herman. *On Thermonuclear War*. Princeton, NJ: Princeton University Press, 1960.

Kaiser, Karl, Georg Leber, Alois Mertes, and Franz-Josef Schulze. "Nuclear Weapons and the Preservation of Peace: A Response to an American Proposal for Renouncing the First Use of Nuclear Weapons," *Foreign Affairs* 60, no. 5 (1982): 1157–1170.

Kaldor, Mary. *New and Old Wars: Organized Violence in a Global Era*. Cambridge: Polity, 1999.

Kampfner, John. *Blair's Wars*. London: Free Press, 2003.

Kaplan, Fred. *The Wizards of Armageddon*. New York: Simon and Schuster, 1983.

Katzenstein, Peter J. *Cultural Norms and National Security: Police and Military in Postwar Japan*. Ithaca, NY: Cornell University Press, 1996.

Katzenstein, Peter J. (ed.). *The Culture of National Security*. New York: Columbia University Press, 1996.

Kaufman, Stuart J. *Modern Hatreds: The Symbolic Politics of Ethnic War*. Ithaca, NY: Cornell University Press, 2001.

Kavanagh, Dennis. *Political Culture*. London: Macmillan, 1972.

Keane, John. *Violence and Democracy*. Cambridge: Cambridge University Press, 2004.

Keck, Margaret E., and Kathryn Sikkink. *Activists Beyond Borders*. Ithaca, NY: Cornell University Press, 1996.

Keeny Jr., Spurgeon M., and Wolfgang K. H. Panofsky. "MAD Versus NUTS," *Foreign Affairs* 60 (Winter 1981–1982): 287–304.

Kelly, Alfred. "Whose War? Whose Nation? Tensions in the Memory of the Franco-German War of 1870–1871," in Manfred F. Boemeke, Roger Chickering, and Stig Forster, eds., *Anticipating Total War: The German and American Experiences, 1871–1914*. Cambridge: Cambridge University Press, 1999.

Kennedy, Edward M., and Mark O. Hatfield. *Freeze! How You Can Help Prevent Nuclear War*. New York: Bantam, 1982.

Kennedy, Michael. *Ireland and the League of Nations, 1923–1946*. Dublin: Irish Academic Press, 1996.

Kier, Elizabeth. "Culture and Military Doctrine: France Between the Wars," *International Security* 19, no. 4 (1995): 65–93.

———. *Imagining War: French and British Military Doctrine Between the Wars*. Princeton, NJ: Princeton University Press, 1997.

Kirgis, Frederic L. "The Formative Years of the American Society of International Law," *American Journal of International Law* 90, no. 4 (1996): 559–589.

Kittichaisaree, Kriangsak. *International Criminal Law*. Oxford: Oxford University Press, 2001.

Klotz, Audie. *Norms in International Relations*. Ithaca, NY: Cornell University Press, 1995.

Knopf, Jeffrey W. *Domestic Society and International Cooperation: The Impact of Protest on US Arms Control Policy*. Cambridge: Cambridge University Press, 1998.

Kofsky, Frank. *Harry S. Truman and the War Scare of 1948*. New York: St. Martin's, 1995.

Koh, Harold Hongju. "Why Do Nations Obey International Law?" *Yale Law Journal* 106 (1997): 2645–2658.

Koskenniemi, Martti. *The Gentle Civilizer of Nations: The Rise and Fall of International Law 1870–1960*. Cambridge: Cambridge University Press, 2001.

Kowert, Paul, and Jeffrey Legro. "Norms, Identity and Their Limits: A Theoretical Reprise," in Peter J. Katzenstein, ed., *The Culture of National Security: Norms and Identity in World Politics*. New York: Columbia University Press, 1996.

Kralev, Nicholas. "US Drops Pledge on Nukes: Won't Rule Out Hitting Any States," *Washington Times,* 22 February 2002.

Kratochwil, Friedrich V. "The Force of Prescriptions," *International Organization* 38, no. 4 (1984): 685–708.

———. *Rules, Norms, and Decisions*. Cambridge: Cambridge University Press, 1989.

Kucia, Charles, and Daryl Kimball. "New Nuclear Policies, New Weapons, New Dangers." Issue Brief, Arms Control Association, 28 April 2003. Available at http://armscontrol.org/.

Kull, Steven, and I. M. Destler. *Misreading the Public: The Myth of a New Isolationism*. Washington, DC: Brookings Institution, 1999.

Lalande, Jean. "La Suisse Change Son Fusil d'Epaule," *Le Point,* 19 August 2004.

Lambeth, Benjamin S. *The Transformation of American Air Power*. Ithaca, NY: Cornell University Press, 2000.

Lantis, Jeffrey S. "Strategic Culture and National Security Policy," *International Studies Review* 4, no. 3 (2002): 87–114.

Lauterpacht, Hersch. "The Problem of Revision of the Law of War," *British Yearbook of International Law* 29 (1952).

Lawrence, Philip K. *Modernity and War: The Creed of Absolute Violence*. New York: St. Martin's, 1997.

Leed, Eric J. *No Man's Land: Combat and Identity in World War One*. Cambridge: Cambridge University Press, 1981.

Leese, Peter. *Shell Shock: Traumatic Neurosis and the British Soldiers of the First World War*. Basingstoke: Palgrave Macmillan, 2002.

Leffler, Melvyn. *A Preponderance of Power: National Security, the Truman Administration, and the Cold War*. Stanford, CA: Stanford University Press, 1992.

Legro, Jeffrey W. *Cooperation Under Fire: Anglo-German Restraint During World War II*. Ithaca, NY: Cornell University Press, 1995.

———. "Whence American Internationalism," *International Organization* 54, no. 2 (2000): 253–289.

———. "Which Norms Matter? Revisiting the 'Failure' of Internationalism," *International Organization* 51, no. 1 (1997): 31–63.

Levi, Michael A. *Fire in the Hole: Nuclear and Non-nuclear Options for Counter-proliferation*. Washington, DC: Carneige Endowment for International Peace, November 2002. Available at http://www.ceip.org/.

Lewis, John Wilson, and Xue Litai. "China's Search for a Modern Air Force," *International Security* 24, no. 1 (1999): 64–94.

Lewis, Michael W. "The Law of Aerial Bombardment in the 1991 Gulf War," *American Journal of International Law* 97, no. 3 (2003): 481–509.

Liulevicius, Vejas Gabriel. *War Land on the Eastern Front: Culture, National Identity and German Occupation in World War I*. Cambridge: Cambridge University Press, 2000.

Lloyd, David W. *Battlefield Tourism: Pilgrimage and the Commemoration of the Great War in Britain, Australia, and Canada, 1919–1939*. Oxford: Berg, 1998.

Lord Robertson, Secretary of State for Defence. *Kosovo: An Account of the Crisis*. London: Ministry of Defence, 1999.

Lustick, Ian S. "History, Historiography and Political Science: Multiple Historical Records and the Problem of Selection Bias," *American Political Science Review* 90, no. 3 (1996): 605–618.

MacAskill, Ewen. "Blair Draws Up Plans to Send Troops to Sudan," *The Guardian*, 22 July 2004.

Mack, Andrew. "Why Big Countries Lose Small Wars: The Politics of Asymmetric Conflict," *World Politics* 26, no. 1 (1975): 175–200.

MacKenzie, Donald. *Inventing Accuracy: A Historical Sociology of Nuclear Missile Guidance*. Cambridge, MA: MIT Press, 1990.

MacKenzie, Donald, and Judy Wajcman. "Introductory Essay," in Donald MacKenzie and Judy Wajcman, eds., *The Social Shaping of Technology*, 2nd ed. Buckingham: Open University Press, 1999.

MacKenzie, Donald, and Judy Wajcman (eds.). *The Social Shaping of Technology*, 2nd ed. Buckingham: Open University Press, 1999.

Macmillan, Alan, Ken Booth, and Russell Trood, "Strategic Culture," in Ken Booth and Russell Trood (eds.), *Strategic Cultures in the Asia-Pacific Region* (New York: St. Martin's, 1999).

Mandelbaum, Michael. "The Anti–Nuclear Weapons Movement," *PS* 17, no. 1 (Winter 1984): 27–28.

———. "Is Major War Obsolete?" *Survival* 40, no. 4 (1998–1999): 20–26.

———. *The Nuclear Revolution: International Politics Before and After Hiroshima*. Cambridge: Cambridge University Press, 1981.

Maoz, Zeev, and Bruce Russett. "Normative and Structural Causes of Democratic Peace," *American Political Science Review* 87, no. 3 (1993): 624–638.

March, James G., and Johan P. Olsen. "The Institutional Dynamics of International Political Orders," *International Organization* 52, no. 4 (1998): 943–969.

———. *Rediscovering Institutions*. New York: Free Press, 1989.

Marwick, Arthur. "Painting and Music During and After the Great War: The Art of Total War," in Roger Chickering and Stig Forster, eds., *Great War, Total War: Combat and Mobilization on the Western Front, 1914–1918*. Cambridge: Cambridge University Press, 2000.

MccGwire, Michael. "Why Did We Bomb Belgrade?" *International Affairs* 76, no. 1 (2000): 1–23.

McDougal, Myres S., and Harold D. Lasswell. "The Identification and Appraisal of Diverse Systems of Public Order," *American Journal of International Law* 53 (1959): 1–29.

McEnaney, Laura. *Civil Defense Begins at Home*. Princeton, NJ: Princeton University Press, 2000.

McInnes, Colin. "A Different Kind of War? September 11 and the United States' Afghan War," *Review of International Studies* 29, no. 2 (2003): 165–184.

———. *Spectator-Sport War: The West and Contemporary Conflict*. Boulder, CO: Lynne Rienner, 2002.

McNamara, Robert S., with Brian VanDeMark. *In Retrospect: The Tragedy and Lessons of Vietnam*. New York: Times, 1995.

McNeill, William. *The Pursuit of Power: Technology, Armed Force, and Society Since AD 1000*. Chicago: University of Chicago Press, 1982.

Mearsheimer, John. J. *The Tragedy of Great Power Politics*. New York: W. W. Norton, 2001.

Meddelsohn, Everett, Merritt Roe Smith, and Peter Weingart (eds.). *Science, Technology and the Military*. Dordrecht: Kluwer, 1998.

Meilinger, Phillip S. "Proselytiser and Prophet: Alexander P. de Seversky and American Airpower," *Journal of Strategic Studies* 18, no. 1 (1995): 7–35.

———. "Trenchard, Slessor, and Royal Air Force Doctrine Before World War II," in Phillip S. Meilinger, ed., *The Paths of Heaven: The Evolution of Airpower Theory*. Maxwell AFB, AL: Air University Press, 1997.

Meilinger, Phillip S. (ed.). *The Paths of Heaven: The Evolution of Airpower Theory*. Maxwell AFB, AL: Air University Press, 1997.

Merridale, Catherine. *Night of Stone: Death and Memory in Russia*. New York: Penguin, 2002.

———. "War, Death, and Remembrance in Soviet Russia," in Jay Winter and Emmanuel Sivan, eds., *War and Remembrance in the Twentieth Century*. Cambridge: Cambridge University Press, 2000.

Meyer, John W., John Boli, George M. Thomas, and Francisco O. Ramirez. "World Society and the Nation-State," *American Journal of Sociology* 193 (1997): 144–181.

Meyer, John W., David Frank, Ann Hironaka, Evan Schofer, and Nancy B. Tuma. "The Structuring of a World Environmental Regime, 1870–1990," *International Organization* 51 (1992): 623–651.

Meyer, John W., Francisco O. Ramirez, and Yasemin Soysal. "World Expansion of Mass Education, 1870–1980," *Sociology of Education* 65, no. 2 (1992): 128–149.

Miles Jr., Rufus E. "Hiroshima: The Strange Myth of Half a Million Lives Saved," *International Security* 10 (1985): 121–140.

Mitchell, Arthur. *Revolutionary Government in Ireland*. Dublin: Gill and Macmillan, 1995.

Morrow, James D. "The Institutional Features of the Prisoners of War Treaties," *International Organization* 55, no. 4 (2001): 971–991.

Mosse, George L. *Fallen Soldiers: Reshaping the Memory of the World Wars*. Oxford: Oxford University Press, 1990.

Mueller, John. "Changing Attitudes Towards War: The Impact of the First World War," *British Journal of Political Science* 21, no. 1 (1991): 1–28.

———. *The Remnants of War*. Ithaca, NY: Cornell University Press, 2004.

———. *Retreat from Doomsday: The Obsolescence of Major War*. New York: Basic, 1989.

Mulcahy, Risteárd. *Richard Mulcahy (1886–1971): A Family Memoir*. Dublin: Aurelian, 1999.

Muller, Jan-Werner (ed.). *Memory and Power in Post-War Europe*. Cambridge: Cambridge University Press, 2002.

Munkler, Herfried. *The New Wars*. Cambridge: Polity, 2005.

Murphy, John F. *The United States and the Rule of Law in International Affairs*. Cambridge: Cambridge University Press, 2004.

Murray, Williamson. "Strategic Bombing: The British, American, and German Experiences," in Williamson Murray and Allan R. Millet, eds., *Military Innovation in the Intrawar Period*. Cambridge: Cambridge University Press, 1996.

Murray, Williamson, and Allan R. Millet (eds.). *Military Innovation in the Intrawar Period*. Cambridge: Cambridge University Press, 1996.

Murray, Williamson, and Robert H. Scales Jr. *The Iraq War: A Military History*. Cambridge, MA: Belknap Press of Harvard University Press, 2003.

Nadelman, Ethan A. "Global Prohibition Regimes: The Evolution of Norms in International Society," *International Organization* 44, no. 4 (1990): 479–526.

National Security Strategy of the United States of America. Washington, DC, 2002. Available at http://www.whitehouse.gov/nsc/nss.html.

Nelson, Robert W. "Low-Yield Earth-Penetrating Nuclear Weapons," *FAS Public Interest Report,* 2001. Available at http://www.fas.org/.

Neustadt, Richard E. *Presidential Power: The Politics of Leadership from FDR to Carter*. New York: John Wiley and Sons, 1980.

Nolan, Janne E. *Guardians of the Arsenal: The Politics of Nuclear Strategy*. New York: Basic, 1989.

Nordlinger, Eric. *Soldiers in Politics*. Englewood Cliffs, NJ: Prentice Hall, 1977.

North Atlantic Military Committee. MC 362 encl. 1, *NATO Rules of Engagement,* 9 November 1999.

North Atlantic Treaty Organization. "The Conduct of the Air Campaign," 30 October 2000. Available at http://www.nato.int/kosovo/repo2000/conduct.htm.

———. "Statement on Kosovo," Washington, DC, summit, 23 April 1999. Available at http://www.nato.int/docu/pr/1999/p99-062e.htm.

Nye, Joseph. "Nuclear Learning and US-Soviet Security Regimes," *International Organization* 41 (1987): 371–402.

O'Connell, J. J. "Guerrilla Warfare as Standard Form," *An t-Óglách* (April 1930): 50–52.

O'Connell, Robert L. *Ride of the Second Horseman*. Oxford: Oxford University Press, 1995.

Office of Technology Assessment, Congress of the United States. *The Effects of Nuclear War*. London: Croom Helm, 1980.

O'Halpin, Eunan. "The Army and the Dáil," in Brian Farrell, ed., *The Creation of the Dáil*. Dublin: Gill and Macmillan, 1994.
———. *Defending Ireland: The Irish State and Its Enemies Since 1922*. Oxford: Oxford University Press, 1999.
Ousby, Ian. *The Road to Verdun: France, Nationalism and the First World War*. London: Jonathan Cape, 2002.
Owen, John M. "How Liberalism Produces Democratic Peace," *International Security* 19, no. 2 (1994): 87–125.
Pape, Robert. "Why Japan Surrendered," *International Security* 18 (1993): 154–201.
Paris, Michael. *Warrior Nation: Images of War in British Popular Culture, 1850–2000*. London: Reaktion, 2000.
Park, Hays W. "'Precision' and 'Area' Bombing: Who Did Which and When?" *Journal of Strategic Studies* 18, no. 1 (1995): 145–174.
Parker, Geoffrey. *The Military Revolution: Military Innovation and the Rise of the West, 1500–1800*, 2nd ed. Cambridge: Cambridge University Press, 1996.
Paul, T. V. "Nuclear Taboo and War Initiation in Regional Conflicts," *Journal of Conflict Resolution* 39, no. 4 (1995): 696–717.
Pellet, Alain. "Brief Remarks on the Unilateral Use of Force," *European Journal of International Law* 11, no. 2 (2000): 385–392.
Peters, Ralph. "The Culture of Future Conflict," *Parameters* (Winter 1995–1996): 18–27.
———. "The New Warrior Class," *Parameters* (Summer 1994): 16–26.
Petrova, Margarita H. "The End of the Cold War: A Battle or Bridging Ground Between Rationalist and Ideational Approaches in International Relations," *European Journal of International Relations* 9, no. 1 (2003): 115–163.
Pick, Daniel. *War Machine: The Rationalisation of Slaughter in the Modern Age*. New Haven, CT: Yale University Press, 1993.
Pike, John E., Bruce G. Blair, and Stephen I. Schwartz. "Defending Against the Bomb," in Stephen I. Schwartz, ed., *Atomic Audit*. Washington, DC: Brookings Institution, 1998.
Porpora, Douglas V. "Cultural Rules and Material Relations," *Sociological Theory* 11, no. 2 (1993): 212–229.
Posen, Barry R. "Nationalism, the Mass Army and Military Power," *International Security* 18, no. 2 (1993): 80–124.
———. *The Sources of Military Doctrine*. Ithaca, NY: Cornell University Press, 1984.
———. "The War for Kosovo: Serbia's Political-Military Strategy," *International Security* 24, no. 4 (2000): 39–84.
Powell, Walter W., and Paul J. DiMaggio (eds.). *The New Institutionalism in Organizational Analysis*. Chicago: University of Chicago Press, 1991.
Price, Richard M. *The Chemical Weapons Taboo*. Ithaca, NY: Cornell University Press, 1997.
———. "Reversing the Gun Sights: Transnational Civil Society Targets Land Mines," *International Organization* 52, no. 3 (1998): 627–631.
Price, Richard, and Nina Tannenwald. "Norms and Deterrence: The Nuclear and Chemical Weapons Taboo," in Peter J. Katzenstein, ed., *The Culture of National Security: Norms and Identity in World Politics*. New York: Columbia University Press, 1996.
Pringle, Peter, and William Arkin. *STOP: Nuclear War from the Inside*. London: Sphere, 1983.
Pye, Lucian W., and Sidney Verba (eds.). *Political Culture and Political Development*. Princeton, NJ: Princeton University Press, 1965.

Ralston, David B. *Importing the European Army: The Introduction of Military Techniques and Institutions into the Extra-European World, 1600–1914.* Chicago: University of Chicago Press, 1990.

Ramirez, Francisco O., and John W. Meyer. "Comparative Education," *Annual Review of Sociology* 6 (1980): 369–399.

Rampton, Sheldon, and John Stauber. *Weapons of Mass Distraction: The Uses of Propaganda in Bush's War on Iraq.* London: Robinson, 2003.

Raymond, John M., and Barbara J. Frischholz. "Lawyers Who Established International Law in the United States, 1776–1914," *American Journal of International Law* 76, no. 4 (1982): 802–829.

Record, Jeffrey. "The Bush Doctrine and War with Iraq," *Parameters* (Spring 2003). Available at http://carlisle-www.army.mil/usawc/Parameters/03spring/record.htm.

———. "Collapsed Countries, Casualty Dread, and the New American Way of War," *Parameters* (Summer 2002). Available at http://carlisle-www.army.mil/usawc/Parameters/02summer/record.htm.

Regan, John. *The Counter-Revolution.* Dublin: Gill and Macmillan, 1999.

Reisman, W. Michael. "Kosovo's Antinomies," *American Journal of International Law* 93, no. 4 (1999): 860–862.

———. "Unilateral Action and the Transformations of the World Constitutive Process: The Special Problem of Humanitarian Intervention," *European Journal of International Law* 11, no. 1 (2000): 3–18.

Report of the Secretary-General's High-Level Panel on Threats, Challenges, and Change. *A More Secure World: Our Shared Responsibility.* New York: United Nations, 2004.

Report of the Secretary-General to the Security Council on the Protection of Civilians in Armed Conflict, 28 May 2004, S/2004/431.

Report to the Congress on the Defeat of Hard and Deeply Buried Targets. Submitted by the Secretary of Defense in conjunction with the Secretary of Energy, July 2001.

Resende-Santo, Joào. "Anarchy and Emulation of Military Systems: Military Organization and Technology in South America, 1870–1930," *Security Studies* 5, no. 3 (1996): 193–260.

Reus-Smit, Christian. *American Power and World Order.* Cambridge: Polity, 2004.

Reus-Smit, Christian (ed.). *The Politics of International Law.* Cambridge: Cambridge University Press, 2004.

Rhem, Kathleen T. "US Military Works to Avoid Civilian Deaths, Collateral Damage," *American Armed Forces Information Service,* 5 March 2003. Available at http://www.defenselink.mil/news/Mar2003/.

Rhodes, Edward. "Constructing Power: Cultural Transformation and Strategic Adjustment in the 1890s," in Peter Trubowitz, Emily O. Goldman, and Edward Rhodes, eds., *The Politics of Strategic Adjustment: Ideas, Institutions and Interests.* New York: Columbia University Press, 1999.

Rhodes, Richard. *Dark Sun: The Making of the Hydrogen Bomb.* New York: Simon and Schuster, 1995.

Ringmar, Erik. *Identity, Interest and Action: A Cultural Explanation of Sweden's Intervention in the Thirty Years War.* Cambridge: Cambridge University Press, 1996.

Risse, Thomas. "'Let's Argue!': Communicative Action in World Politics," *International Organization* 54, no. 1 (2000): 1–39.

Risse, Thomas, Stephen C. Ropp, and Kathryn Sikkink (eds.). *The Power of Human Rights: International Norms and Domestic Change.* Cambridge: Cambridge University Press, 1999.

Risse, Thomas, and Kathryn Sikkink. "The Socialization of International Human Rights Norms into Domestic Practices: Introduction," in Thomas Risse, Stephen C. Ropp, and Kathryn Sikkink, eds., *The Power of Human Rights.* Cambridge: Cambridge University Press, 1999.

Risse-Kappen, Thomas. *Cooperation Among Democracies: The European Influence on US Foreign Policy.* Princeton, NJ: Princeton University Press, 1995.

Roberts, Adam. "Law and the Use of Force After Iraq," *Survival* 45, no. 2 (2003): 31–56.

———. "NATO's 'Humanitarian War' over Kosovo," *Survival* 41, no. 3 (1999): 102–123.

———. "The Price of Protection," *Survival* 44, no. 4 (2002–2003): 157–161.

———. "The United Nations and Humanitarian Intervention," in Jennifer M. Welsh, ed., *Humanitarian Intervention and International Relations.* Oxford: Oxford University Press, 2004.

Roberts, Adam, and Richard Guelff. "Editors Introduction," in Adam Roberts and Richard Guelff, eds., *Documents on the Laws of War,* 3rd ed. Oxford: Oxford University Press, 1999.

Roberts, Adam, and Richard Guelff (eds.). *Documents on the Laws of War,* 3rd ed. Oxford: Oxford University Press, 1999.

Roberts, Lee, Riyadh Lafta, Richard Garfield, Jamal Khudhairi, and Gilbert Burnham. "Mortality Before and After the 2003 Invasion of Iraq: Cluster Sample Survey," *The Lancet,* 29 October 2004. Available at http://image.thelancet.com/extras/04art10342web.pdf.

Robinson, Piers. *The CNN Effect: The Myth of News, Foreign Policy and Intervention.* London: Routledge, 2002.

Rogers, A. P. V. *Law on the Battlefield.* Manchester: Manchester University Press, 1996.

Rohkramer, Thomas. "Heroes and Would-Be Heroes: Veterans' and Reservists' Associations in Imperial Germany," in Manfred F. Boemeke, Roger Chickering, and Stig Forster, eds., *Anticipating Total War: The German and American Experiences, 1871–1914.* Cambridge: Cambridge University Press, 1999.

Roht-Arriaza, Naomi. "'Soft Law' in a 'Hybrid Organization': The International Organization for Standardization," in Dinah Shelton, ed., *Commitment and Compliance: The Role of Non-Binding Norms in the International Legal System.* Oxford: Oxford University Press, 2000.

Roman, Peter J. "Ike's Hair-Trigger: US Nuclear Predelegation, 1953–1960," *Security Studies* 7 (1998): 121–164.

Rosen, Stephen Peter. *Societies and Military Power: India and Its Armies.* Ithaca, NY: Cornell University Press, 1996.

———. *Winning the Next War: Innovation and the Modern Military.* Ithaca, NY: Cornell University Press, 1991.

Rosenbaum, Walter A. *Political Culture.* London: Nelson, 1975.

Rosenberg, David Alan. "American Atomic Strategy and the Hydrogen Bomb Decision," *Journal of American History* 66, no. 1 (1979): 62–87.

———. "The Origins of Overkill: Nuclear Weapons and American Strategy, 1945–1960," *International Security* 7 (1983): 3–71.

———. "A Smoking Radiating Ruin at the End of Two Hours: Documents on American Plans for Nuclear War with the Soviet Union," *International Security* 6, no. 3 (1981–1982): 3–17.

Ross, Steven T. *American War Plans, 1945–1950.* London: Frank Cass, 1996.

Rubin, Alfred. *Ethics and Authority in International Law.* Cambridge: Cambridge University Press, 1997.

Rudolph, Christopher. "Constructing an Atrocities Regime: The Politics of War Crimes Tribunals," *International Organization* 55, no. 3 (2001): 655–691.

Russell, Edmund. *War and Nature: Fighting Humans and Insects with Chemicals from World War I to Silent Spring.* Cambridge: Cambridge University Press, 2001.

Russett, Bruce. *Grasping the Democratic Peace.* Princeton, NJ: Princeton University Press, 1993.

Sagan, Scott D. "The Commitment Trap: Why the United States Should Not Use Nuclear Threats to Deter Biological and Chemical Weapons Attacks," *International Security* 24, no. 4 (2000): 85–115.

———. *Moving Targets: Nuclear Strategy and National Security.* Princeton, NJ: Princeton University Press, 1989.

Schachter, Oscar. "Self-Defense and the Rule of Law," *American Journal of International Law* 83, no. 2 (1989): 259–277.

Schaffer, Ronald. *Wings of Judgment: American Bombing in World War II.* Oxford: Oxford University Press, 1985.

Schama, Simon. *The Embarrassment of Riches: An Interpretation of Dutch Culture in the Golden Age.* London: Fontana, 1991.

Schell, Jonathan. *The Fate of the Earth.* New York: Avon, 1982.

Schimmelfennig, Frank. *The EU, NATO and the Integration of Europe: Rules and Rhetoric.* Cambridge: Cambridge University Press, 2003.

Schroeder, Paul. "History and International Relations Theory: Not Use or Abuse, but Fit or Misfit," *International Security* 22, no. 1 (1997): 64–74.

Schudson, Michael (ed.). *Memory Distortion: How Minds, Brains and Societies Reconstruct the Past.* Cambridge, MA: Harvard University Press, 1995.

Schulzinger, Robert D. *A Time for War: The United States and Vietnam, 1941–1975.* Oxford: Oxford University Press, 1997.

Schwartz, David N. *NATO's Nuclear Dilemmas.* Washington, DC: Brookings Institution, 1983.

Schwartz, Stephen I. (ed.). *Atomic Audit: The Costs and Consequences of US Nuclear Weapons Since 1945.* Washington, DC: Brookings Institution, 1998.

Schweller, Randall L. *Deadly Imbalances: Tripolarity and Hitler's Strategy of World Conquest.* New York: Columbia University Press, 1997.

Scott, Shirley V. "Is There Room for International Law in *Realpolitik*? Accounting for the US 'Attitude' Towards International Law," *Review of International Studies* 30, no. 1 (2004): 71–88.

Scott, W. Richard. *Organizations: Rational, Natural, and Open Systems,* 3rd ed. Englewood Cliffs, NJ: Prentice Hall, 1992.

Scott, W. Richard, John W. Meyer, and Associates. *Institutional Environments and Organizations: Structural Complexity and Individualism.* Thousand Oaks, CA: Sage, 1994.

Searle, John R. *The Social Construction of Social Reality.* New York: Free Press, 1995.

Secretary-General Address to the General Assembly. New York, 23 September 2003. Available at http://www.un.org/webcast/ga/58/statements/sgeng030923.htm.

Shah, Anup. "Media, Propaganda and Iraq," 30 March 2003. Available at http://www.globalissues.org/HumanRights/Media/Propaganda.

Shaw, Malcolm N. *International Law,* 5th ed. Cambridge: Cambridge University Press, 2003.

Shaw, Martin. *War and Genocide.* Cambridge: Polity, 2003.

Shelton, Dinah (ed.). *Commitment and Compliance: The Role of Non-Binding Norms in the International Legal System.* Oxford: Oxford University Press, 2000.

Shephard, Ben. *A War of Nerves: Soldiers and Psychiatrists, 1914–1994*. London: Pimlico, 2002.

Sherry, Michael S. *Preparing for the Next War: American Plans for Postwar Defense, 1941–1945*. New Haven, CT: Yale University Press, 1977.

———. *The Rise of American Air Power: The Creation of Armageddon*. New Haven, CT: Yale University Press, 1987.

Showalter, Dennis E. "From Deterrence to Doomsday Machine: The German Way of War, 1890–1914," *Journal of Military History* 64 (July 2000): 679–710.

Shulman, Mark. "Institutionalizing a Political Idea: Navalism and the Emergence of American Sea Power," in Peter Trubowitz, Emily O. Goldman, and Edward Rhodes, eds., *The Politics of Strategic Adjustment: Ideas, Institutions and Interests*. New York: Columbia University Press, 1999.

Simma, Bruno. "NATO, the UN and Use of Force: Legal Aspects," *European Journal of International Law* 10 (1999): 1–22.

Simon, Jeffrey. *Central European Civil-Military Relations and NATO Expansion*. Washington, DC: National Defense University Press, 1995.

Singer, P. W. "Corporate Warriors: The Rise of the Privatized Military Industry and Its Ramifications for International Security," *International Security* 26, no. 3 (2001–2002): 186–220.

Slaughter, Anne-Marie. *A New World Order*. Princeton, NJ: Princeton University Press, 2004.

Smith, M. L. R. *Fighting for Ireland*. London: Routledge, 1997.

Smith, Merrit Roe, and Leo Marx (eds.). *Does Technology Drive History? The Dilemma of Technological Determinism*. Cambridge, MA: MIT Press, 1994.

Smith, Thomas W. "The New Law of War: Legitimating Hi-Tech and Infrastructural Violence," *International Studies Quarterly* 46, no. 3 (2002): 355–374.

Snyder, Jack. *Myths of Empire*. Ithaca, NY: Cornell University Press, 1991.

———. "Richness, Rigor and Relevance in the Study of Soviet Foreign Policy," *International Security* 9, no. 3 (1984–1985): 89–108.

Sokolsky, Richard. "Demystifying the US Nuclear Posture Review," *Survival* 44, no. 3 (2002): 133–148.

Spinardi, Graham. *From Polaris to Trident: The Development of US Fleet Ballistic Missile Technology*. Cambridge: Cambridge University Press, 1994.

Steinisch, Imgard. "Different Path to War: A Comparative Study of Militarism and Imperialism in the United States and Imperial Germany, 1871–1914," in Manfred F. Boemeke, Roger Chickering, and Stig Forster, eds., *Anticipating Total War: The German and American Experiences, 1871–1914*. Cambridge: Cambridge University Press, 1999.

Steinmo, Sven, Kathleen Thelen, and Frank Longstreth (eds.). *Structuring Politics: Historical Institutionalism in Comparative Politics*. Cambridge: Cambridge University Press, 1992.

Stigler, Andrew L. "A Clear Victory of Air Power: NATO's Empty Threat to Invade Kosovo," *International Security* 27, no. 3 (2002–2003): 124–157.

Stone, John. "The British Army and the Tank," in Theo Farrell and Terry Terriff, eds., *The Sources of Military Change: Culture, Politics, Technology*. Boulder, CO: Lynne Rienner, 2002.

———. *The Tank Debate: Armour and Anglo-American Military Tradition*. Amsterdam: Harwood, 2000.

Strachan, Hew. *The First World War, Vol. 1: To Arms*. Oxford: Oxford University Press. 2001.

————. "Germany in the First World War: The Problem of Strategy," *German History* 12, no. 2 (1994): 237–249.

Strang, David, and Patricia Chang. "The International Labour Organization and the Welfare State: Institutional Effects on National Welfare Spending, 1960–1980," *International Organization* 47 (1993): 235–262.

Supplementary Volume to the Report of the International Commission on Intervention and State Sovereignty. *The Responsibility to Protect: Research, Bibliography, Background.* Ottawa, ON: International Research Development Centre, 2001.

Swidler, Ann. "Culture in Action: Symbols and Strategies," *American Sociological Review* 51, no. 2 (1986): 273–286.

Synder, Glenn. *Alliance Politics.* Ithaca, NY: Cornell University Press, 1997.

Tannenwald, Nina. "The Nuclear Taboo: The United States and the Normative Basis of Nuclear Non-use," *International Organization* 53, no. 3 (1999): 433–468.

Taylor, Brian. "Russia's Passive Army: Rethinking Military Coups," *Comparative Political Studies* 34, no. 8 (2001): 924–952.

Teitler, G. *The Genesis of the Professional Officers' Corps.* Beverly Hills, CA: Sage, 1977.

Terriff, Terry. *The Nixon Administration and the Making of US Nuclear Strategy.* Ithaca, NY: Cornell University Press, 1995.

Thomas, Ward. *The Ethics of Destruction: Norms and Force in International Relations.* Ithaca, NY: Cornell University Press, 2001.

Thomson, Janice. *Mercenaries, Pirates and Sovereigns.* Princeton, NJ: Princeton University Press, 1994.

Tilly, Charles. "Reflections on the History of European State-making," in Charles Tilly, ed., *The Formation of Nation States in Western Europe.* Princeton, NJ: Princeton University Press, 1975.

Tilly, Charles (ed.). *The Formation of Nation States in Western Europe.* Princeton, NJ: Princeton University Press, 1975.

Townshend, Charles. "The Irish Republican Army and the Development of Guerrilla Warfare, 1916–1921," *English Historical Review* 94 (1987): 318–345.

————. *Political Violence in Ireland.* Oxford: Oxford University Press, 1983.

Trachtenberg, Marc. *History and Strategy.* Princeton, NJ: Princeton University Press, 1991.

Trask, David F. "Military Imagination in the United States, 1815–1917," in Manfred F. Boemeke, Roger Chickering, and Stig Forster, eds., *Anticipating Total War: The German and American Experiences, 1871–1914.* Cambridge: Cambridge University Press, 1999.

Travers, Tim. "Could the Tanks of 1918 Have Been War-Winners for the British Expeditionary Force?" *Journal of Contemporary History* 27, no. 3 (1992): 389–406.

Trubowitz, Peter. "Geography and Strategy: The Politics of American Naval Expansion," in Peter Trubowitz, Emily O. Goldman, and Edward Rhodes, eds., *The Politics of Strategic Adjustment: Ideas, Institutions and Interests.* New York: Columbia University Press, 1999.

Trubowitz, Peter, Emily O. Goldman, and Edward Rhodes (eds.). *The Politics of Strategic Adjustment: Ideas, Institutions and Interests.* New York: Columbia University Press, 1999.

Union of Concerned Scientists. "The Troubling Science of Bunker-Busting Nuclear Weapons," April 2003. Available at http://ucsusa.org/.

US Army. AR 3504-41 *Training in Units.* 19 March 1993.

Usborne, David. "WMD Just a Convenient Excuse for War, Admits Wolfowitz," *The Independent,* 30 May 2003.

US Department of Defense. "DOD News: Background Briefing on Targeting," 5 March 2003. Available at http://www.defenselink.mil/news/Mar2003/.

———. News Briefing, Lt.-Gen. Michael Moseley, CFACC, 5 April 2003 (Pentagon–Saudi Arabia Two-Way Briefing). Available at http://www.usinfo.state.gov/topical/pol/terror/texts/03040502.htm.

US Department of Defense and the US Atomic Energy Commission. *The Effects of Atomic Weapons.* New York: McGraw-Hill, 1950.

US General Accounting Office (GAO). *Kosovo Air Operations: Need to Maintain Alliance Cohesion Resulted in Doctrinal Departures.* GAO-01-784. Washington, DC: GAO, July 2001.

———. *Strategic Weapons: Nuclear Weapons Targeting Process.* GAO/NSIAD-91-319FS. Washington, DC: GAO, September 1991.

Valiulis, Maryann Gialanella. *Potrait of a Revolutionary: General Richard Mulcahy and the Founding of the Irish State.* Dublin: Irish Academic Press, 1992.

Verhey, Jeffrey. *The Spirit of 1914: Militarism, Myth and Mobilization in Germany.* Cambridge: Cambridge University Press, 2000.

Vick, Alan, et al. *Aerospace Operations in Urban Environments: Exploring New Concepts.* RAND report MR-1187-AF, 2000. Available at http://www.rand.org/publications/MR/MR1187/.

Villelabeita, Ibon. "Marines Say Iraq Abuse Case Could Hurt Cease-Fire," *Reuters,* 19 May 2004. Available at http://www.reuters.com/.

von Trotha, Trutz. "'The Fellows Can Just Starve': On Wars of 'Pacification' in the African Colonies of Imperial Germany and the Concept of 'Total War,'" in Manfred F. Boemeke, Roger Chickering, and Stig Forster, eds., *Anticipating Total War: The German and American Experiences, 1871–1914.* Cambridge: Cambridge University Press, 1999.

Walt, Stephen M. *The Origins of Alliances.* Ithaca, NY: Cornell University Press, 1987.

Waltz, Kenneth N. "Structural Realism After the Cold War," *International Security* 25, no. 1 (2000): 30–39.

———. *Theory of International Politics.* Reading, MA: Addison-Wesley, 1979.

Warden III, John A. "Success in Modern War: A Response to Robert Pape's *Bombing to Win,*" *Security Studies* 7, no. 2 (1997–1998): 172–190.

Weart, Spencer R. *Nuclear Fear: A History of Images.* Cambridge, MA: Harvard University Press, 1988.

Welch, Stephen. *The Concept of Political Culture.* Basingstoke: Macmillan, 1993.

Welsh, Jennifer M. (ed.). *Humanitarian Intervention and International Relations.* Oxford: Oxford University Press, 2004.

Wendt, Alexander. "Anarchy Is What States Make of It: The Social Construction of Power Politics," *International Organization* 46, no. 2 (1992): 392–425.

———. "On Constitution and Causation in International Relations," *Review of International Relations* 24, Special Issue (1998): 101–117.

———. "Constructing International Politics," *International Security* 20, no. 1 (1995): 73–74.

———. *Social Theory of International Politics.* Cambridge: Cambridge University Press, 1999.

Wendt, Alexander, and Michael Barnett. "Dependent State Formation and Third World Militarization," *Review of International Studies* 19, no. 4 (1993): 321–347.

Weyland, Kurt. "The American Bias in Organization Theory," *Governance* 8, no. 1 (1995): 113–124.

Wheeler, Nicholas J. "The Humanitarian Responsibilities of Sovereignty: Explaining the Development of a New Norm of Military Intervention for Humanitarian Purposes in International Society," in Jennifer M. Welsh, ed., *Humanitarian Intervention and International Relations*. Oxford: Oxford University Press, 2004.

———. "The Kosovo Bombing Campaign," in Christian Reus-Smit, ed., *The Politics of International Law*. Cambridge: Cambridge University Press, 2004.

———. *Saving Strangers: Humanitarian Intervention in International Society*. Oxford: Oxford University Press, 2000.

Wheeler, Nicholas J., and Tim Dunne. *Moral Britannia? Evaluating the Ethical Dimension in Labour's Foreign Policy*. London: Foreign Policy Centre, 2004.

White, N. D., and A. Abass. "Countermeasures and Sanctions," in Malcolm Evans, ed., *International Law*. Oxford: Oxford University Press, 2003.

Widavsky, Aaron. "Choosing Preferences by Constructing Institutions: A Cultural Theory of Preference Formation," *American Political Science Review* 81, no. 1 (1987): 3–21.

Williams, Paul. "The Rise and Fall of the 'Ethical Dimension': Presentation and Practice in New Labour's Foreign Policy," *Cambridge Review of International Affairs* 15, no. 1 (2002): 53–63.

Williamson Jr., Samuel R., and Steven L. Reardon. *The Origins of US Nuclear Strategy, 1945–1953*. New York: St. Martin's, 1993.

Winograd, Eugene, and Ulric Neisser (eds.). *Affect and Accuracy in Recall: Studies of Flashblub Memories*. Cambridge: Cambridge University Press, 1992.

Winter, Denis. *Death's Men: Soldiers of the Great War*. London: Penguin, 1978.

Winter, Jay. *Sites of Memory, Sites of Mourning: The Great War in European Cultural History*. Cambridge: Cambridge University Press, 1995.

Winter, Jay, and Emmanuel Sivan. "Setting the Framework," in Jay Winter and Emmanuel Sivan, eds., *War and Remembrance in the Twentieth Century*. Cambridge: Cambridge University Press, 2000.

Winter, Jay, and Emmanuel Sivan (eds.). *War and Remembrance in the Twentieth Century*. Cambridge: Cambridge University Press, 2000.

Wirtz, James J. *The Tet Offensive*. Ithaca, NY: Cornell University Press, 1991.

Wittner, Lawrence S. *The Struggle Against the Bomb: 3 Volumes*. Stanford, CA: Stanford University Press, 1993.

Wohl, Robert. *A Passion for Wings: Aviation and Western Imagination, 1908–1918*. New Haven, CT: Yale University Press, 1994.

Wolcott, James. "Color Me Khaki," *Vanity Fair* (September 2004): 70–72.

Woodward, Bob. *Plan of Attack*. New York: Simon and Schuster, 2004.

World Bank. *World Development Indicators 2004*. Available at http://www.worldbank.org/data/wdi2004/index.htm.

Wright, Evan. *Generation Kill: Living Dangerous on the Road to Baghdad with the Ultraviolent Marines of Bravo Company*. Bantam Press, 2004.

Wright, Patrick. *Tank: The Progress of a Monstrous War Machine*. London: Faber and Faber, 2000.

Yost, David S. "The New NATO and Collective Security," *Survival* 40, no. 2 (1998): 135–160.

Young, Peter. "Defence and the New Irish State, 1919–1939," *The Irish Sword* 19 (1993–1994): 1–10.

Zahar, Marie-Joelle. "Fanatics, Mercenaries, Brigands and Politicians: Militia Decision-Making and Civil Conflict Resolution." Ph.D. diss., McGill University, 1999.

Zhukov, Georgi K. *Marshall Zhukov's Greatest Battles.* London: Sphere, 1971.

Zisk, Kimberly Martin. *Engaging the Enemy: Organization Theory and Soviet Military Development, 1955–1991.* Princeton, NJ: Princeton University Press, 1993.

Zucchino, David. *Thunder Run: Three Days in the Battle for Baghdad.* London: Atlantic, 2005.

Index

215

About the Book

A lthough the horrors of war are manifest, academic debate is dominated by accounts that reinforce the concept of warfare as a rational project. Seeking to explain this paradox—to uncover the motivations at the core of warring communities—Theo Farrell explores the cultural forces that have shaped modern Western conflict.

Farrell finds that the norms of war—shared beliefs about what is right and what works—are created and embraced not only by polities and military organizations, but also by constituencies throughout civil society. Culture, he demonstrates, accounts for all core areas of military activity at every level, sometimes with puzzling results.

Tracing the lineage of the modern military and ranging from historical examples to charged contemporary issues, this provocative book goes to the heart of the relationship between society and war.

Theo Farrell is Reader in War in the Modern World at King's College London. He is author of *Weapons Without a Cause: The Politics of Weapons Acquisition in the United States* and coeditor (with Terry Terriff) of *The Sources of Military Change: Culture, Politics, Technology.*